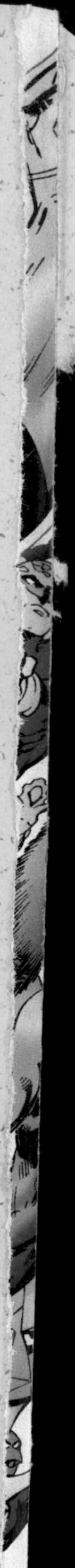

THE SINESTRO CORPS WAR

volume one

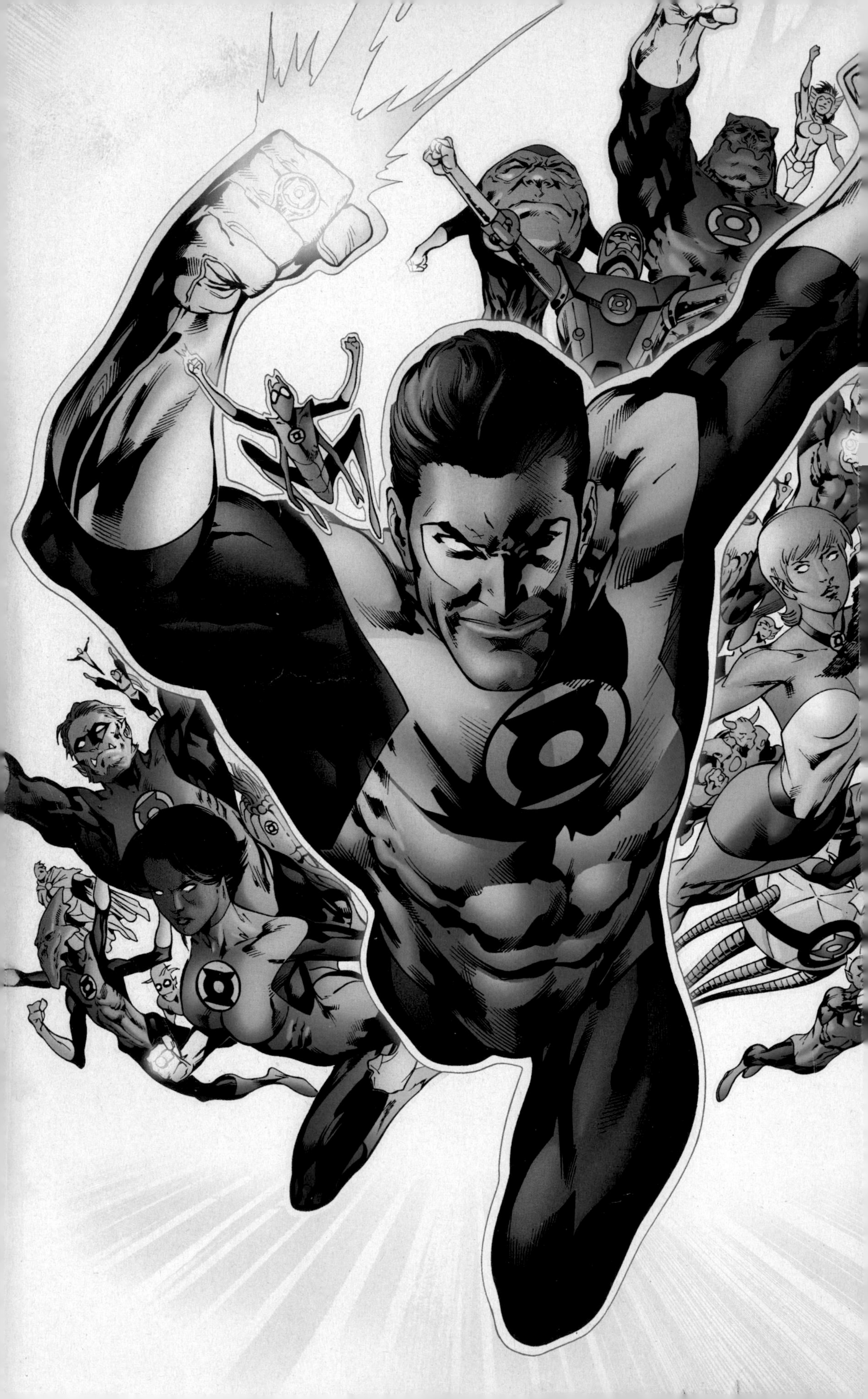

GREEN LANTERN

THE SINESTRO CORPS WAR

Geoff Johns   Dave Gibbons
Writers

Ethan Van Sciver   Ivan Reis   Patrick Gleason   Angel Unzeta
Pencillers

Ethan Van Sciver   Oclair Albert   Prentis Rollins   Drew Geraci
Inkers

Moose Baumann   Guy Major
Colorists

Rob Leigh   Phil Balsman
Letterers

DC COMICS

Dan DiDio Senior VP-Executive Editor
Eddie Berganza Peter Tomasi
Editors-original series
Adam Schlagman Elisabeth V. Gehrlein
Assistant Editors-original series
Bob Joy Editor-collected edition
Robbin Brosterman Senior Art Director
Paul Levitz President & Publisher
Georg Brewer VP-Design & DC Direct Creative
Richard Bruning Senior VP-Creative Director
Patrick Caldon Executive VP-Finance & Operations
Chris Caramalis VP-Finance
John Cunningham VP-Marketing
Terri Cunningham VP-Managing Editor
Alison Gill VP-Manufacturing
David Hyde VP-Publicity
Hank Kanalz VP-General Manager, WildStorm
Jim Lee Editorial Director-WildStorm
Paula Lowitt Senior VP-Business & Legal Affairs
MaryEllen McLaughlin VP-Advertising &
Custom Publishing
John Nee Senior VP-Business Development
Gregory Noveck Senior VP-Creative Affairs
Sue Pohja VP-Book Trade Sales
Steve Rotterdam Senior VP-Sales & Marketing
Cheryl Rubin Senior VP-Brand Management
Jeff Trojan VP-Business Development, DC Direct
Bob Wayne VP-Sales

Cover art by Ethan Van Sciver and Moose Bauman.

GREEN LANTERN: THE SINESTRO CORPS WAR
Volume 1
Published by DC Comics. Cover and compilation copyright © 2008
DC Comics. All Rights Reserved.

Originally published in single magazine form in GREEN LANTERN 21-23,
GREEN LANTERN CORPS 14-15, GREEN LANTERN: SINESTRO CORPS
SPECIAL. Copyright © 2007 DC Comics. All Rights Reserved.
All characters, their distinctive likenesses and related elements
featured in this publication are trademarks of DC Comics.
The stories, characters and incidents featured in this publication are
entirely fictional. DC Comics does not read or accept unsolicited
submissions of ideas, stories or artwork.

DC Comics, 1700 Broadway, New York, NY 10019
A Warner Bros. Entertainment Company
Printed in Canada. First Printing.

Hardcover ISBN: 978-1-4012-1650-4
Softcover ISBN: 978-1-4012-1870-6

GREEN LANTERN: SINESTRO CORPS SPECIAL
Ethan Van Sciver
Moose Baumann

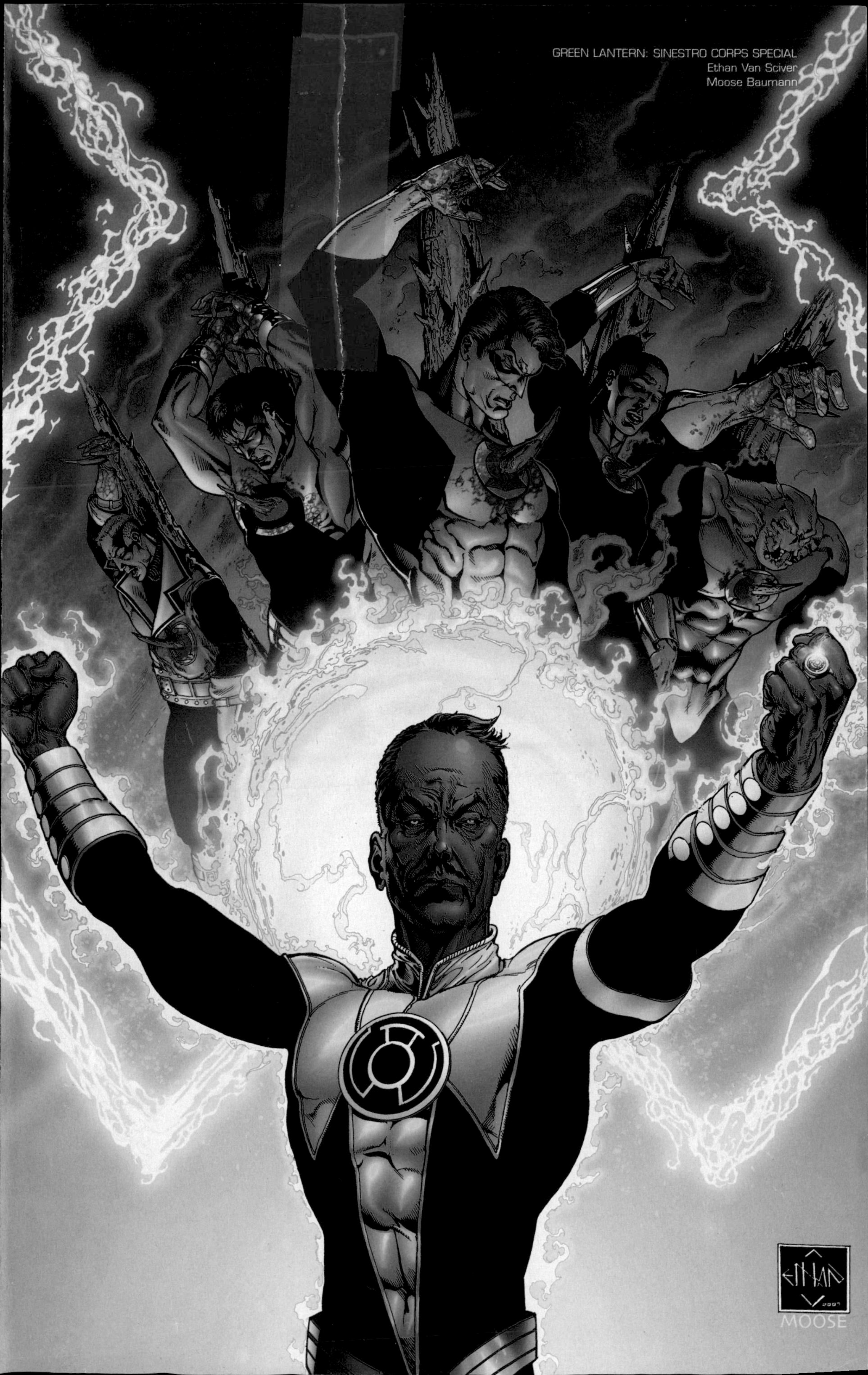

THE SINESTRO CORPS WAR
Prologue
THE SECOND REBIRTH
Writer: **Geoff Johns**
Artist: **Ethan Van Sciver**
Colorist: **Moose Baumann**

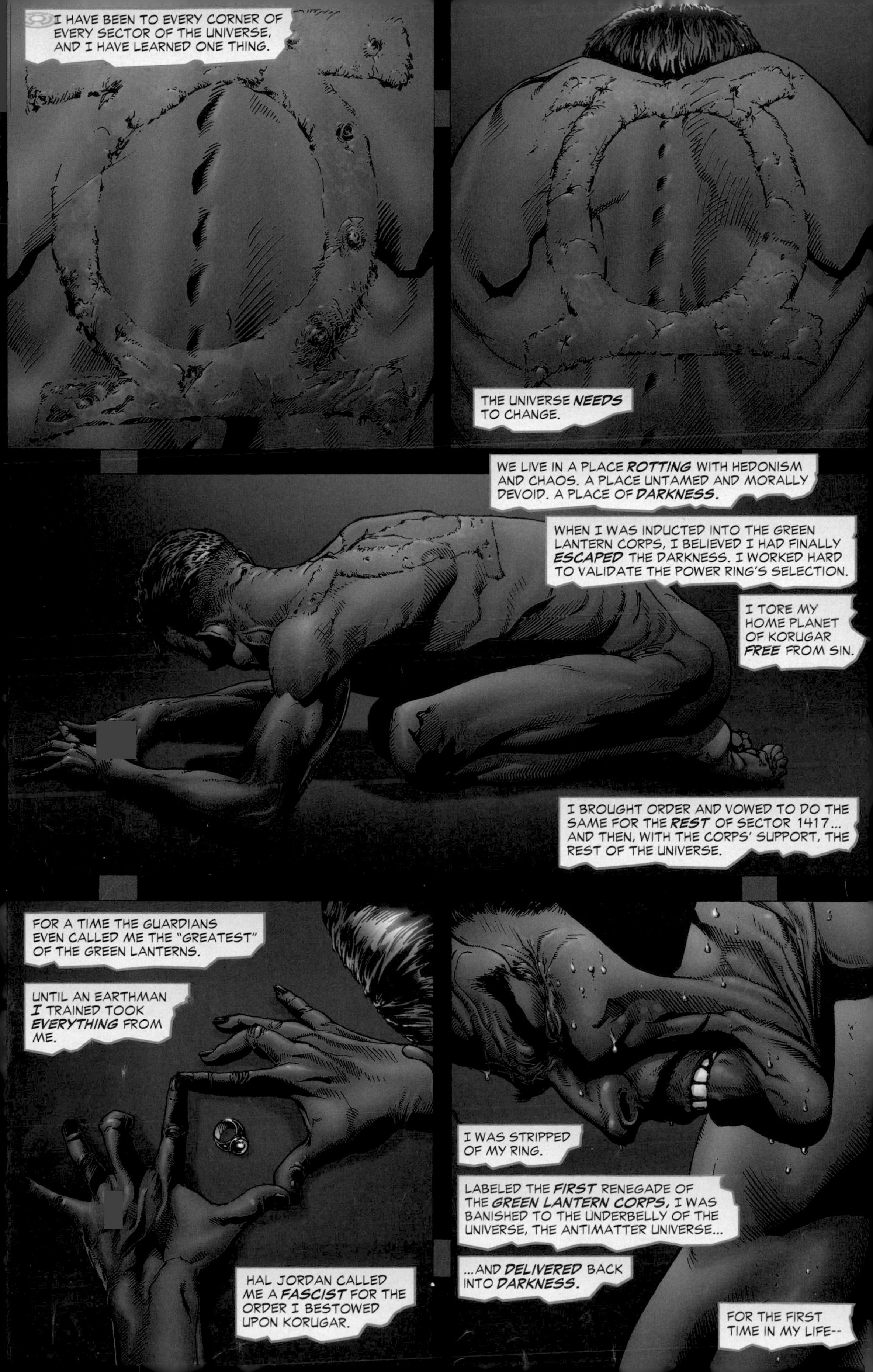
I HAVE BEEN TO EVERY CORNER OF EVERY SECTOR OF THE UNIVERSE, AND I HAVE LEARNED ONE THING.
THE UNIVERSE NEEDS TO CHANGE.
WE LIVE IN A PLACE ROTTING WITH HEDONISM AND CHAOS. A PLACE UNTAMED AND MORALLY DEVOID. A PLACE OF DARKNESS.
WHEN I WAS INDUCTED INTO THE GREEN LANTERN CORPS, I BELIEVED I HAD FINALLY ESCAPED THE DARKNESS. I WORKED HARD TO VALIDATE THE POWER RING'S SELECTION.
I TORE MY HOME PLANET OF KORUGAR FREE FROM SIN.
I BROUGHT ORDER AND VOWED TO DO THE SAME FOR THE REST OF SECTOR 1417... AND THEN, WITH THE CORPS' SUPPORT, THE REST OF THE UNIVERSE.
FOR A TIME THE GUARDIANS EVEN CALLED ME THE "GREATEST" OF THE GREEN LANTERNS.
UNTIL AN EARTHMAN I TRAINED TOOK EVERYTHING FROM ME.
HAL JORDAN CALLED ME A FASCIST FOR THE ORDER I BESTOWED UPON KORUGAR.
I WAS STRIPPED OF MY RING.
LABELED THE FIRST RENEGADE OF THE GREEN LANTERN CORPS, I WAS BANISHED TO THE UNDERBELLY OF THE UNIVERSE, THE ANTIMATTER UNIVERSE...
...AND DELIVERED BACK INTO DARKNESS.
FOR THE FIRST TIME IN MY LIFE--

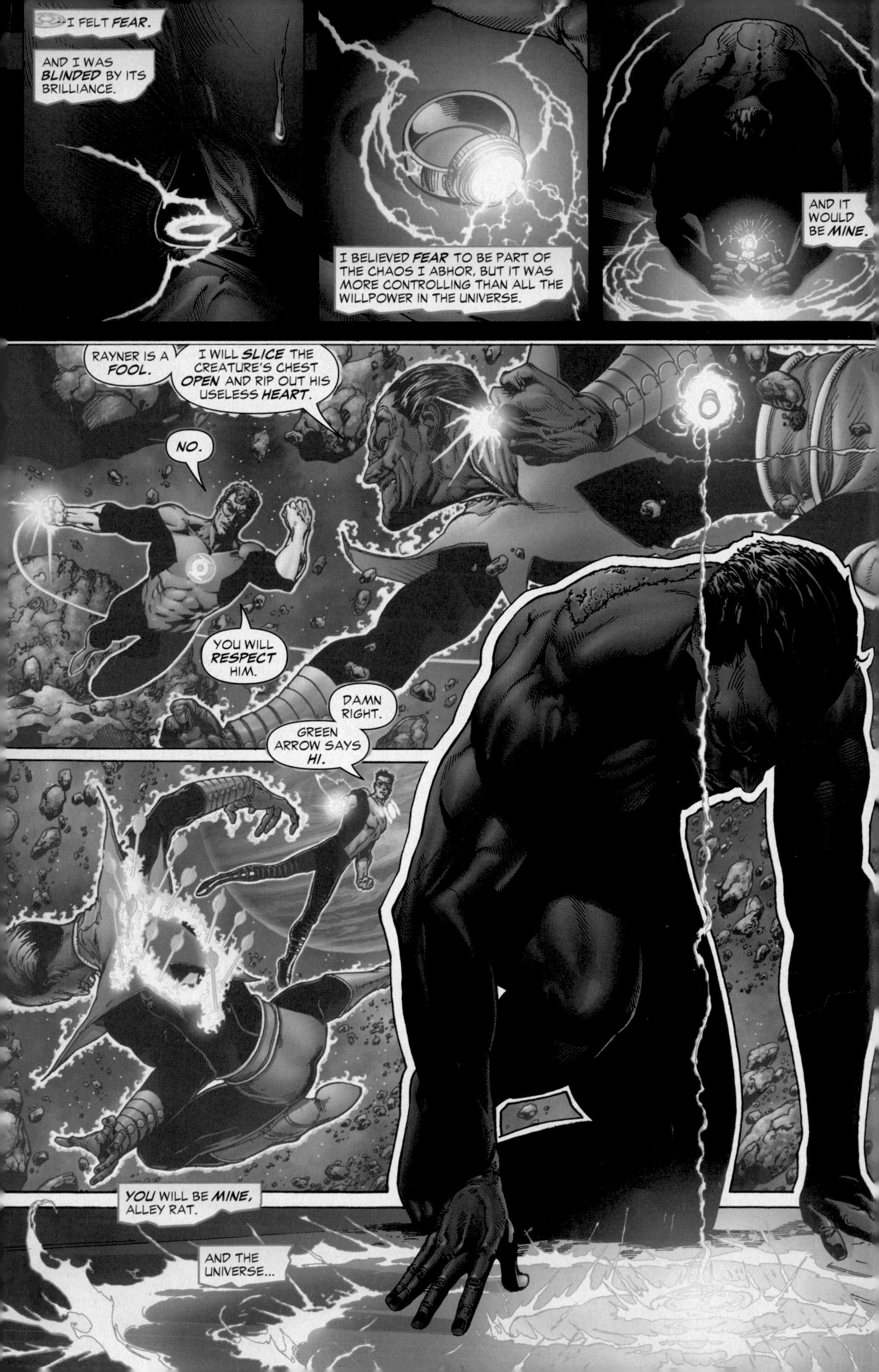

...I FELT FEAR.
AND I WAS BLINDED BY ITS BRILLIANCE.
I BELIEVED FEAR TO BE PART OF THE CHAOS I ABHOR, BUT IT WAS MORE CONTROLLING THAN ALL THE WILLPOWER IN THE UNIVERSE.
AND IT WOULD BE MINE.
RAYNER IS A FOOL.
I WILL SLICE THE CREATURE'S CHEST OPEN AND RIP OUT HIS USELESS HEART.
NO.
YOU WILL RESPECT HIM.
DAMN RIGHT.
GREEN ARROW SAYS HI.
YOU WILL BE MINE, ALLEY RAT.
AND THE UNIVERSE...

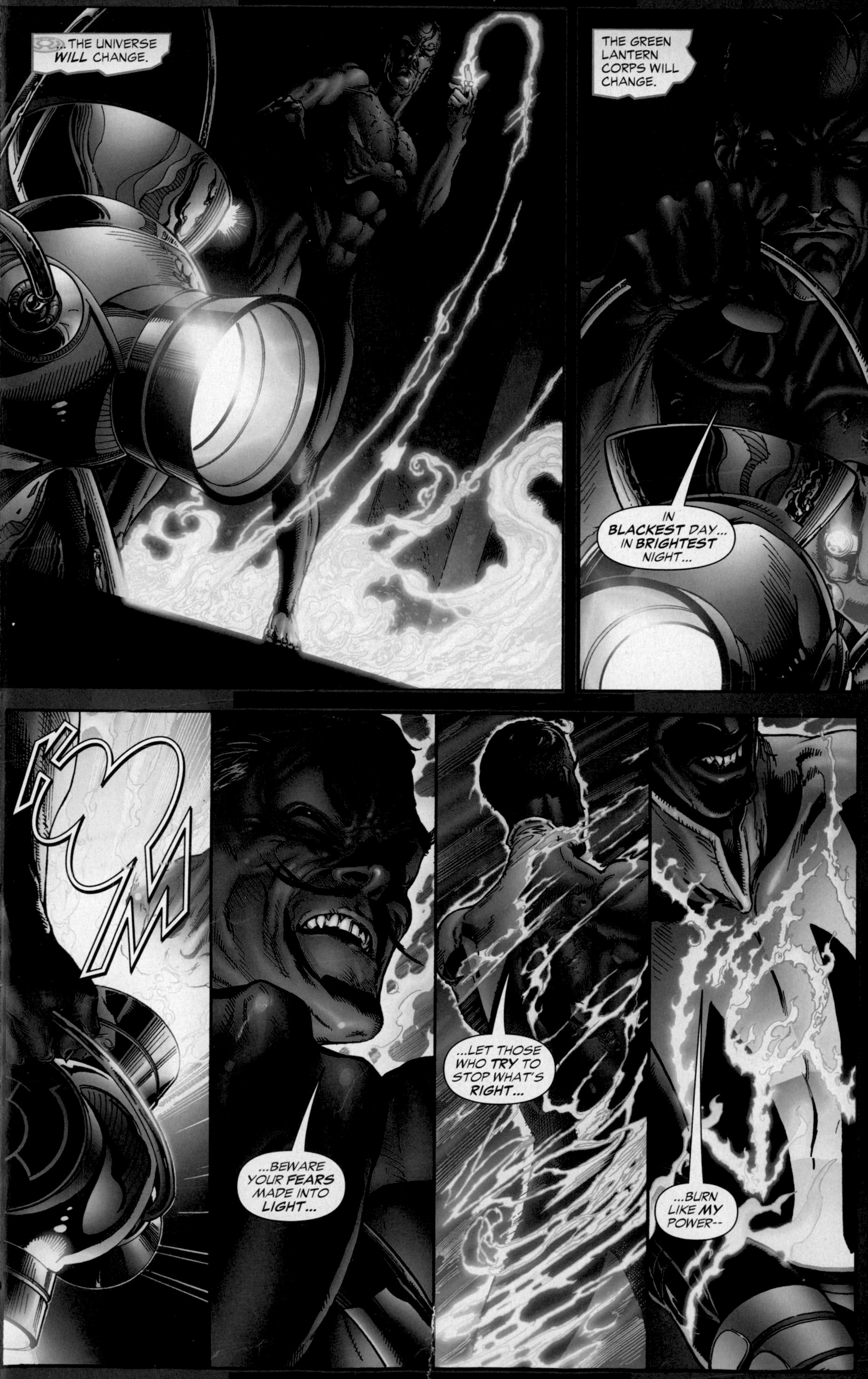
...THE UNIVERSE WILL CHANGE.
THE GREEN LANTERN CORPS WILL CHANGE.
IN BLACKEST DAY... IN BRIGHTEST NIGHT...
...BEWARE YOUR FEARS MADE INTO LIGHT...
...LET THOSE WHO TRY TO STOP WHAT'S RIGHT...
...BURN LIKE MY POWER--

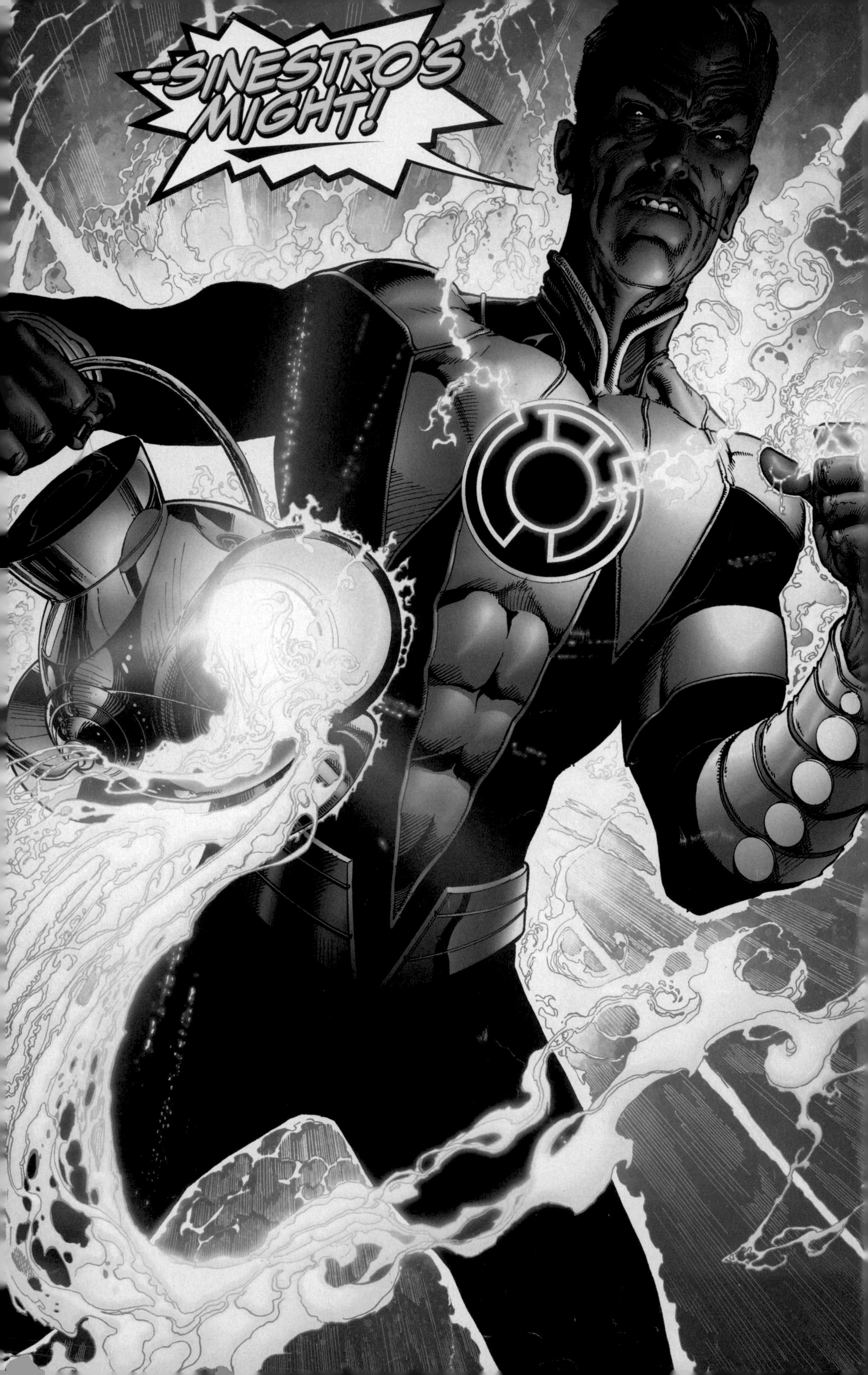
--SINESTRO'S MIGHT!

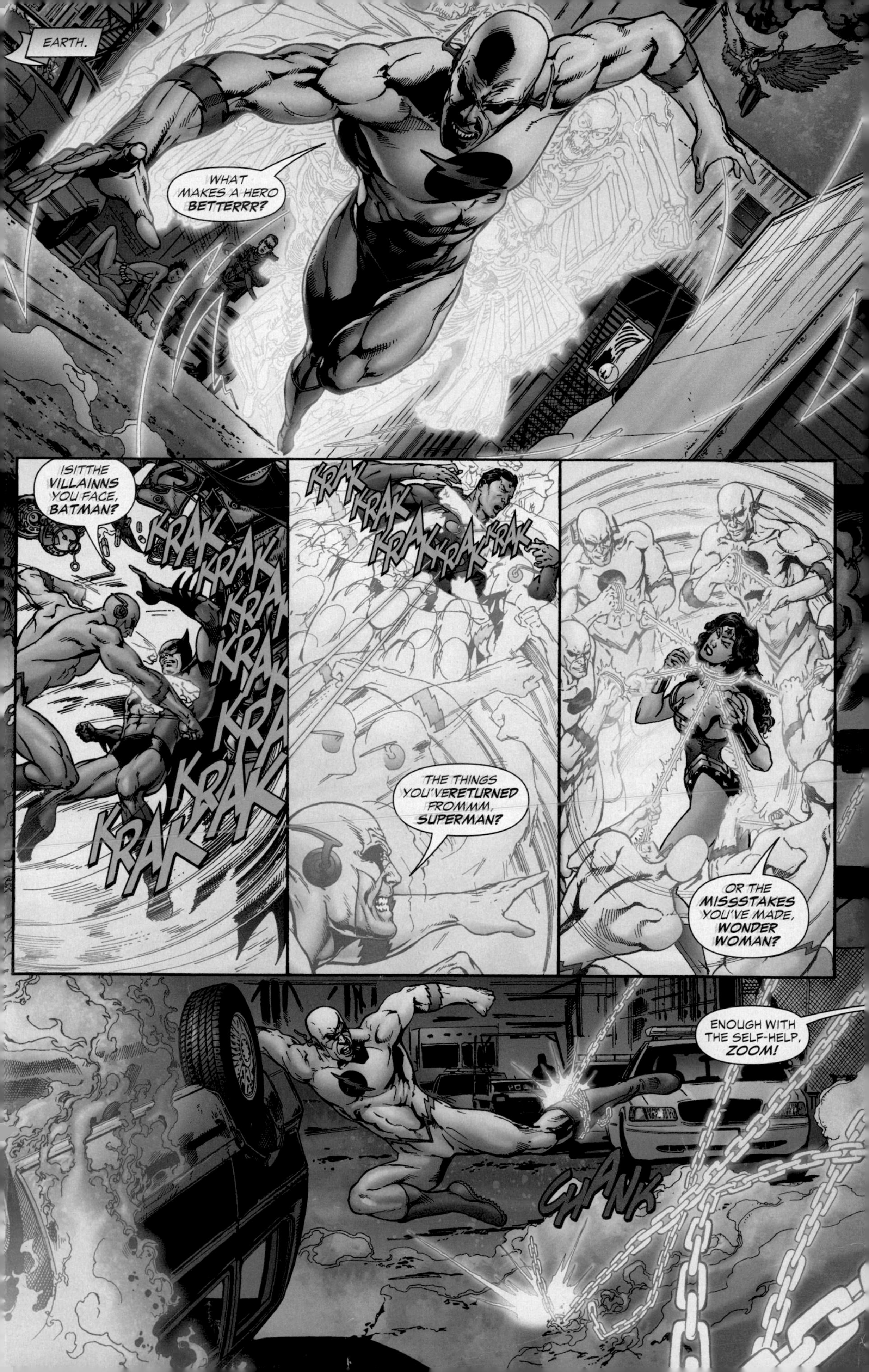
EARTH.
WHAT MAKES A HERO BETTERRR?
ISITTHE VILLAINNS YOU FACE, BATMAN?
KRAK KRAK KRAK KRAK KRAK KRAK KRAK KRAK KRAK
KRAK KRAK KRAK KRAK KRAK
THE THINGS YOU'VERETURNED FROMMM, SUPERMAN?
OR THE MISSSTAKES YOU'VE MADE, WONDER WOMAN?
ENOUGH WITH THE SELF-HELP, ZOOM!
CHANK

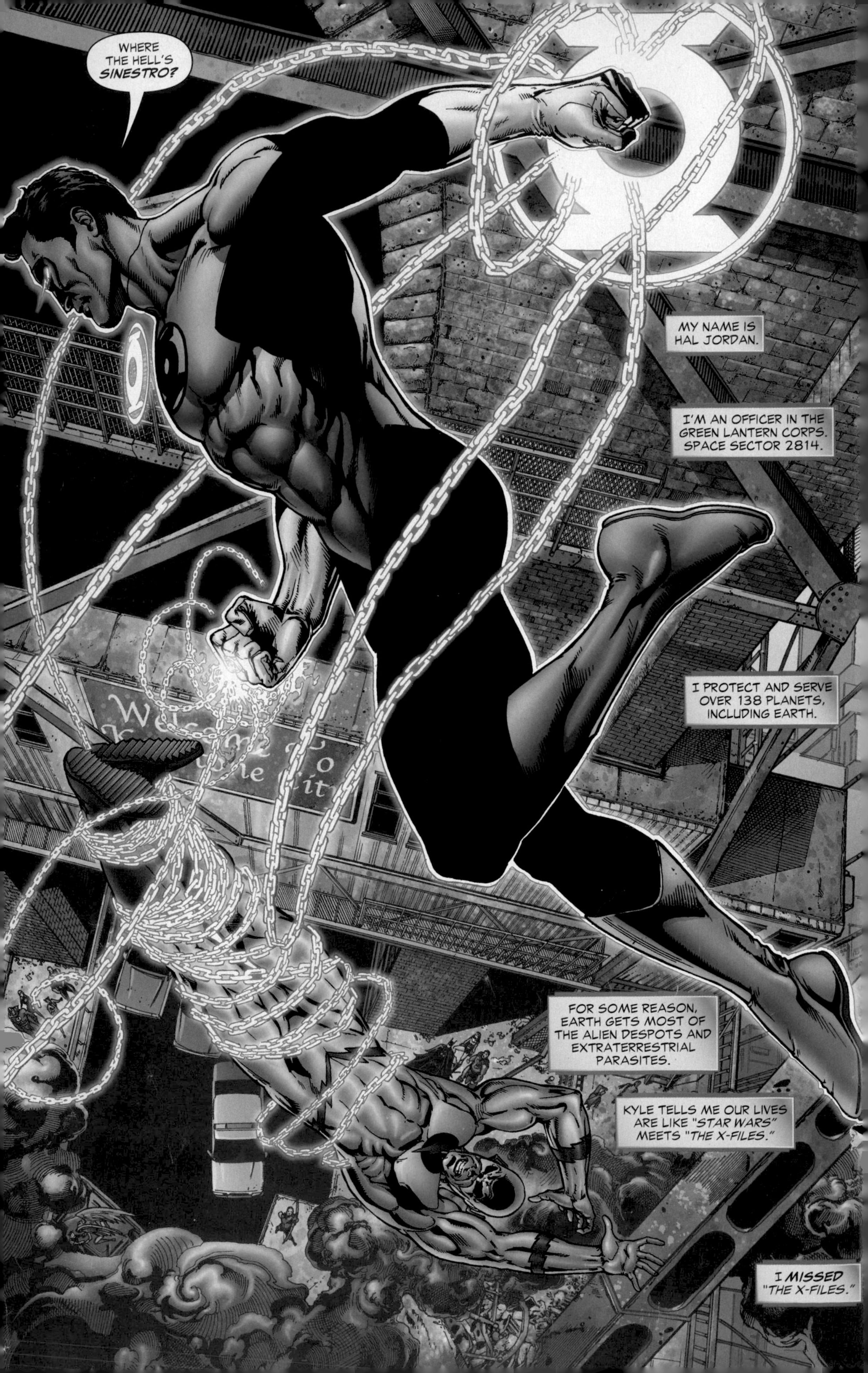
WHERE THE HELL'S *SINESTRO?*
MY NAME IS HAL JORDAN.
I'M AN OFFICER IN THE GREEN LANTERN CORPS. SPACE SECTOR 2814.
I PROTECT AND SERVE OVER 138 PLANETS, INCLUDING EARTH.
FOR SOME REASON, EARTH GETS MOST OF THE ALIEN DESPOTS AND EXTRATERRESTRIAL PARASITES.
KYLE TELLS ME OUR LIVES ARE LIKE "*STAR WARS*" MEETS "*THE X-FILES*."
I *MISSED* "*THE X-FILES*."

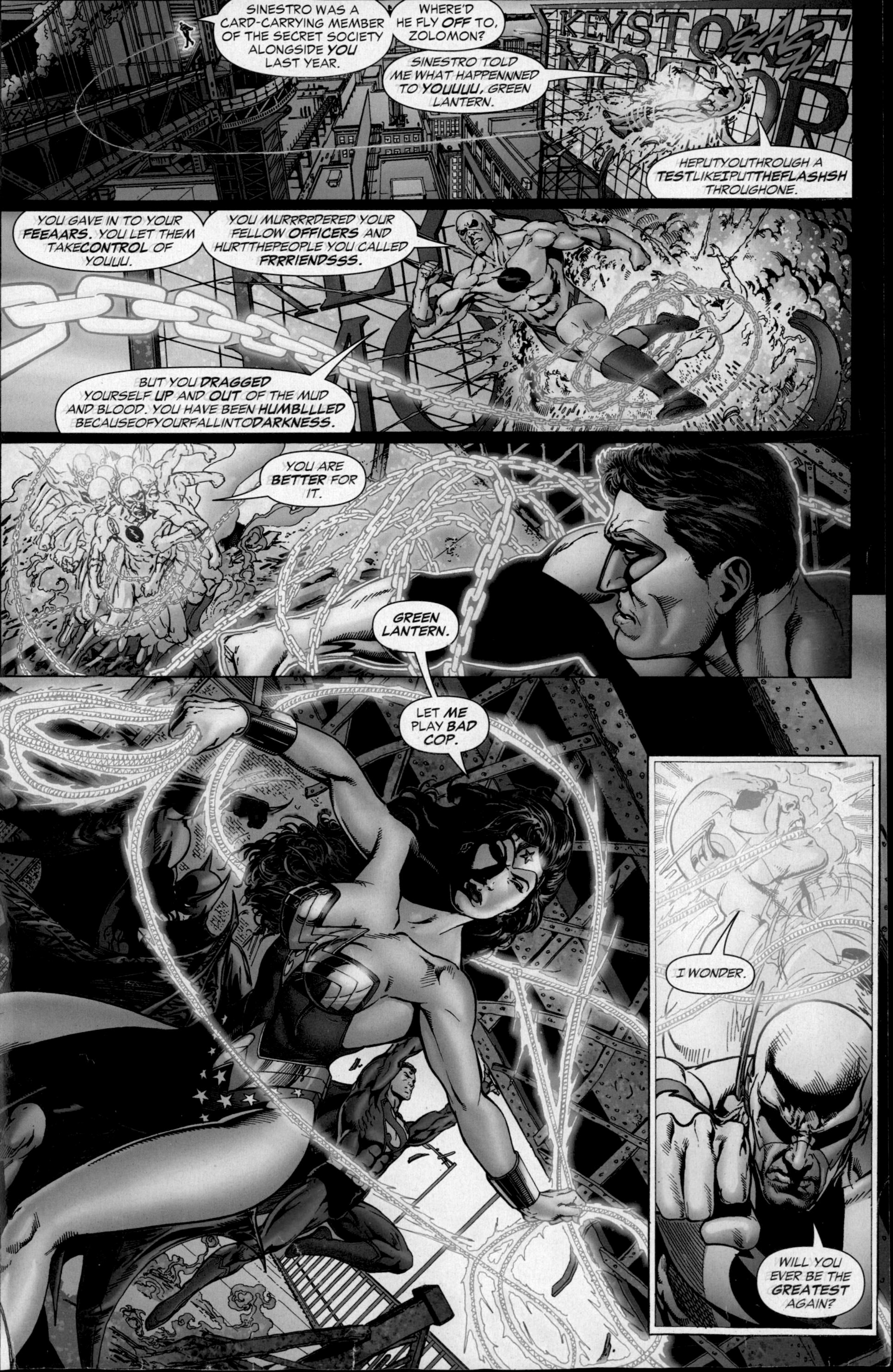
SINESTRO WAS A CARD-CARRYING MEMBER OF THE SECRET SOCIETY ALONGSIDE YOU LAST YEAR.
WHERE'D HE FLY OFF TO, ZOLOMON?
SINESTRO TOLD ME WHAT HAPPENNED TO YOUUUU, GREEN LANTERN.
KRASH
HEPUTYOUTHROUGH A TESTLIKEIPUTTHEFLASHSH THROUGHONE.
YOU GAVE IN TO YOUR FEEAARS. YOU LET THEM TAKECONTROL OF YOUUU.
YOU MURRRRDERED YOUR FELLOW OFFICERS AND HURTTHEPEOPLE YOU CALLED FRRRIENDSSS.
BUT YOU DRAGGED YOURSELF UP AND OUT OF THE MUD AND BLOOD. YOU HAVE BEEN HUMBLLLED BECAUSEOFYOURFALLINTODARKNESS.
YOU ARE BETTER FOR IT.
GREEN LANTERN.
LET ME PLAY BAD COP.
I WONDER.
WILL YOU EVER BE THE GREATEST AGAIN?

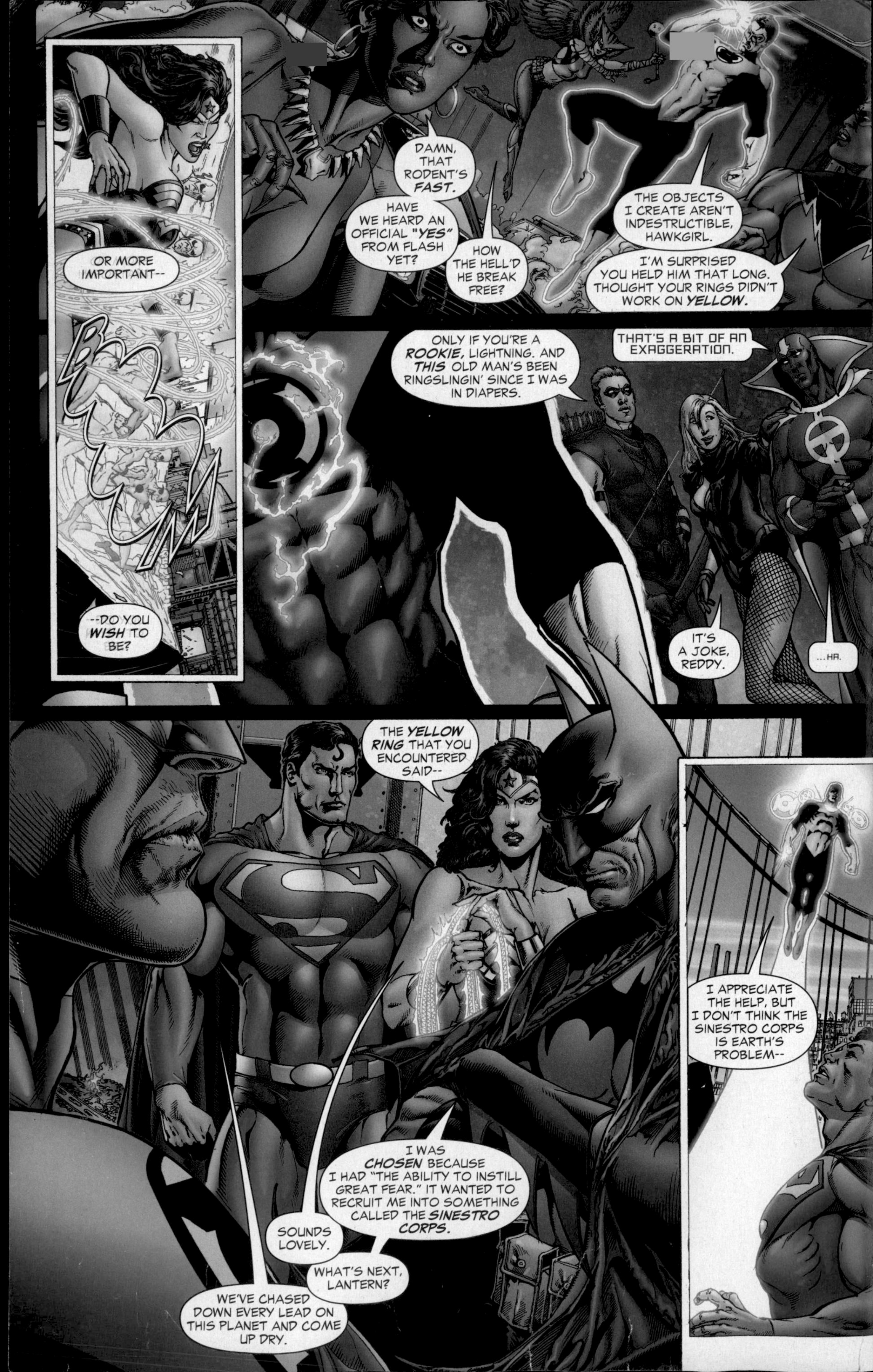

OR MORE IMPORTANT--
--DO YOU WISH TO BE?
DAMN, THAT RODENT'S FAST.
HAVE WE HEARD AN OFFICIAL "YES" FROM FLASH YET?
HOW THE HELL'D HE BREAK FREE?
THE OBJECTS I CREATE AREN'T INDESTRUCTIBLE, HAWKGIRL.
I'M SURPRISED YOU HELD HIM THAT LONG. THOUGHT YOUR RINGS DIDN'T WORK ON YELLOW.
ONLY IF YOU'RE A ROOKIE, LIGHTNING. AND THIS OLD MAN'S BEEN RINGSLINGIN' SINCE I WAS IN DIAPERS.
THAT'S A BIT OF AN EXAGGERATION.
IT'S A JOKE, REDDY.
...HA.
THE YELLOW RING THAT YOU ENCOUNTERED SAID--
I WAS CHOSEN BECAUSE I HAD "THE ABILITY TO INSTILL GREAT FEAR." IT WANTED TO RECRUIT ME INTO SOMETHING CALLED THE SINESTRO CORPS.
SOUNDS LOVELY.
WHAT'S NEXT, LANTERN?
WE'VE CHASED DOWN EVERY LEAD ON THIS PLANET AND COME UP DRY.
I APPRECIATE THE HELP, BUT I DON'T THINK THE SINESTRO CORPS IS EARTH'S PROBLEM--

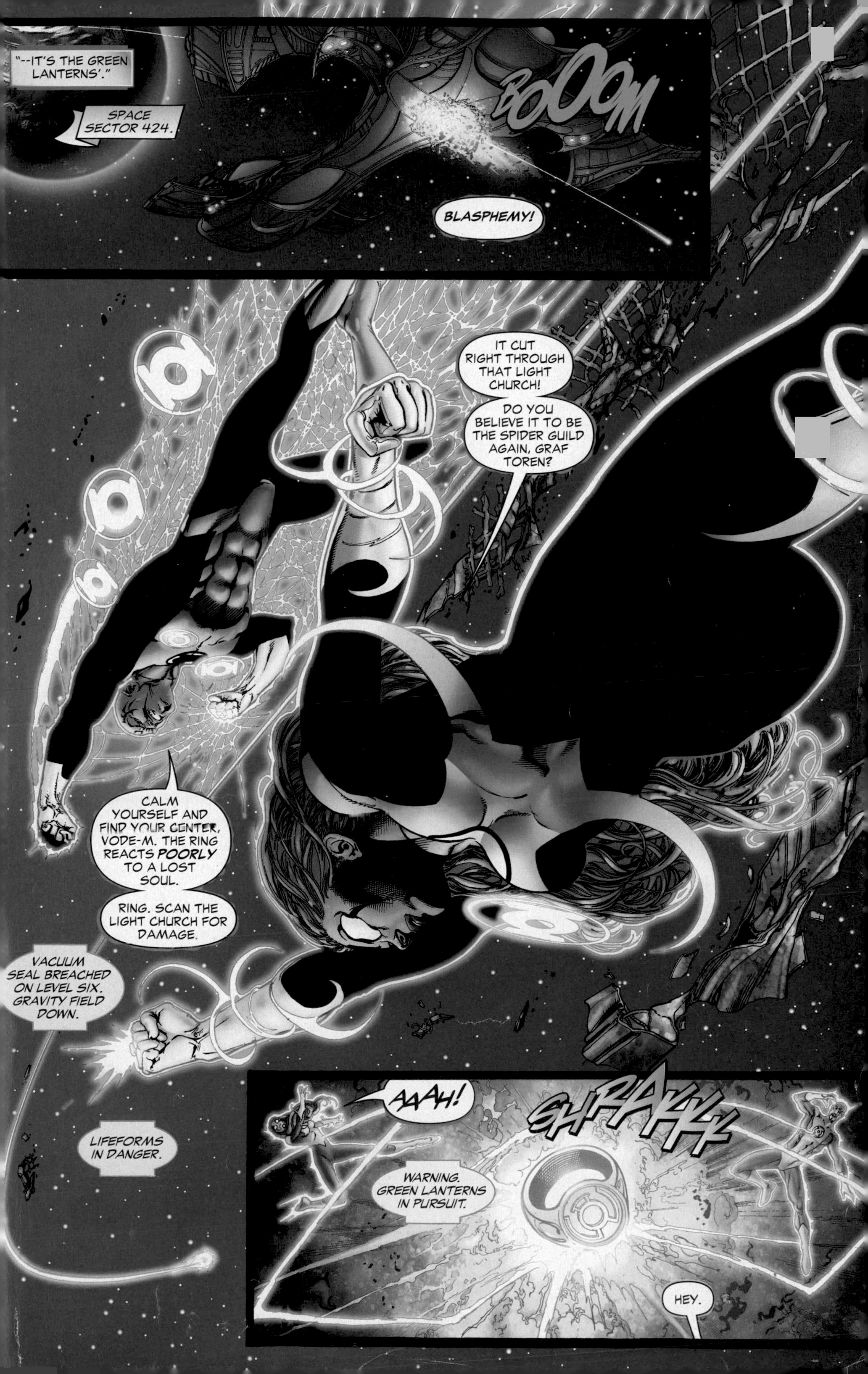
"--IT'S THE GREEN LANTERNS'."
SPACE SECTOR 424.
BOOOM
BLASPHEMY!
IT CUT RIGHT THROUGH THAT LIGHT CHURCH!
DO YOU BELIEVE IT TO BE THE SPIDER GUILD AGAIN, GRAF TOREN?
CALM YOURSELF AND FIND YOUR CENTER, VODE-M. THE RING REACTS POORLY TO A LOST SOUL.
RING. SCAN THE LIGHT CHURCH FOR DAMAGE.
VACUUM SEAL BREACHED ON LEVEL SIX. GRAVITY FIELD DOWN.
LIFEFORMS IN DANGER.
AAAH!
SHRAKKK
WARNING. GREEN LANTERNS IN PURSUIT.
HEY.

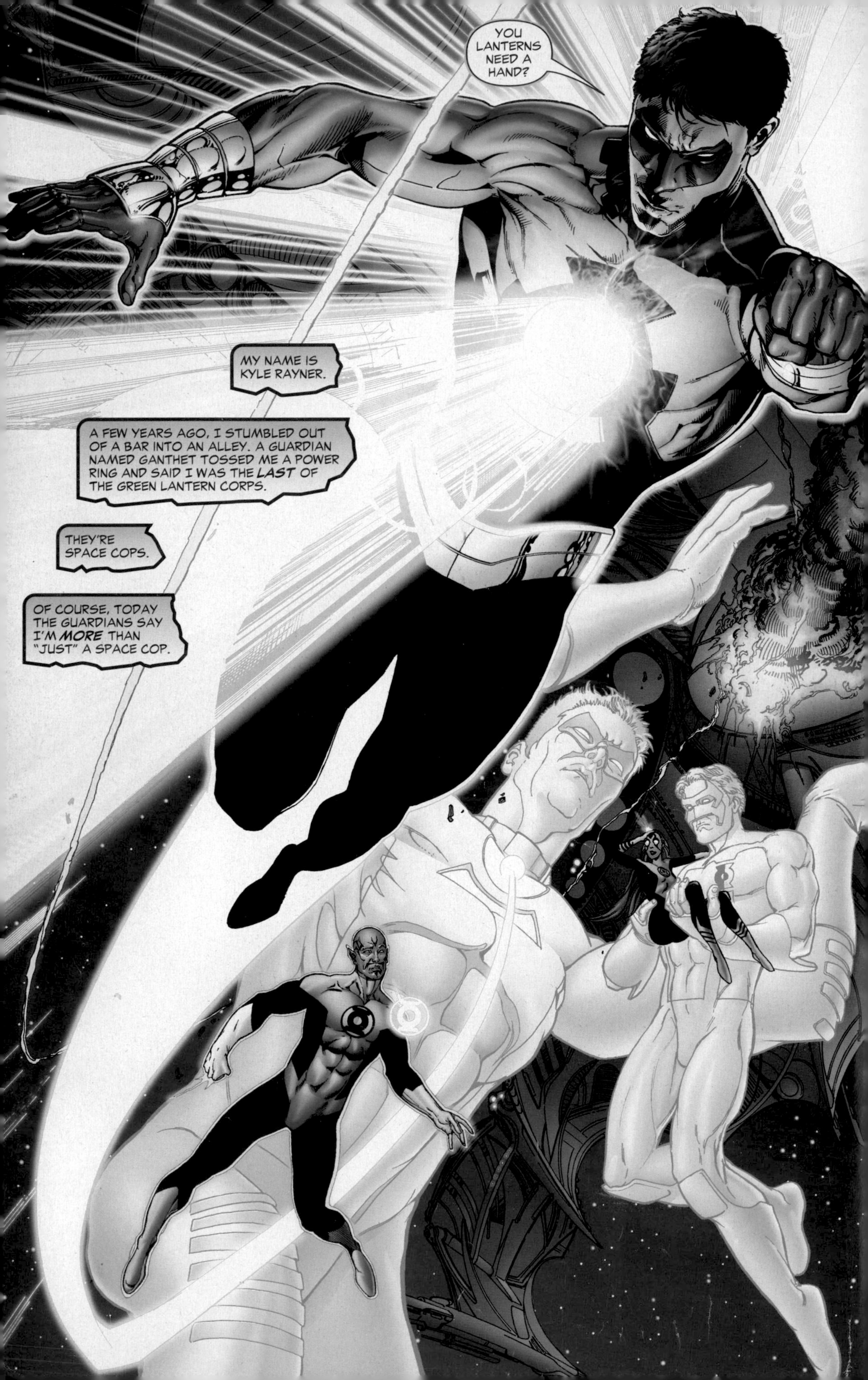
YOU LANTERNS NEED A HAND?
MY NAME IS KYLE RAYNER.
A FEW YEARS AGO, I STUMBLED OUT OF A BAR INTO AN ALLEY. A GUARDIAN NAMED GANTHET TOSSED ME A POWER RING AND SAID I WAS THE LAST OF THE GREEN LANTERN CORPS.
THEY'RE SPACE COPS.
OF COURSE, TODAY THE GUARDIANS SAY I'M MORE THAN "JUST" A SPACE COP.

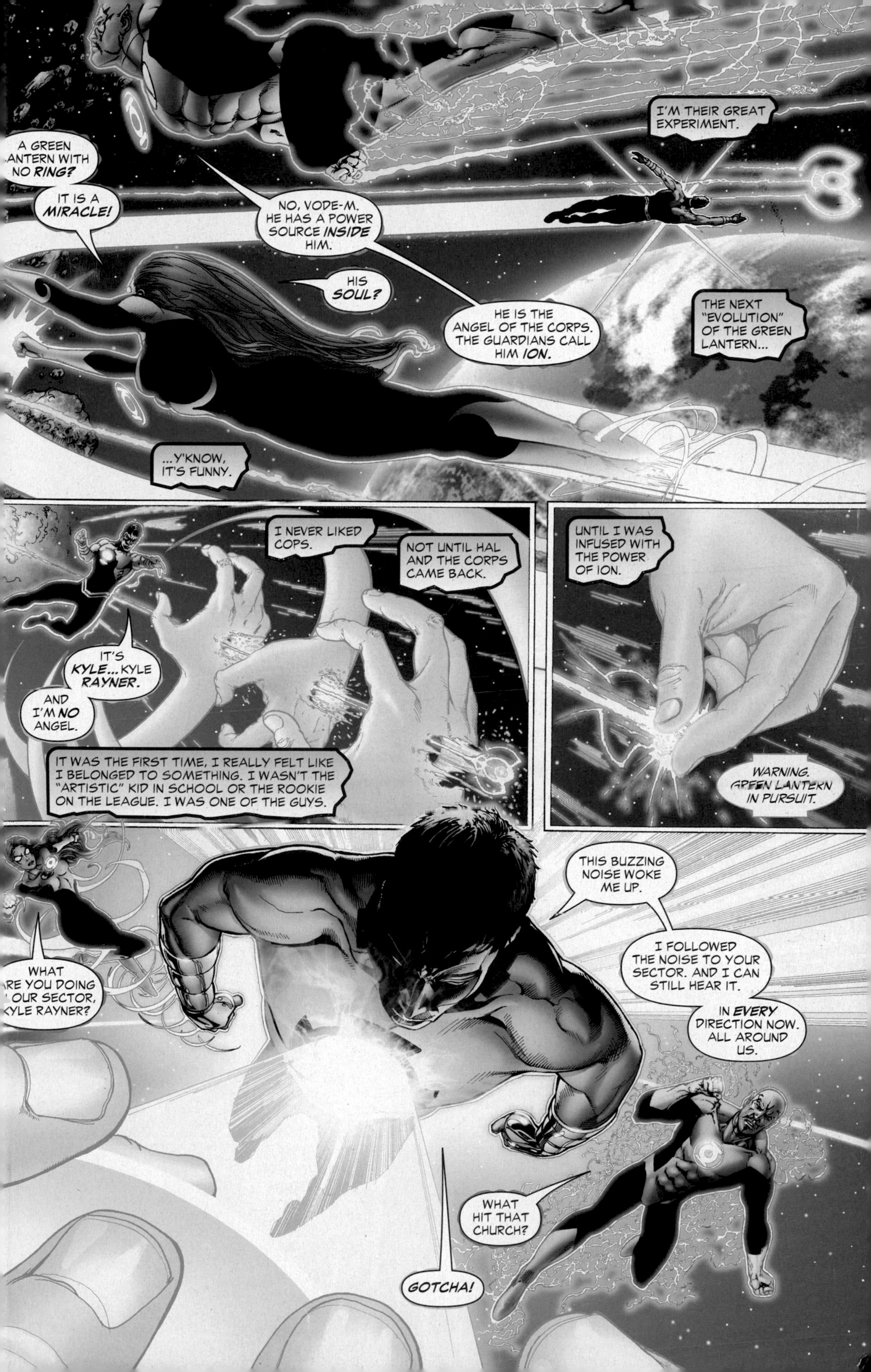
A GREEN LANTERN WITH NO RING?
IT IS A MIRACLE!
NO, VODE-M. HE HAS A POWER SOURCE INSIDE HIM.
HIS SOUL?
HE IS THE ANGEL OF THE CORPS. THE GUARDIANS CALL HIM ION.
I'M THEIR GREAT EXPERIMENT.
THE NEXT "EVOLUTION" OF THE GREEN LANTERN...
...Y'KNOW, IT'S FUNNY.
I NEVER LIKED COPS.
NOT UNTIL HAL AND THE CORPS CAME BACK.
IT'S KYLE... KYLE RAYNER.
AND I'M NO ANGEL.
IT WAS THE FIRST TIME, I REALLY FELT LIKE I BELONGED TO SOMETHING. I WASN'T THE "ARTISTIC" KID IN SCHOOL OR THE ROOKIE ON THE LEAGUE. I WAS ONE OF THE GUYS.
UNTIL I WAS INFUSED WITH THE POWER OF ION.
WARNING. GREEN LANTERN IN PURSUIT.
WHAT ARE YOU DOING OUR SECTOR, KYLE RAYNER?
THIS BUZZING NOISE WOKE ME UP.
I FOLLOWED THE NOISE TO YOUR SECTOR. AND I CAN STILL HEAR IT.
IN EVERY DIRECTION NOW. ALL AROUND US.
WHAT HIT THAT CHURCH?
GOTCHA!

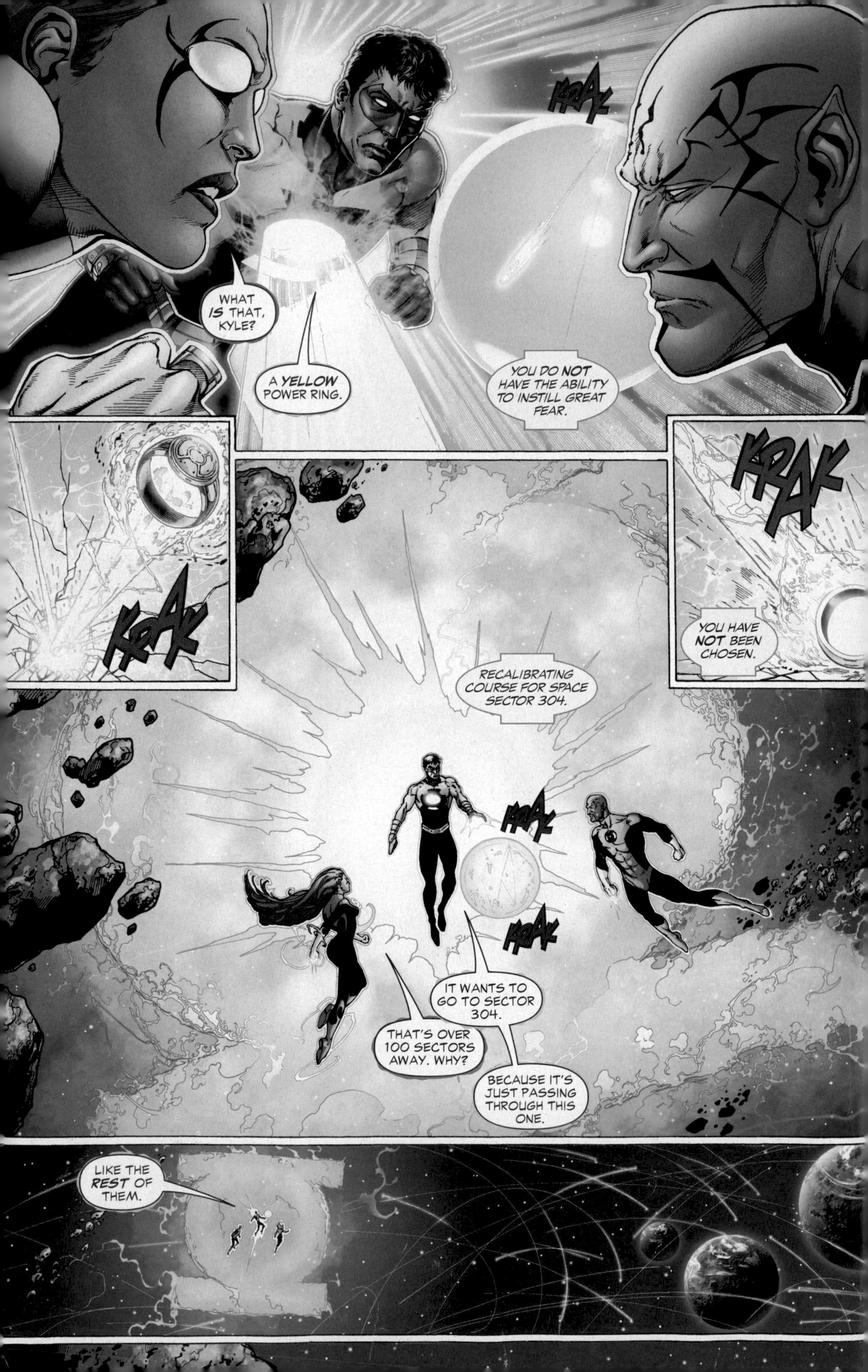
KRAK
WHAT IS THAT, KYLE?
A YELLOW POWER RING.
YOU DO NOT HAVE THE ABILITY TO INSTILL GREAT FEAR.
KRAK
KRAK
YOU HAVE NOT BEEN CHOSEN.
RECALIBRATING COURSE FOR SPACE SECTOR 304.
KRAK
KRAK
IT WANTS TO GO TO SECTOR 304.
THAT'S OVER 100 SECTORS AWAY. WHY?
BECAUSE IT'S JUST PASSING THROUGH THIS ONE.
LIKE THE REST OF THEM.

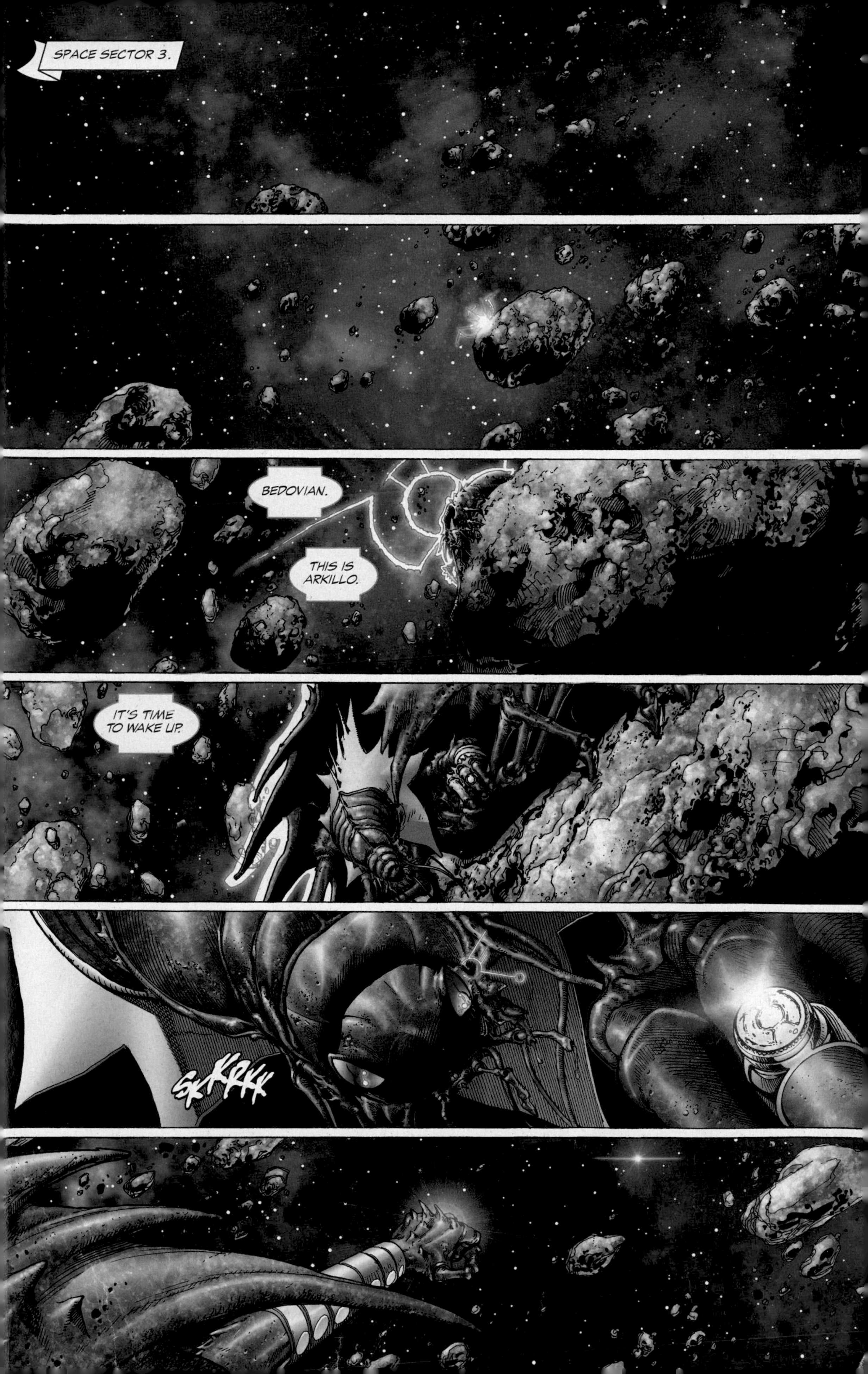
SPACE SECTOR 3.
BEDOVIAN.
THIS IS ARKILLO.
IT'S TIME TO WAKE UP.
SKKRKK

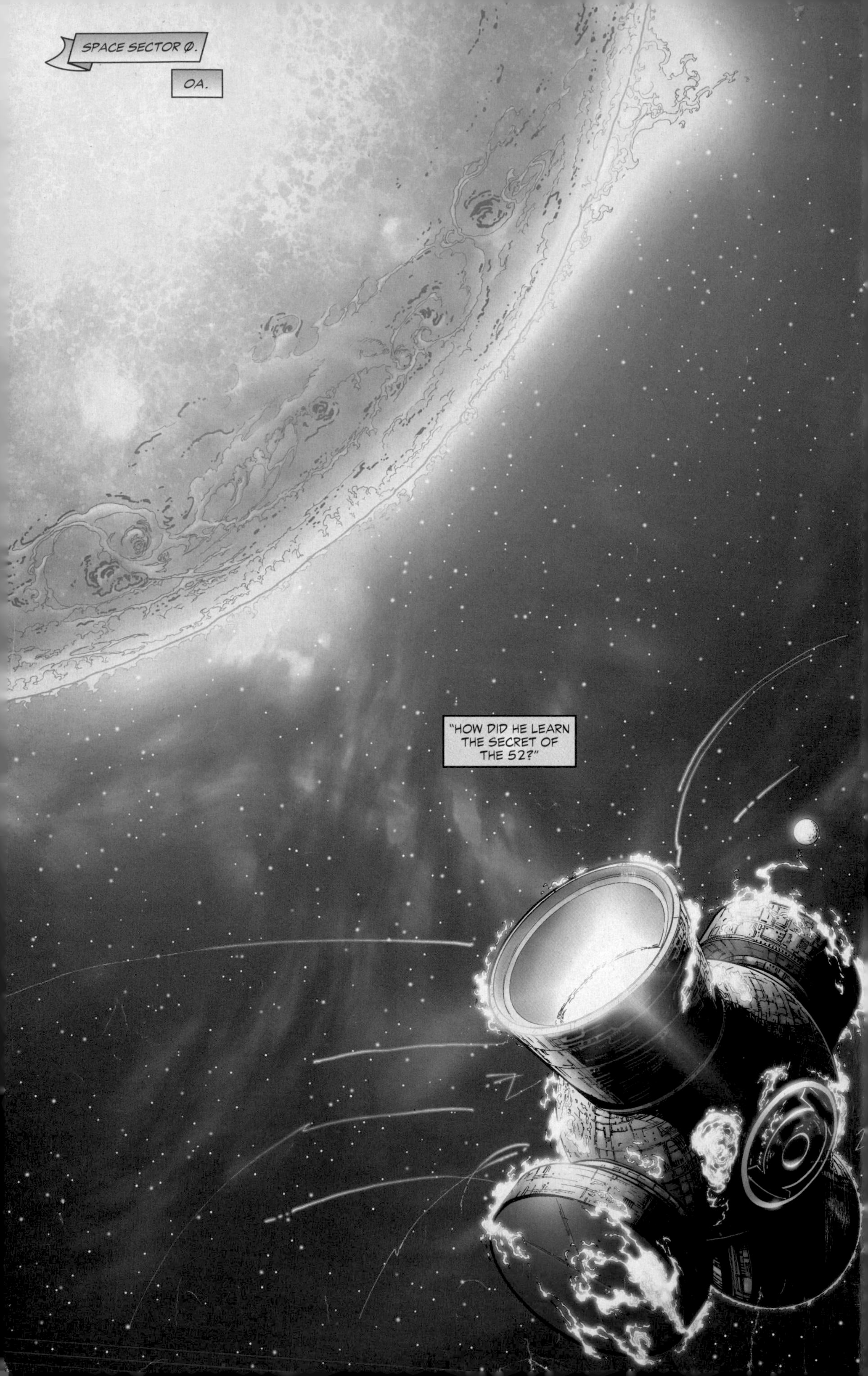
SPACE SECTOR Ø.
OA.
"HOW DID HE LEARN THE SECRET OF THE 52?"

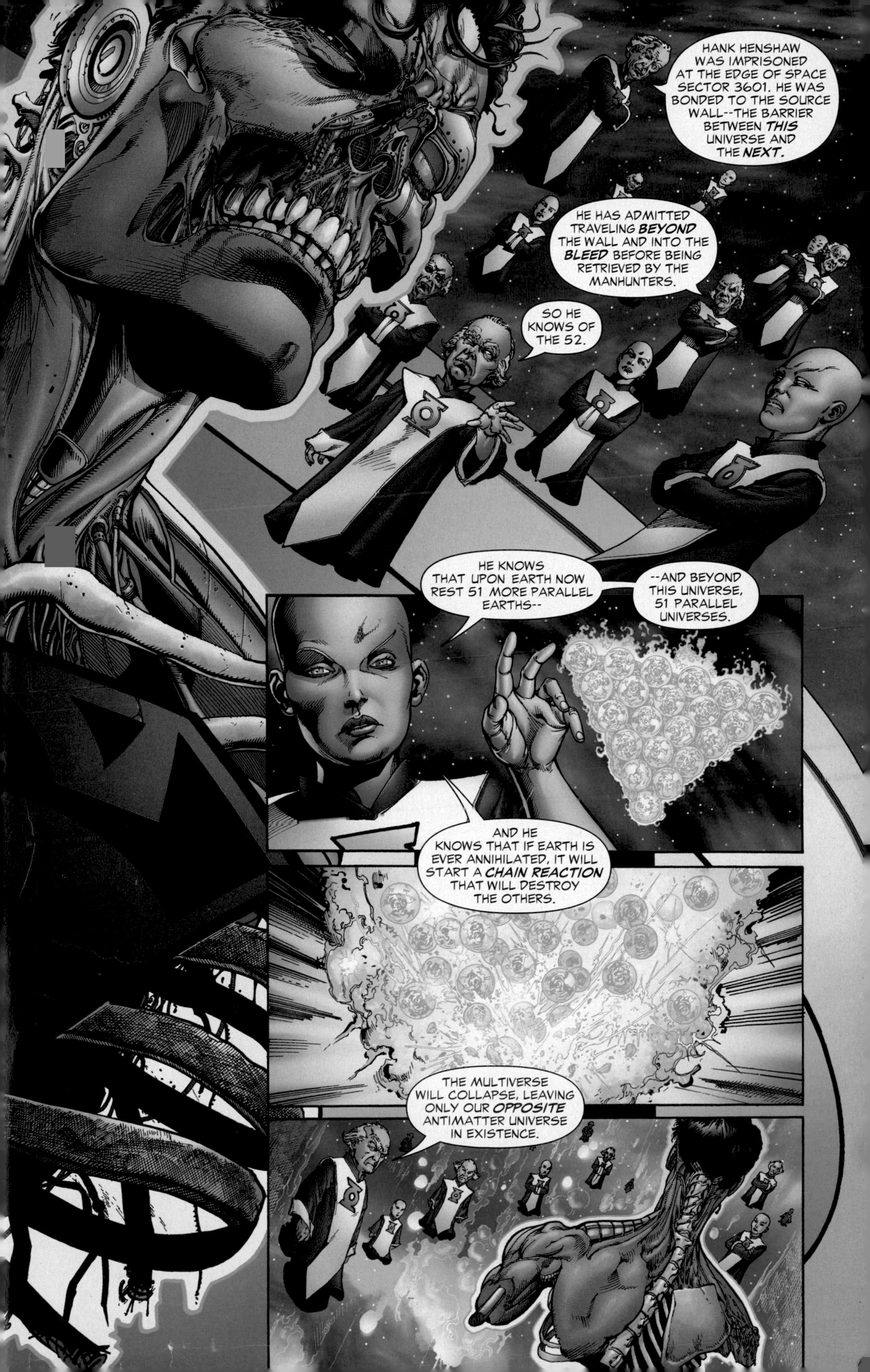
HANK HENSHAW WAS IMPRISONED AT THE EDGE OF SPACE SECTOR 3601. HE WAS BONDED TO THE SOURCE WALL--THE BARRIER BETWEEN *THIS* UNIVERSE AND THE *NEXT.*
HE HAS ADMITTED TRAVELING *BEYOND* THE WALL AND INTO THE *BLEED* BEFORE BEING RETRIEVED BY THE MANHUNTERS.
SO HE KNOWS OF THE 52.
HE KNOWS THAT UPON EARTH NOW REST 51 MORE PARALLEL EARTHS--
--AND BEYOND THIS UNIVERSE, 51 PARALLEL UNIVERSES.
AND HE KNOWS THAT IF EARTH IS EVER ANNIHILATED, IT WILL START A *CHAIN REACTION* THAT WILL DESTROY THE OTHERS.
THE MULTIVERSE WILL COLLAPSE, LEAVING ONLY OUR *OPPOSITE* ANTIMATTER UNIVERSE IN EXISTENCE.

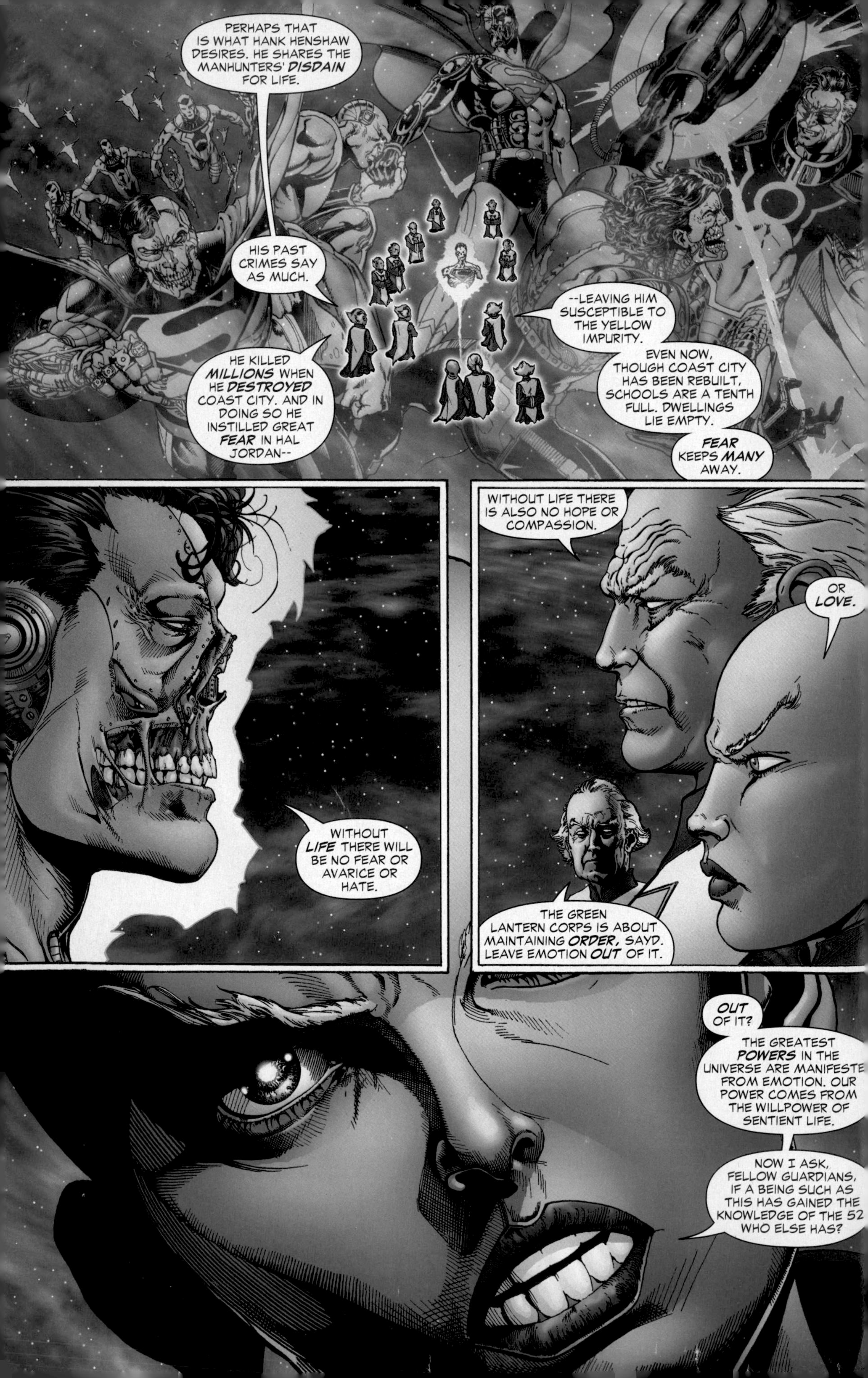
PERHAPS THAT IS WHAT HANK HENSHAW DESIRES. HE SHARES THE MANHUNTERS' DISDAIN FOR LIFE.
HIS PAST CRIMES SAY AS MUCH.
HE KILLED MILLIONS WHEN HE DESTROYED COAST CITY. AND IN DOING SO HE INSTILLED GREAT FEAR IN HAL JORDAN--
--LEAVING HIM SUSCEPTIBLE TO THE YELLOW IMPURITY.
EVEN NOW, THOUGH COAST CITY HAS BEEN REBUILT, SCHOOLS ARE A TENTH FULL. DWELLINGS LIE EMPTY.
FEAR KEEPS MANY AWAY.
WITHOUT LIFE THERE WILL BE NO FEAR OR AVARICE OR HATE.
WITHOUT LIFE THERE IS ALSO NO HOPE OR COMPASSION.
OR LOVE.
THE GREEN LANTERN CORPS IS ABOUT MAINTAINING ORDER, SAYD. LEAVE EMOTION OUT OF IT.
OUT OF IT?
THE GREATEST POWERS IN THE UNIVERSE ARE MANIFESTE FROM EMOTION. OUR POWER COMES FROM THE WILLPOWER OF SENTIENT LIFE.
NOW I ASK, FELLOW GUARDIANS, IF A BEING SUCH AS THIS HAS GAINED THE KNOWLEDGE OF THE 52 WHO ELSE HAS?

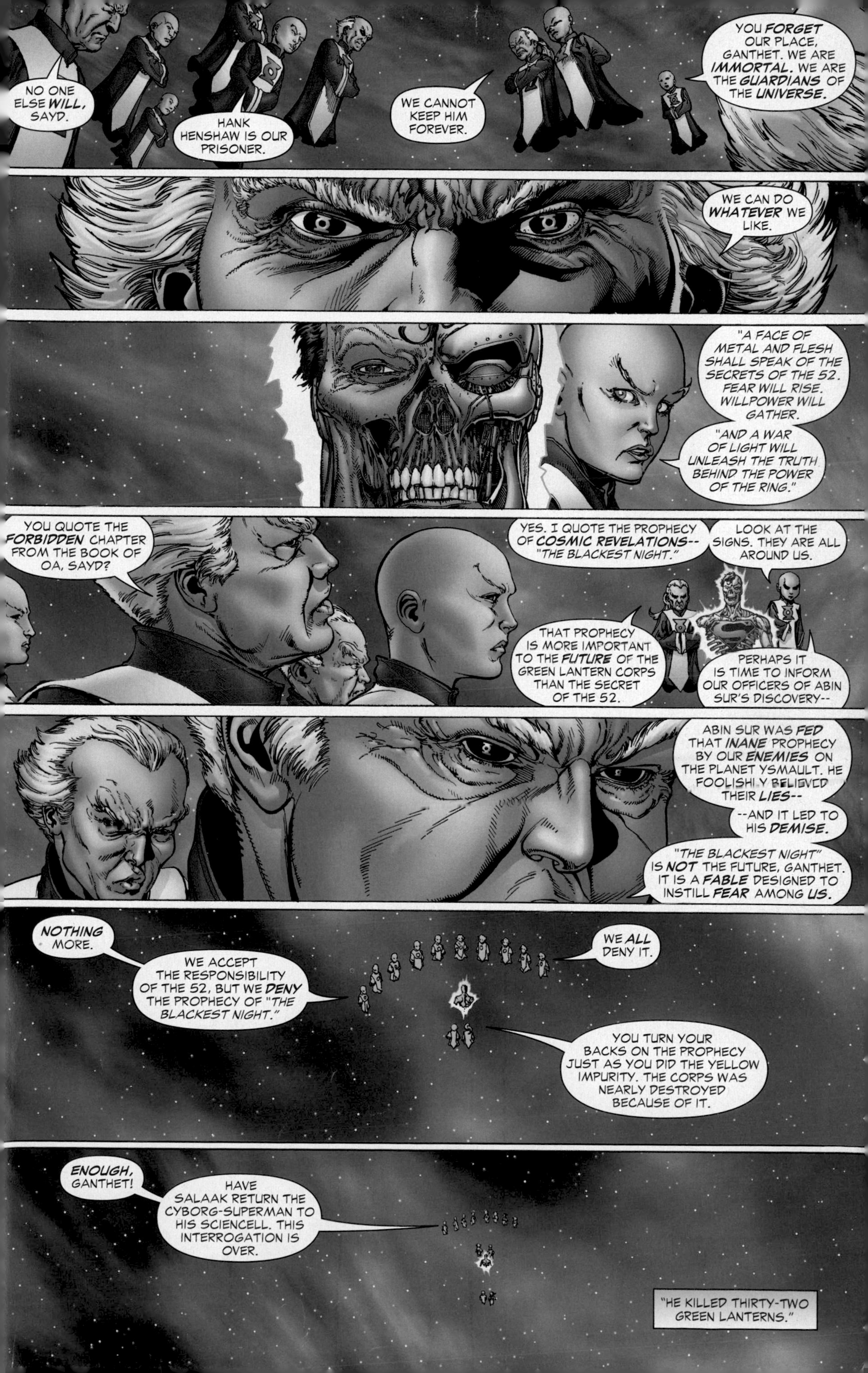
NO ONE ELSE WILL, SAYD.
HANK HENSHAW IS OUR PRISONER.
WE CANNOT KEEP HIM FOREVER.
YOU FORGET OUR PLACE, GANTHET. WE ARE IMMORTAL. WE ARE THE GUARDIANS OF THE UNIVERSE.
WE CAN DO WHATEVER WE LIKE.
"A FACE OF METAL AND FLESH SHALL SPEAK OF THE SECRETS OF THE 52. FEAR WILL RISE. WILLPOWER WILL GATHER.
"AND A WAR OF LIGHT WILL UNLEASH THE TRUTH BEHIND THE POWER OF THE RING."
YOU QUOTE THE FORBIDDEN CHAPTER FROM THE BOOK OF OA, SAYD?
YES. I QUOTE THE PROPHECY OF COSMIC REVELATIONS-- "THE BLACKEST NIGHT."
LOOK AT THE SIGNS. THEY ARE ALL AROUND US.
THAT PROPHECY IS MORE IMPORTANT TO THE FUTURE OF THE GREEN LANTERN CORPS THAN THE SECRET OF THE 52.
PERHAPS IT IS TIME TO INFORM OUR OFFICERS OF ABIN SUR'S DISCOVERY--
ABIN SUR WAS FED THAT INANE PROPHECY BY OUR ENEMIES ON THE PLANET YSMAULT. HE FOOLISHLY BELIEVED THEIR LIES--
--AND IT LED TO HIS DEMISE.
"THE BLACKEST NIGHT" IS NOT THE FUTURE, GANTHET. IT IS A FABLE DESIGNED TO INSTILL FEAR AMONG US.
NOTHING MORE.
WE ACCEPT THE RESPONSIBILITY OF THE 52, BUT WE DENY THE PROPHECY OF "THE BLACKEST NIGHT."
WE ALL DENY IT.
YOU TURN YOUR BACKS ON THE PROPHECY JUST AS YOU DID THE YELLOW IMPURITY. THE CORPS WAS NEARLY DESTROYED BECAUSE OF IT.
ENOUGH, GANTHET!
HAVE SALAAK RETURN THE CYBORG-SUPERMAN TO HIS SCIENCELL. THIS INTERROGATION IS OVER.
"HE KILLED THIRTY-TWO GREEN LANTERNS."

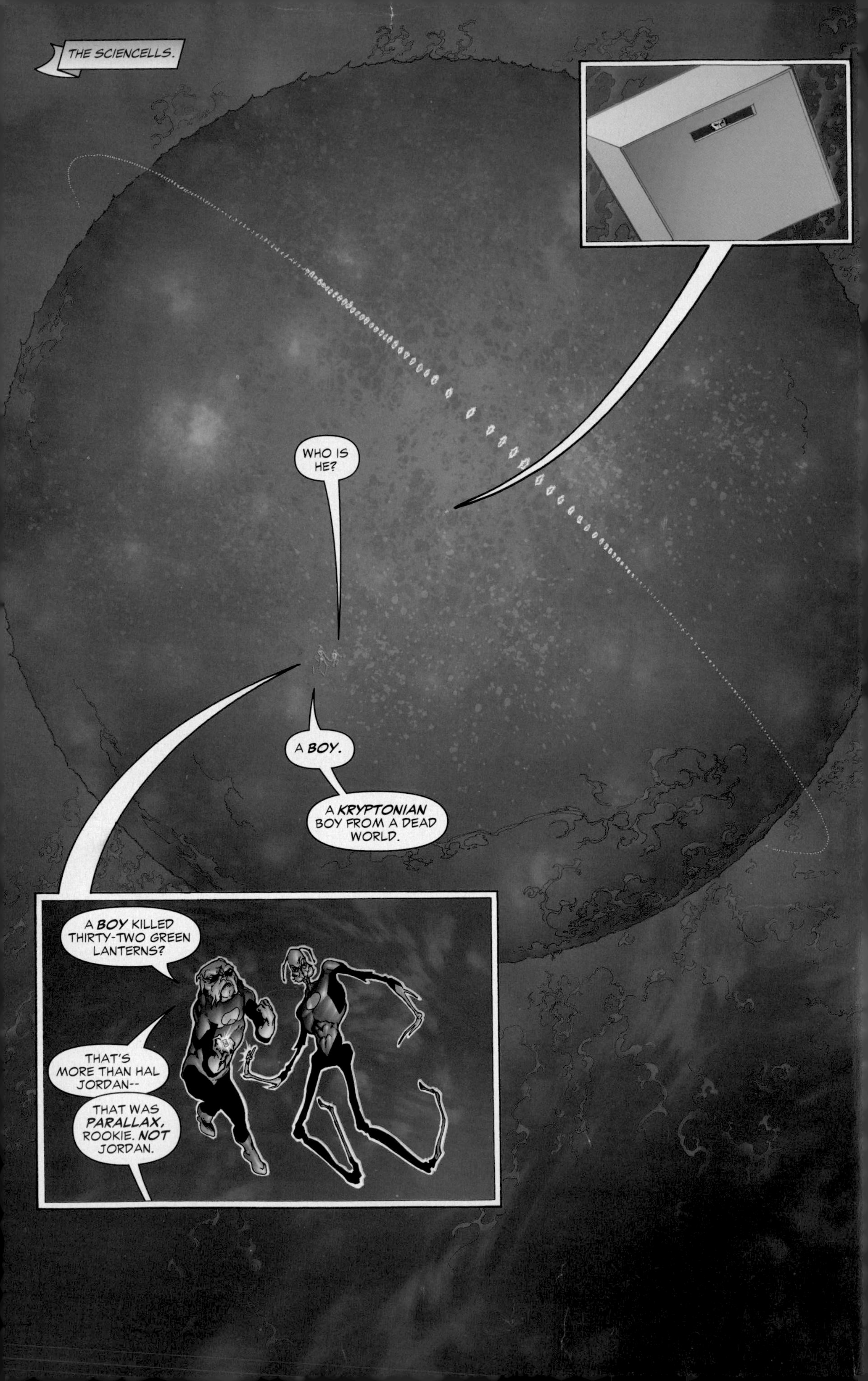
THE SCIENCELLS.
WHO IS HE?
A BOY.
A KRYPTONIAN BOY FROM A DEAD WORLD.
A BOY KILLED THIRTY-TWO GREEN LANTERNS?
THAT'S MORE THAN HAL JORDAN--
THAT WAS PARALLAX, ROOKIE. NOT JORDAN.

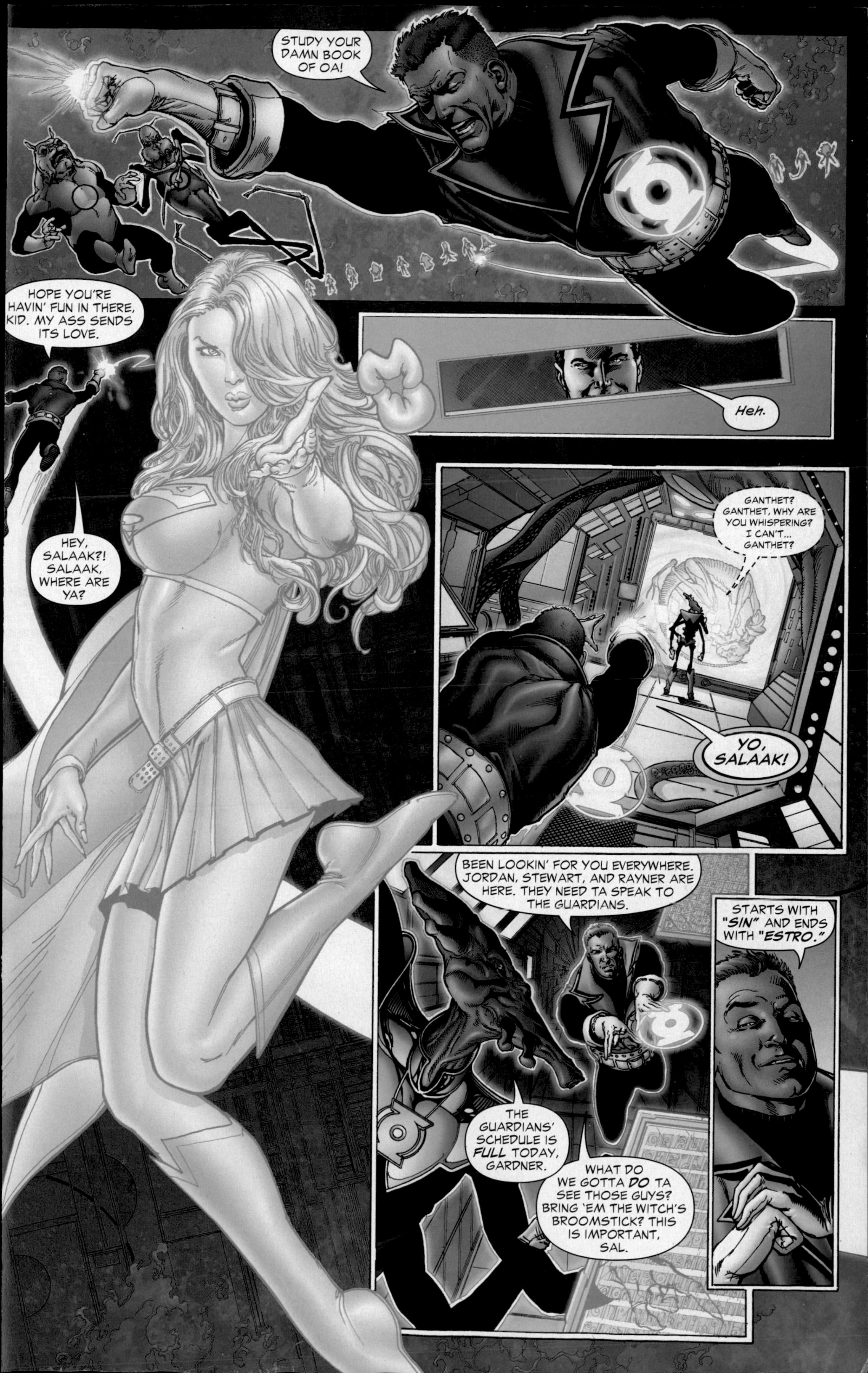
STUDY YOUR DAMN BOOK OF OA!
HOPE YOU'RE HAVIN' FUN IN THERE, KID. MY ASS SENDS ITS LOVE.
Heh.
HEY, SALAAK?! SALAAK, WHERE ARE YA?
GANTHET? GANTHET, WHY ARE YOU WHISPERING? I CAN'T... GANTHET?
YO, SALAAK!
BEEN LOOKIN' FOR YOU EVERYWHERE. JORDAN, STEWART, AND RAYNER ARE HERE. THEY NEED TA SPEAK TO THE GUARDIANS.
THE GUARDIANS' SCHEDULE IS FULL TODAY, GARDNER.
WHAT DO WE GOTTA DO TA SEE THOSE GUYS? BRING 'EM THE WITCH'S BROOMSTICK? THIS IS IMPORTANT, SAL.
STARTS WITH "SIN" AND ENDS WITH "ESTRO."

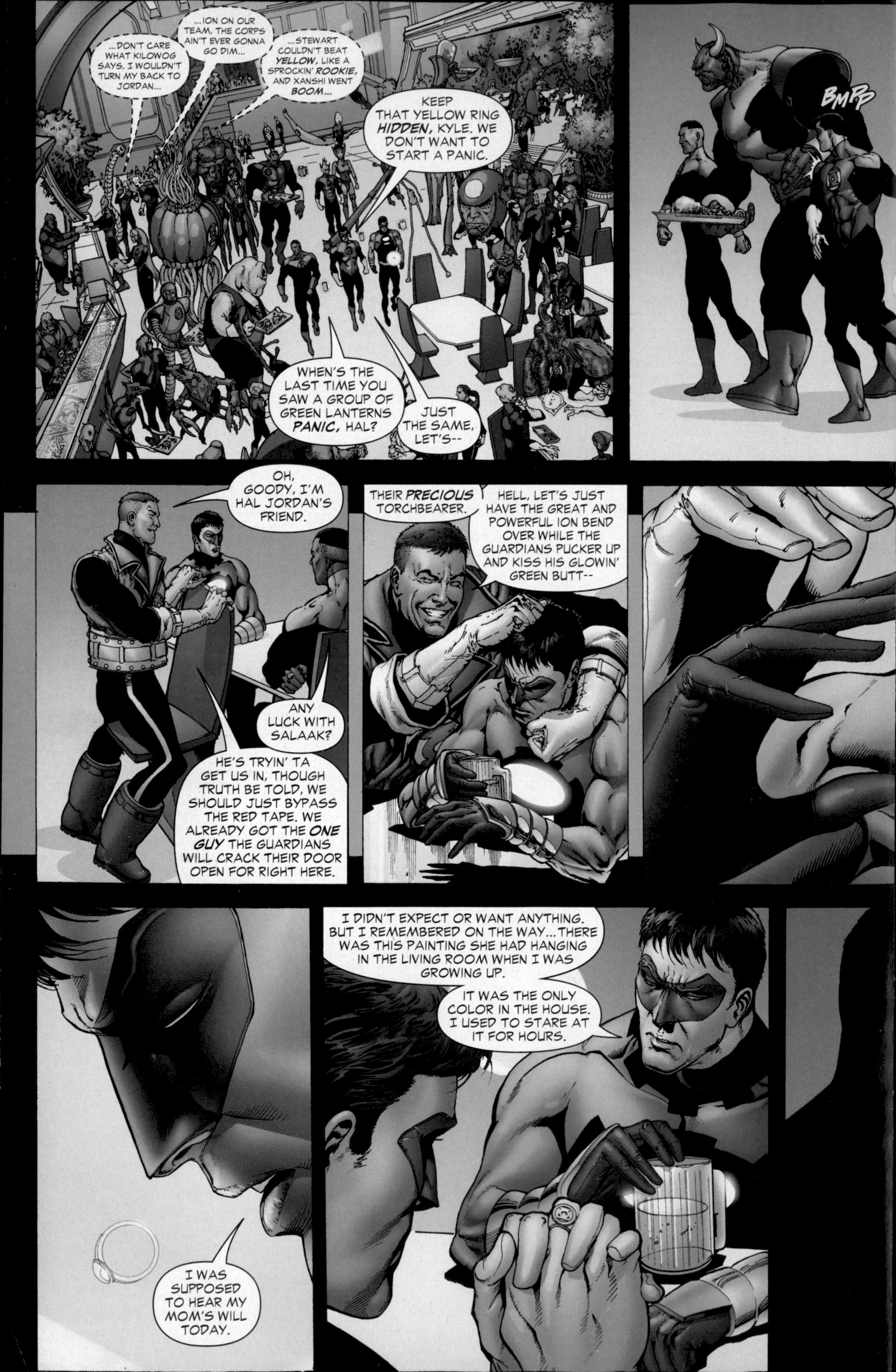
...DON'T CARE WHAT KILOWOG SAYS, I WOULDN'T TURN MY BACK TO JORDAN...
...ION ON OUR TEAM, THE CORPS AIN'T EVER GONNA GO DIM...
...STEWART COULDN'T BEAT YELLOW, LIKE A SPROCKIN' ROOKIE, AND XANSHI WENT BOOM...
KEEP THAT YELLOW RING HIDDEN, KYLE. WE DON'T WANT TO START A PANIC.
WHEN'S THE LAST TIME YOU SAW A GROUP OF GREEN LANTERNS PANIC, HAL?
JUST THE SAME, LET'S--
BMPP
OH, GOODY, I'M HAL JORDAN'S FRIEND.
ANY LUCK WITH SALAAK?
HE'S TRYIN' TA GET US IN, THOUGH TRUTH BE TOLD, WE SHOULD JUST BYPASS THE RED TAPE. WE ALREADY GOT THE ONE GUY THE GUARDIANS WILL CRACK THEIR DOOR OPEN FOR RIGHT HERE.
THEIR PRECIOUS TORCHBEARER.
HELL, LET'S JUST HAVE THE GREAT AND POWERFUL ION BEND OVER WHILE THE GUARDIANS PUCKER UP AND KISS HIS GLOWIN' GREEN BUTT--
I WAS SUPPOSED TO HEAR MY MOM'S WILL TODAY.
I DIDN'T EXPECT OR WANT ANYTHING. BUT I REMEMBERED ON THE WAY... THERE WAS THIS PAINTING SHE HAD HANGING IN THE LIVING ROOM WHEN I WAS GROWING UP.
IT WAS THE ONLY COLOR IN THE HOUSE. I USED TO STARE AT IT FOR HOURS.

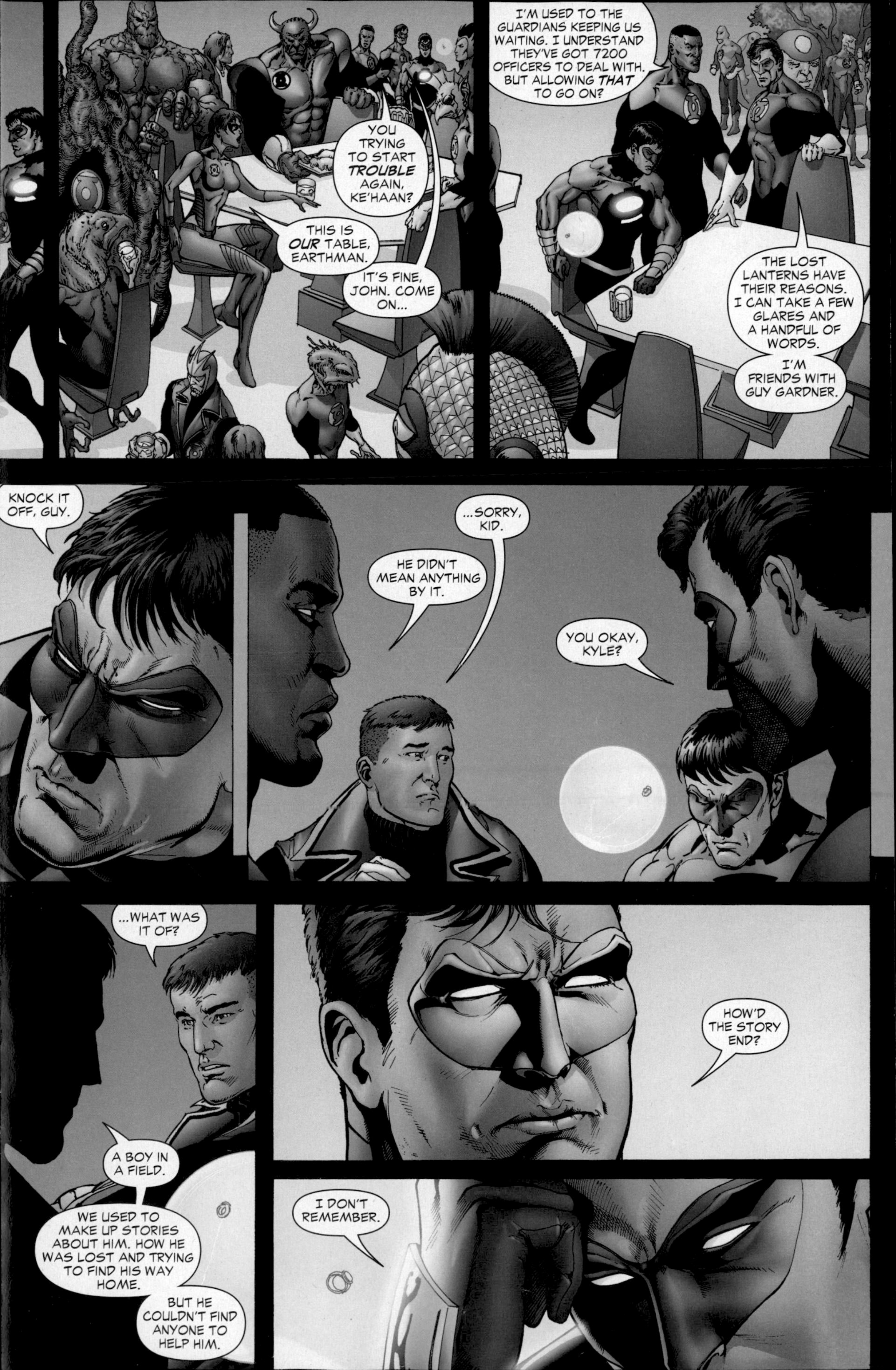
YOU TRYING TO START TROUBLE AGAIN, KE'HAAN?
THIS IS OUR TABLE, EARTHMAN.
IT'S FINE, JOHN. COME ON...
I'M USED TO THE GUARDIANS KEEPING US WAITING. I UNDERSTAND THEY'VE GOT 7200 OFFICERS TO DEAL WITH. BUT ALLOWING THAT TO GO ON?
THE LOST LANTERNS HAVE THEIR REASONS. I CAN TAKE A FEW GLARES AND A HANDFUL OF WORDS.
I'M FRIENDS WITH GUY GARDNER.
KNOCK IT OFF, GUY.
...SORRY, KID.
HE DIDN'T MEAN ANYTHING BY IT.
YOU OKAY, KYLE?
...WHAT WAS IT OF?
A BOY IN A FIELD.
WE USED TO MAKE UP STORIES ABOUT HIM. HOW HE WAS LOST AND TRYING TO FIND HIS WAY HOME.
BUT HE COULDN'T FIND ANYONE TO HELP HIM.
HOW'D THE STORY END?
I DON'T REMEMBER.

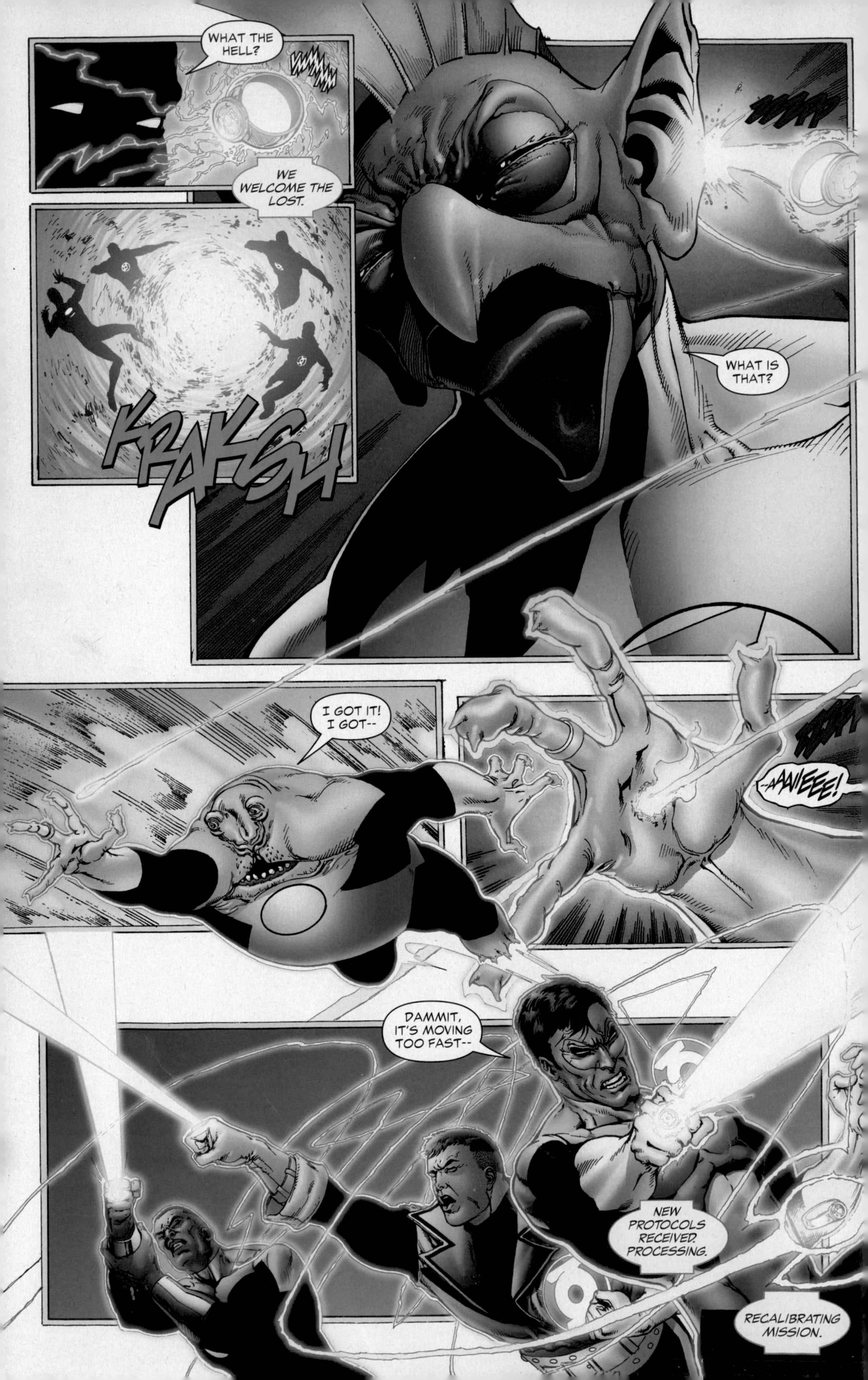

WHAT THE HELL?
VMMMMM
WE WELCOME THE LOST.
KRAKSH
WHAT IS THAT?
I GOT IT! I GOT--
--AAAIEEE!
DAMMIT, IT'S MOVING TOO FAST--
NEW PROTOCOLS RECEIVED. PROCESSING.
RECALIBRATING MISSION.

ION
TARGETED.

ION
CAPTURED.

PREPARE
TO TRANSPORT
SENTIENT
BEING.

GAAAAAHHHH!

KYLE!

BOOOOOMMMMM

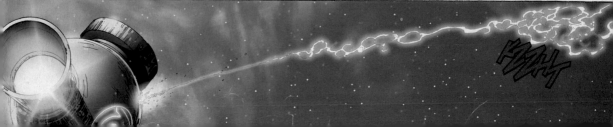

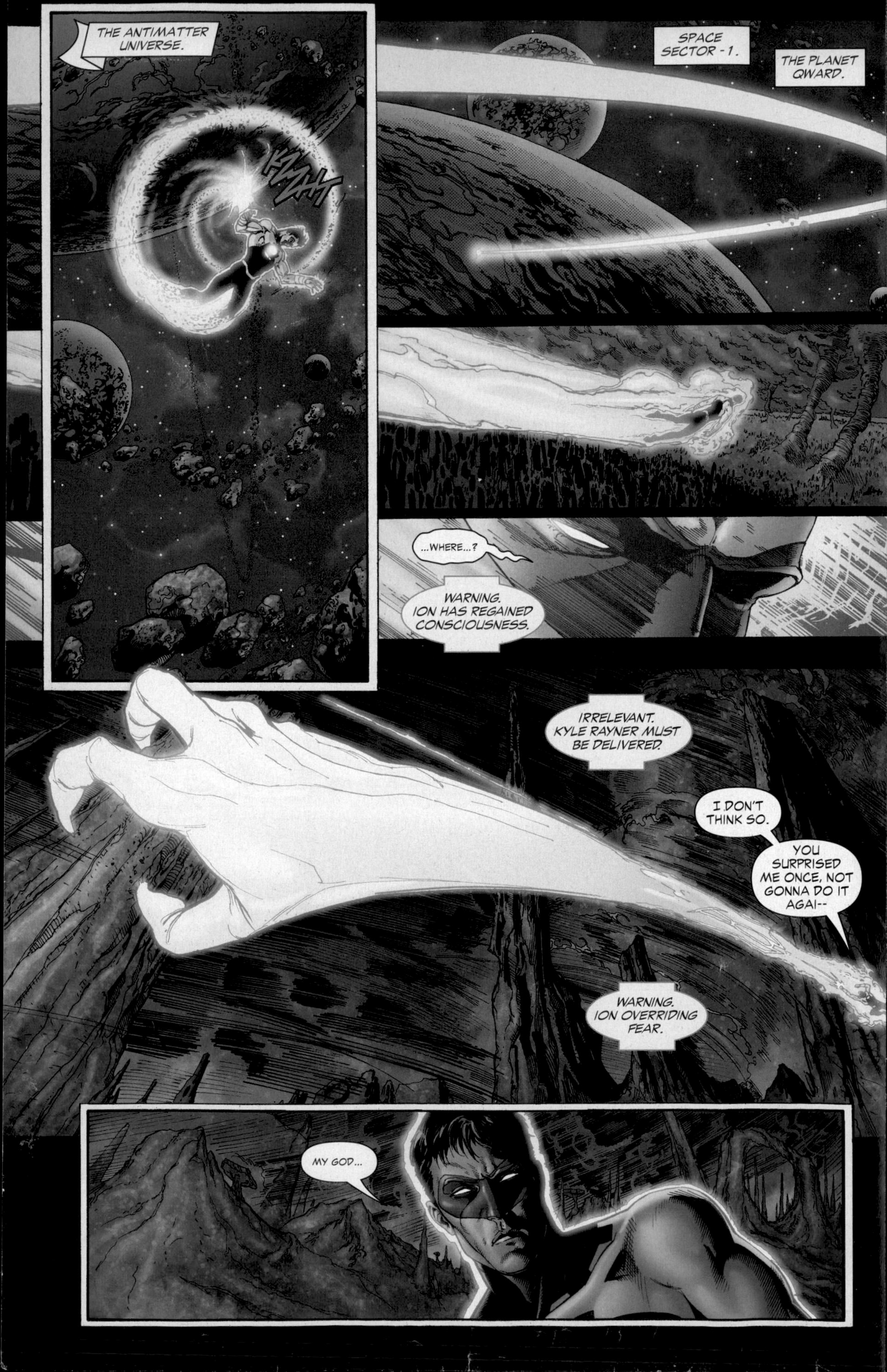
THE ANTIMATTER UNIVERSE.
KWAAK
SPACE SECTOR -1.
THE PLANET QWARD.
...WHERE...?
WARNING. ION HAS REGAINED CONSCIOUSNESS.
IRRELEVANT. KYLE RAYNER MUST BE DELIVERED.
I DON'T THINK SO.
YOU SURPRISED ME ONCE, NOT GONNA DO IT AGAI--
WARNING. ION OVERRIDING FEAR.
MY GOD...

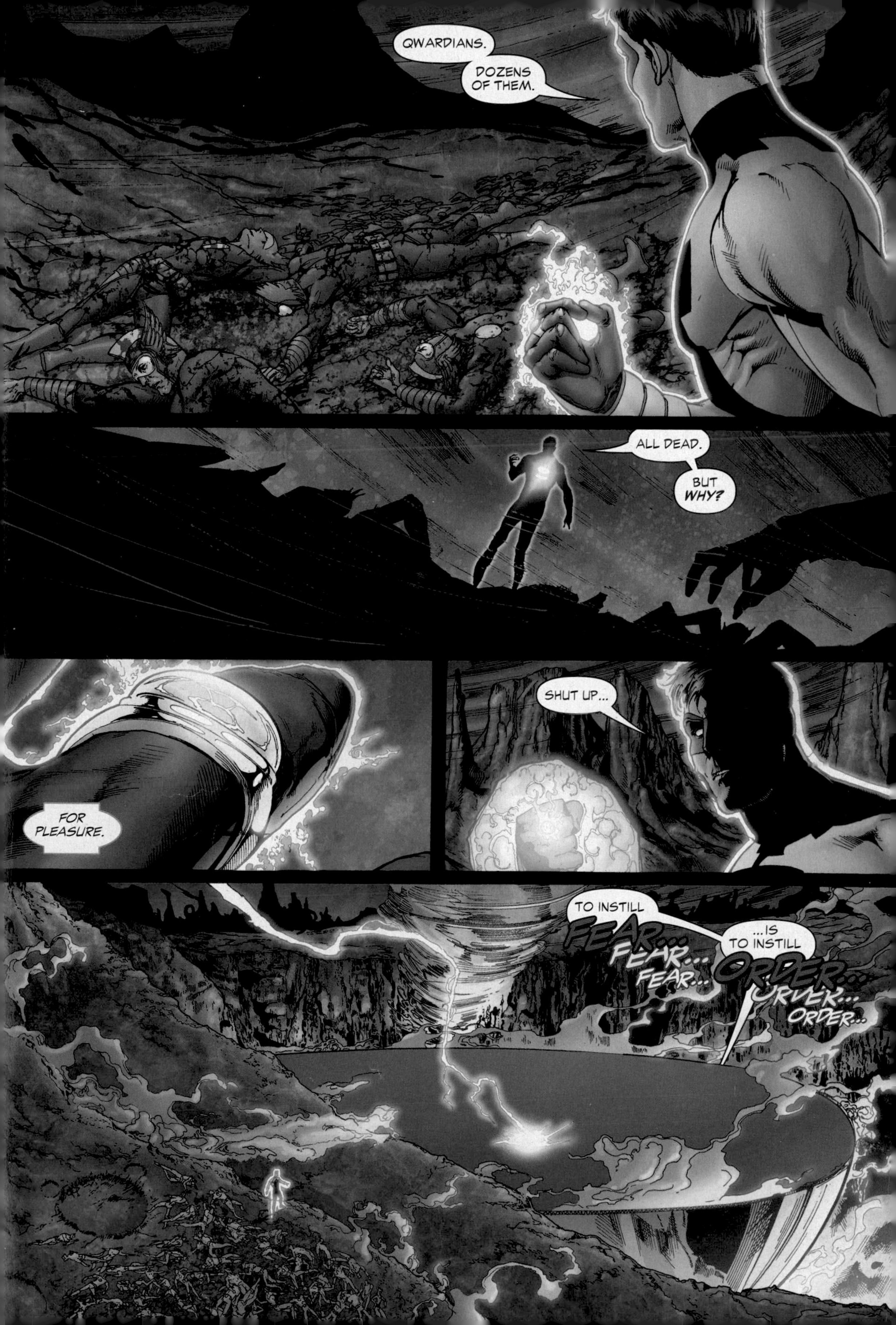
QWARDIANS.
DOZENS OF THEM.
ALL DEAD.
BUT *WHY?*
FOR PLEASURE.
SHUT UP...
TO INSTILL
FEAR... FEAR... FEAR...
...IS TO INSTILL
ORDER... ORDER... ORDER...

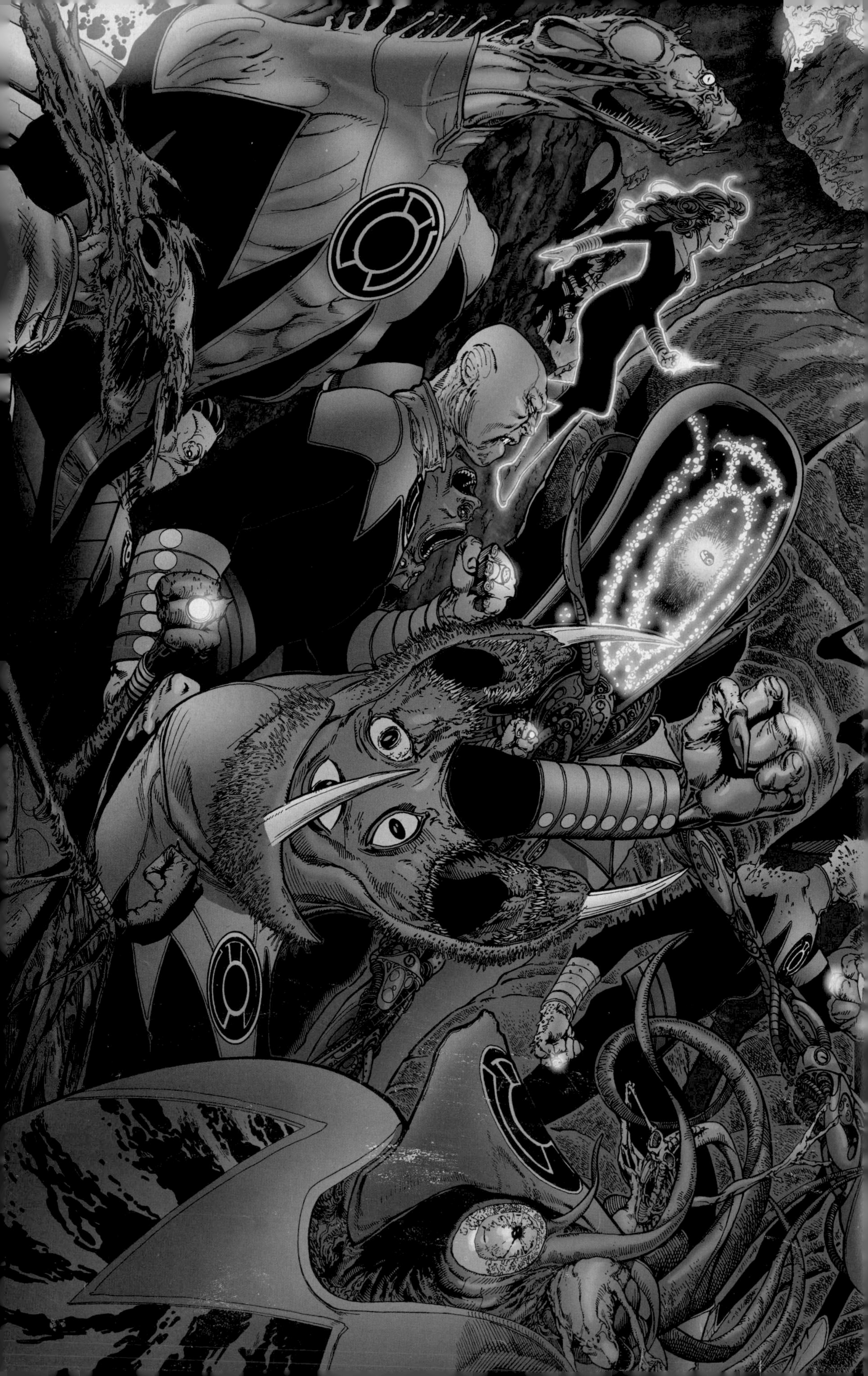

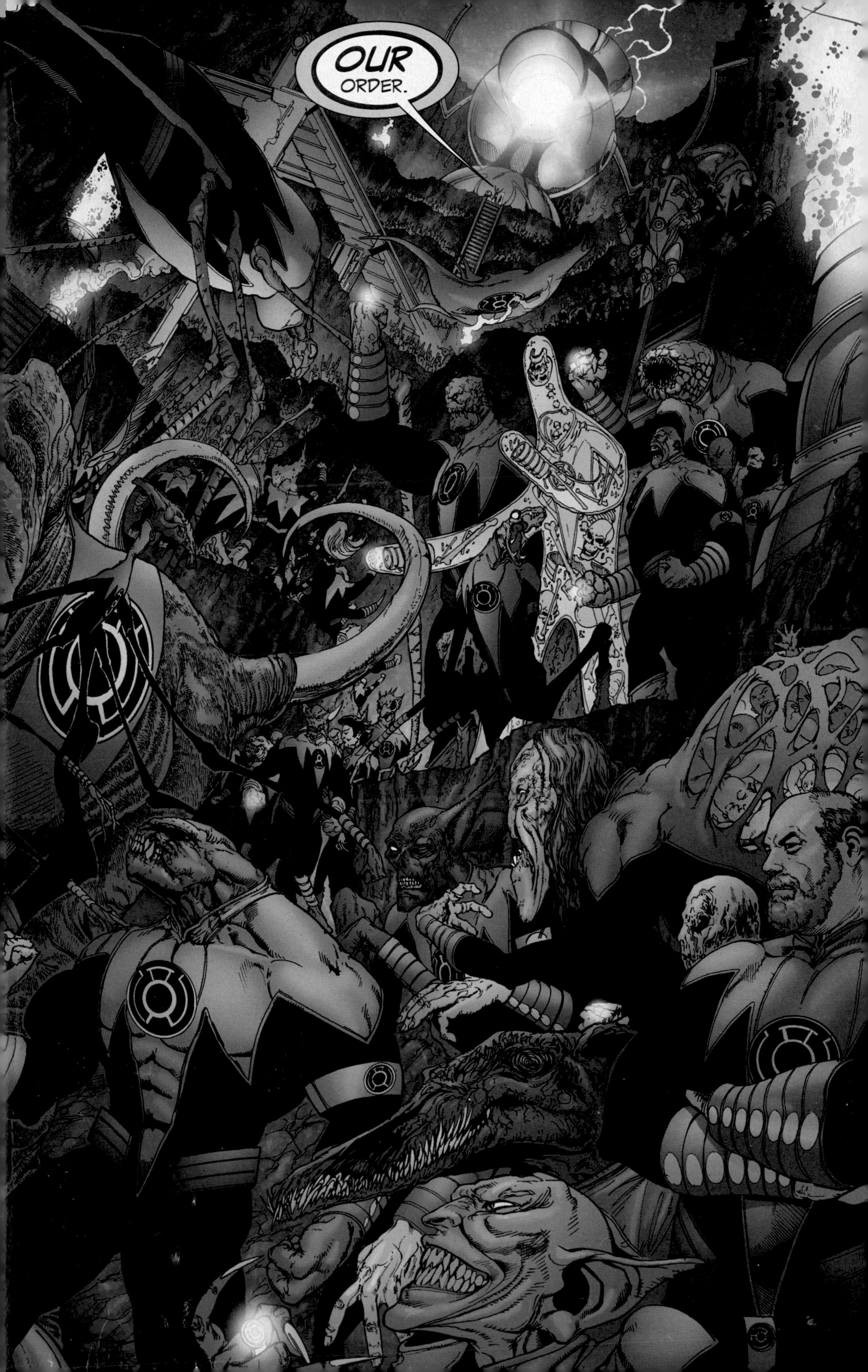
OUR ORDER.

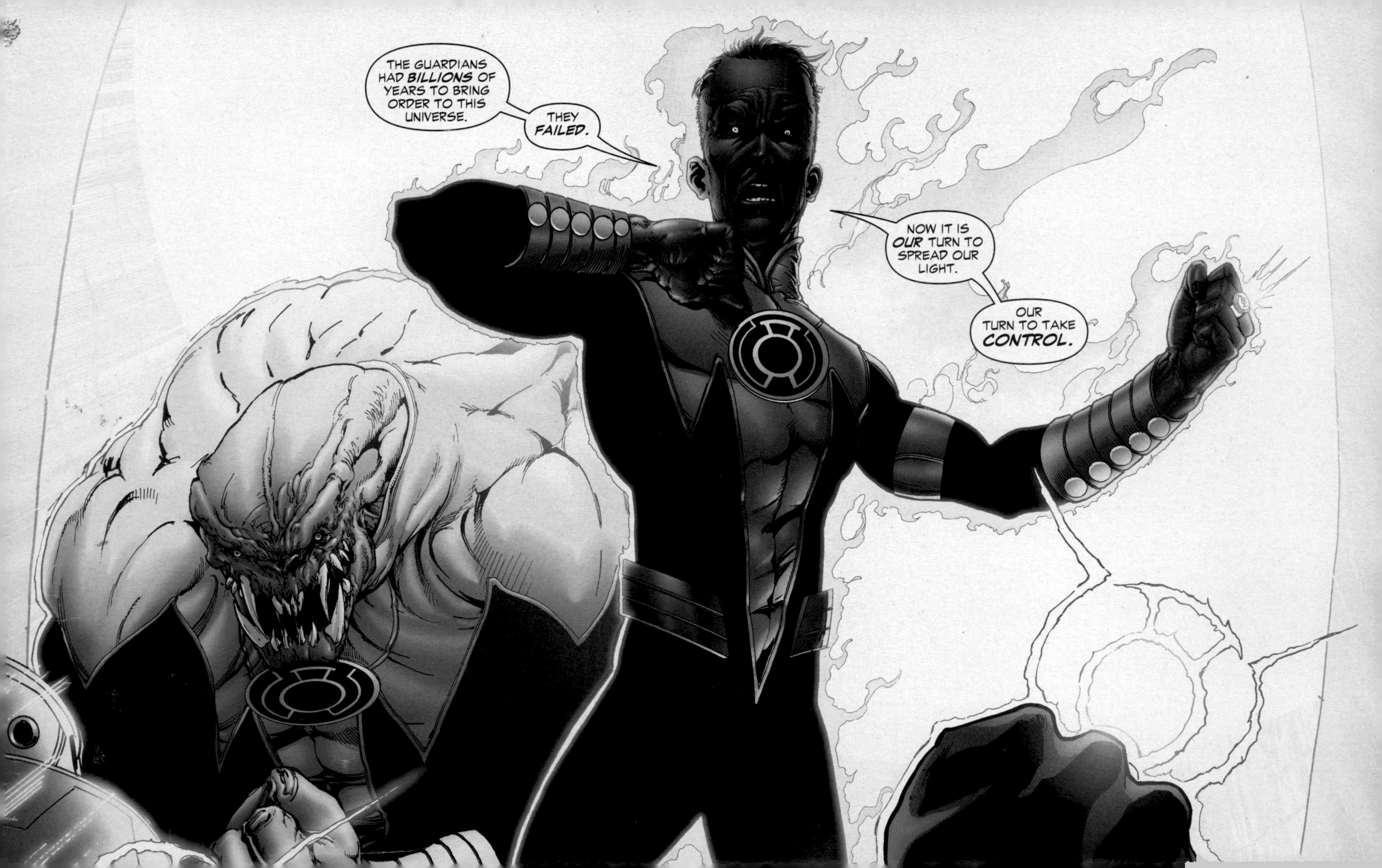
THE GUARDIANS HAD BILLIONS OF YEARS TO BRING ORDER TO THIS UNIVERSE.
THEY FAILED.
NOW IT IS OUR TURN TO SPREAD OUR LIGHT.
OUR TURN TO TAKE CONTROL.

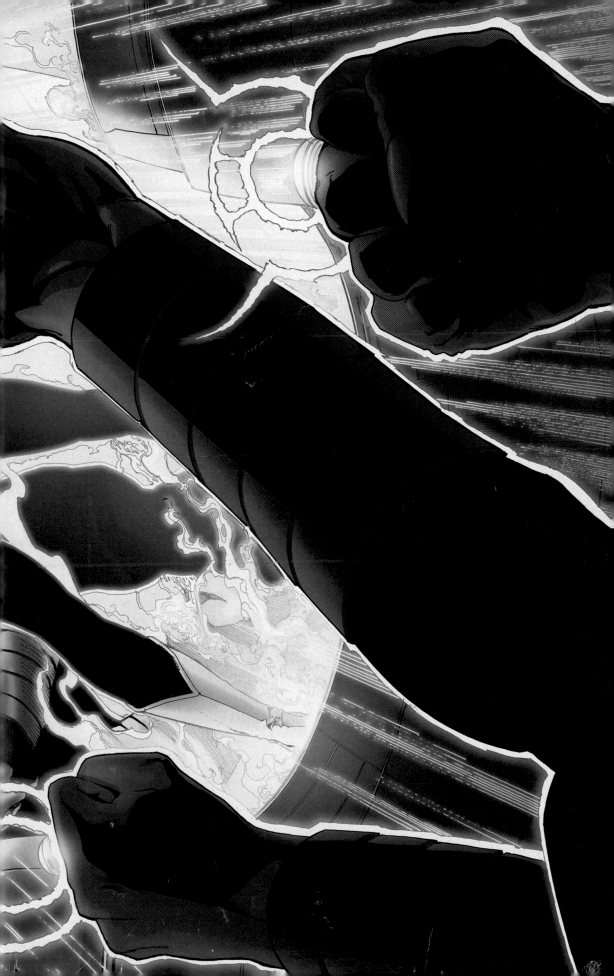

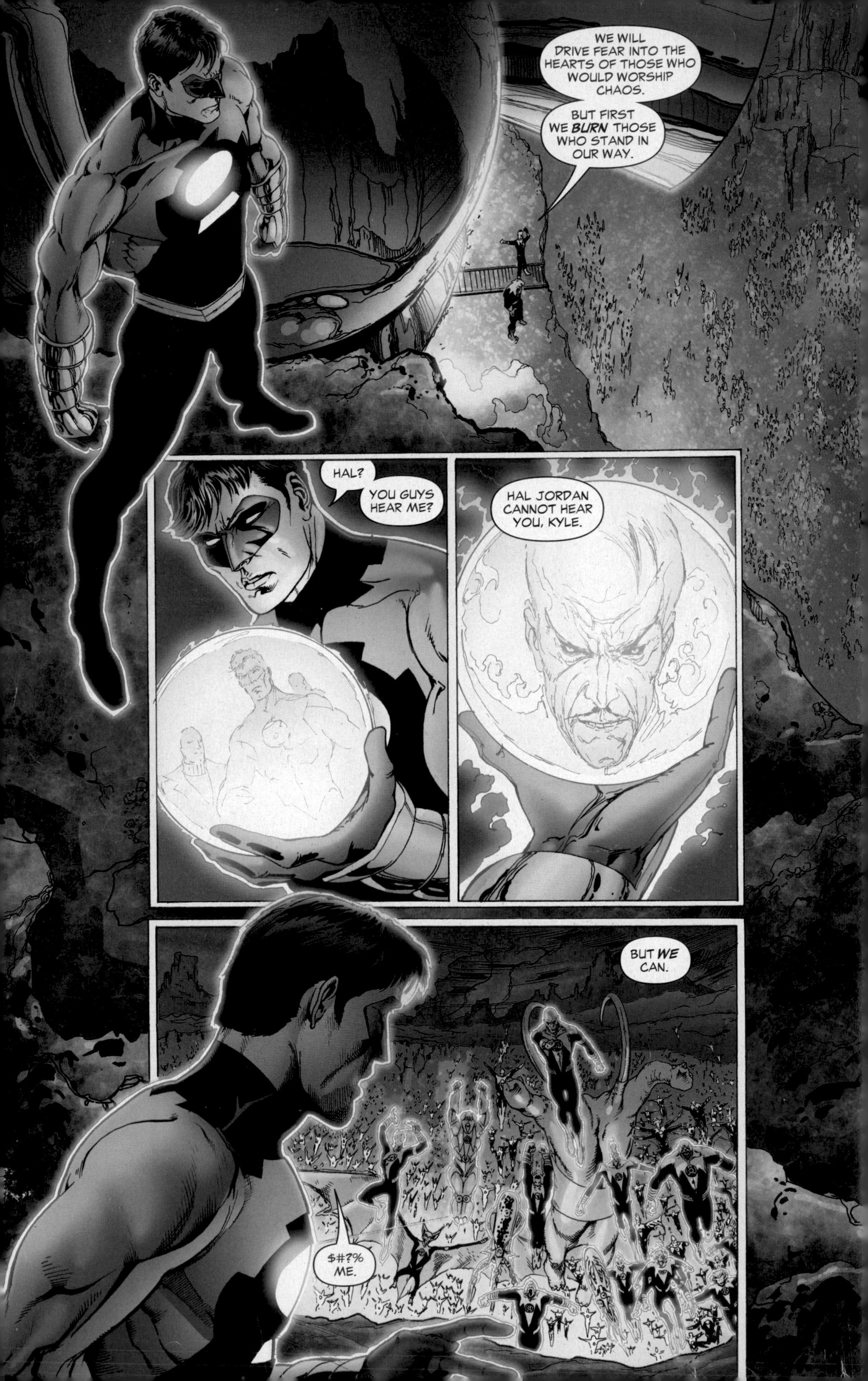
WE WILL DRIVE FEAR INTO THE HEARTS OF THOSE WHO WOULD WORSHIP CHAOS.
BUT FIRST WE BURN THOSE WHO STAND IN OUR WAY.
HAL?
YOU GUYS HEAR ME?
HAL JORDAN CANNOT HEAR YOU, KYLE.
BUT WE CAN.
$#?% ME.

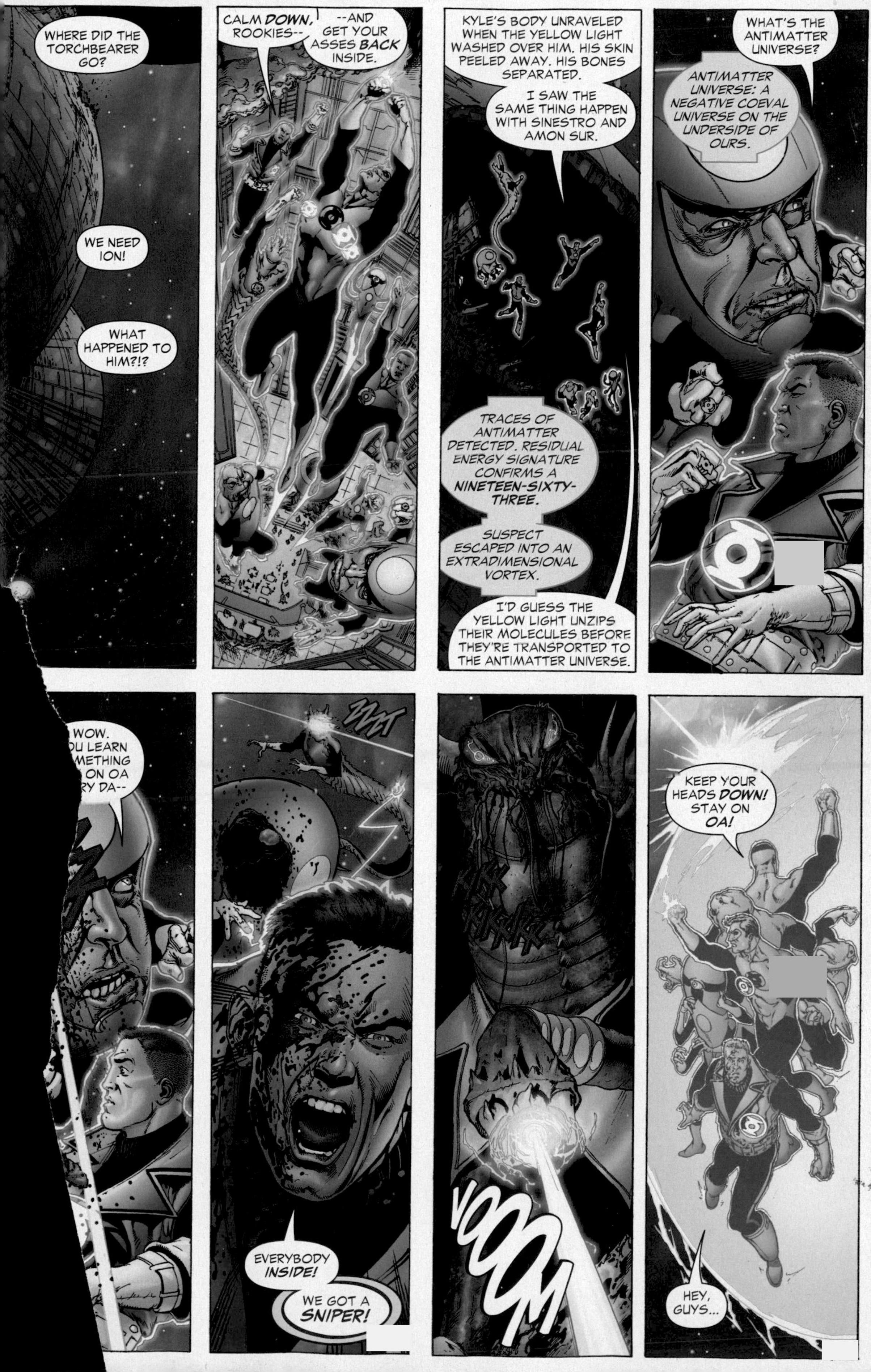
WHERE DID THE TORCHBEARER GO?
WE NEED ION!
WHAT HAPPENED TO HIM?!?
CALM DOWN, ROOKIES--
--AND GET YOUR ASSES BACK INSIDE.
KYLE'S BODY UNRAVELED WHEN THE YELLOW LIGHT WASHED OVER HIM. HIS SKIN PEELED AWAY. HIS BONES SEPARATED.
I SAW THE SAME THING HAPPEN WITH SINESTRO AND AMON SUR.
TRACES OF ANTIMATTER DETECTED. RESIDUAL ENERGY SIGNATURE CONFIRMS A NINETEEN-SIXTY-THREE.
SUSPECT ESCAPED INTO AN EXTRADIMENSIONAL VORTEX.
I'D GUESS THE YELLOW LIGHT UNZIPS THEIR MOLECULES BEFORE THEY'RE TRANSPORTED TO THE ANTIMATTER UNIVERSE.
WHAT'S THE ANTIMATTER UNIVERSE?
ANTIMATTER UNIVERSE: A NEGATIVE COEVAL UNIVERSE ON THE UNDERSIDE OF OURS.
WOW. OU LEARN METHING ON OA RY DA--
EVERYBODY INSIDE!
WE GOT A SNIPER!
VOOOM
KEEP YOUR HEADS DOWN! STAY ON OA!
HEY, GUYS...

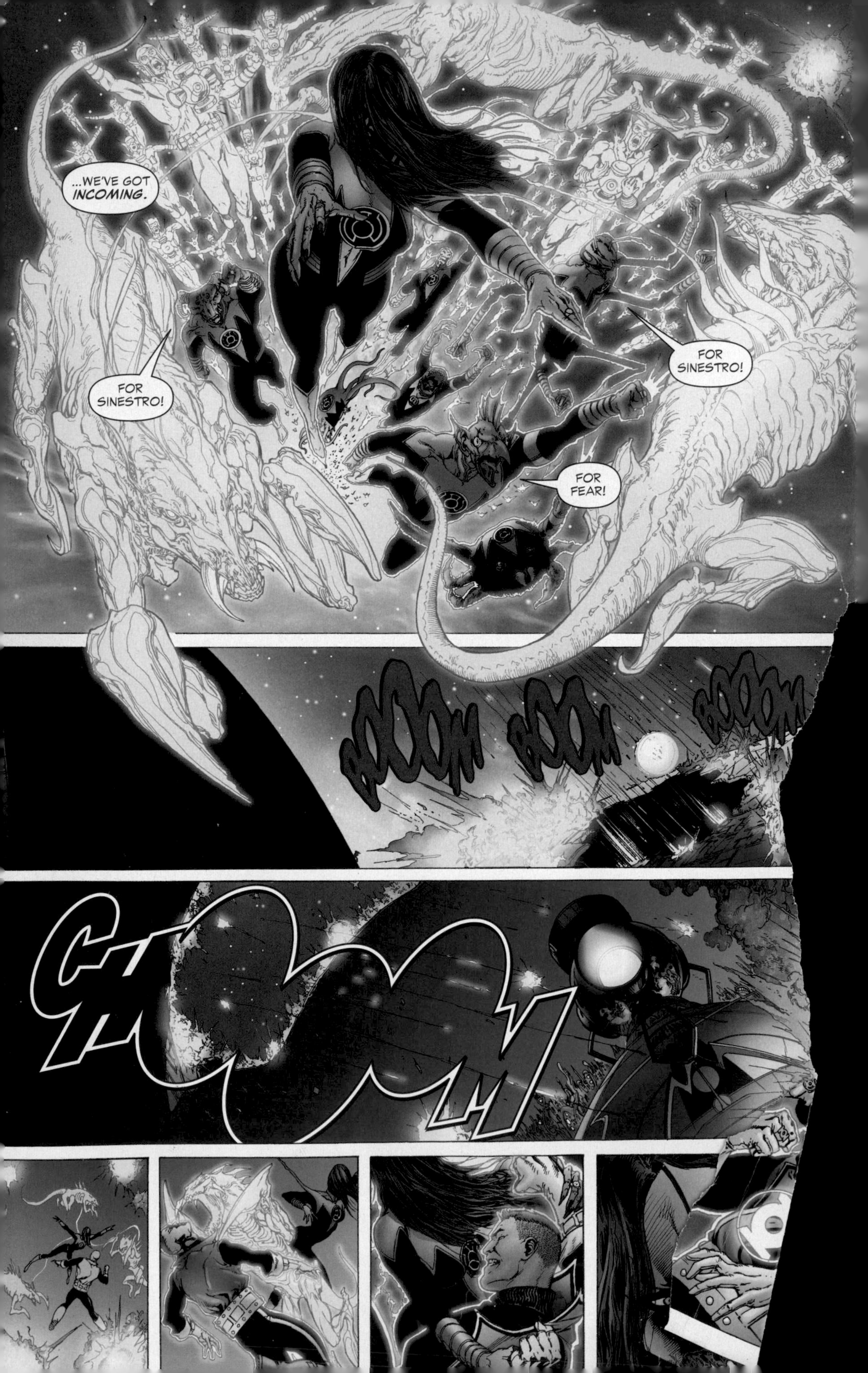
...WE'VE GOT INCOMING.
FOR SINESTRO!
FOR SINESTRO!
FOR FEAR!
BOOOM BOOM BOOOM
CHOOM

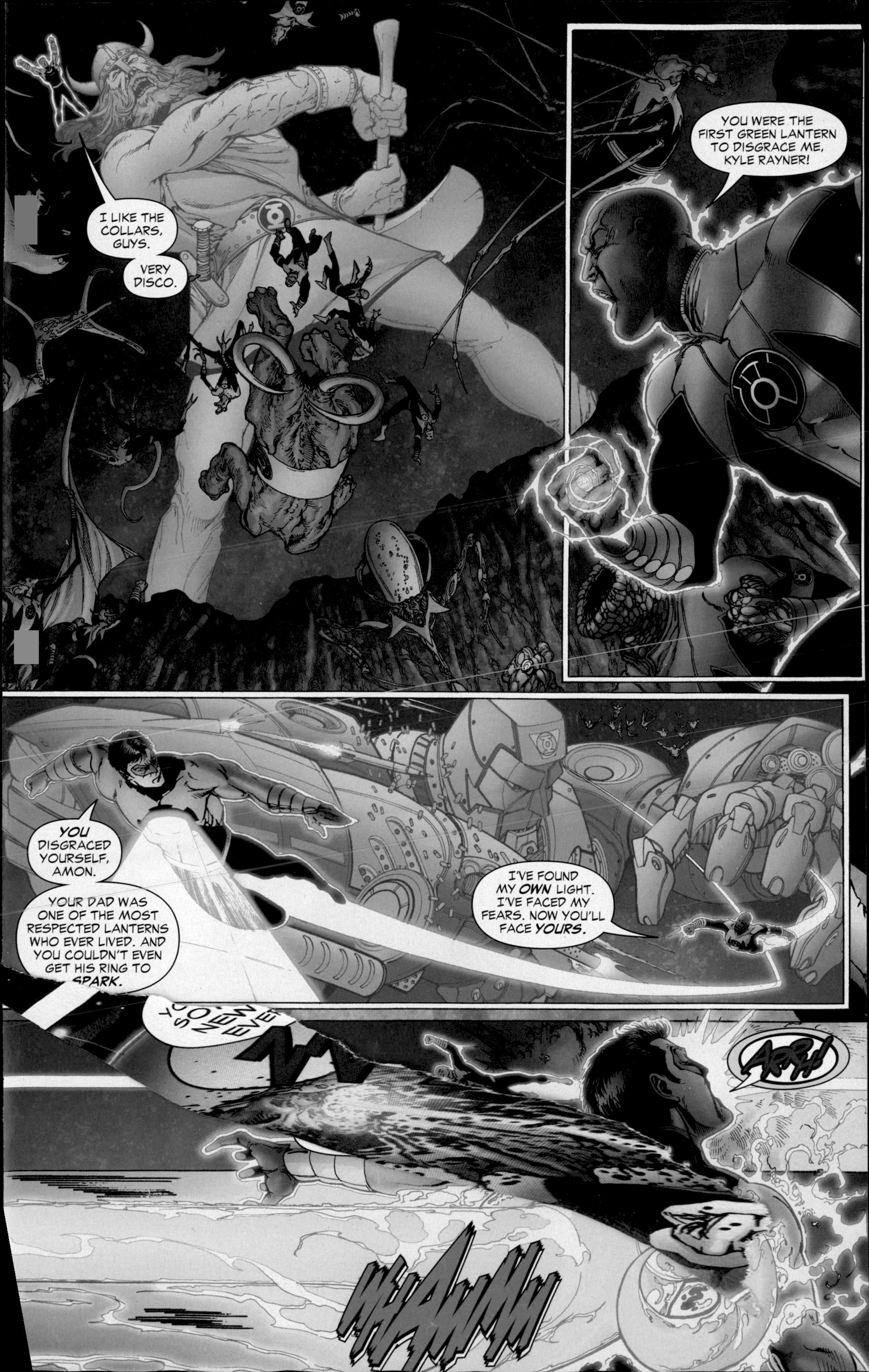
I LIKE THE COLLARS, GUYS.
VERY DISCO.
YOU WERE THE FIRST GREEN LANTERN TO DISGRACE ME, KYLE RAYNER!
YOU DISGRACED YOURSELF, AMON.
YOUR DAD WAS ONE OF THE MOST RESPECTED LANTERNS WHO EVER LIVED. AND YOU COULDN'T EVEN GET HIS RING TO SPARK.
I'VE FOUND MY OWN LIGHT. I'VE FACED MY FEARS. NOW YOU'LL FACE YOURS.
ARRH!
WHAMM

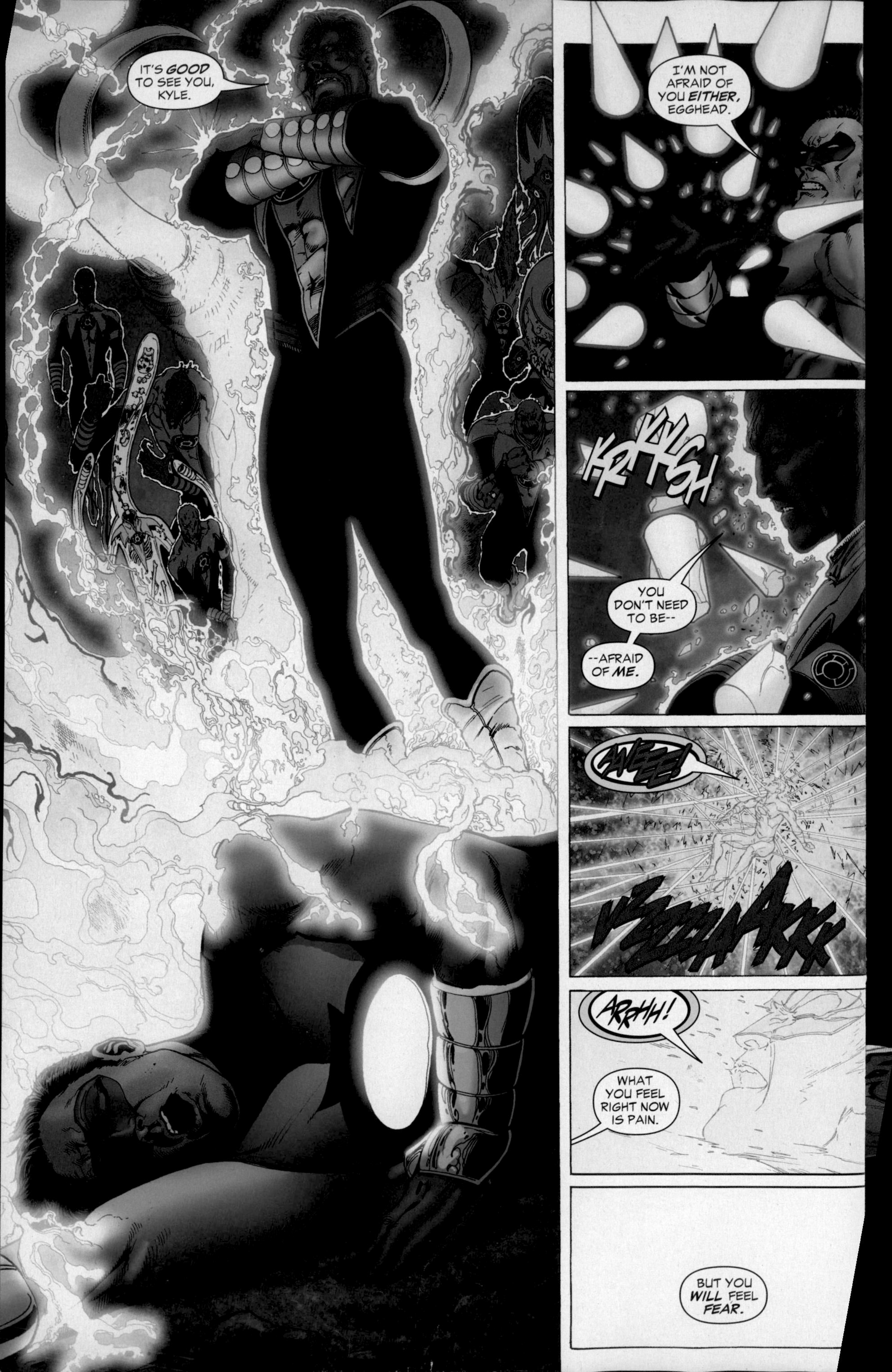
IT'S GOOD TO SEE YOU, KYLE.
I'M NOT AFRAID OF YOU EITHER, EGGHEAD.
KRKKSH
YOU DON'T NEED TO BE--
--AFRAID OF ME.
AAEEE!
VZZZAAKKK
ARRHH!
WHAT YOU FEEL RIGHT NOW IS PAIN.
BUT YOU WILL FEEL FEAR.

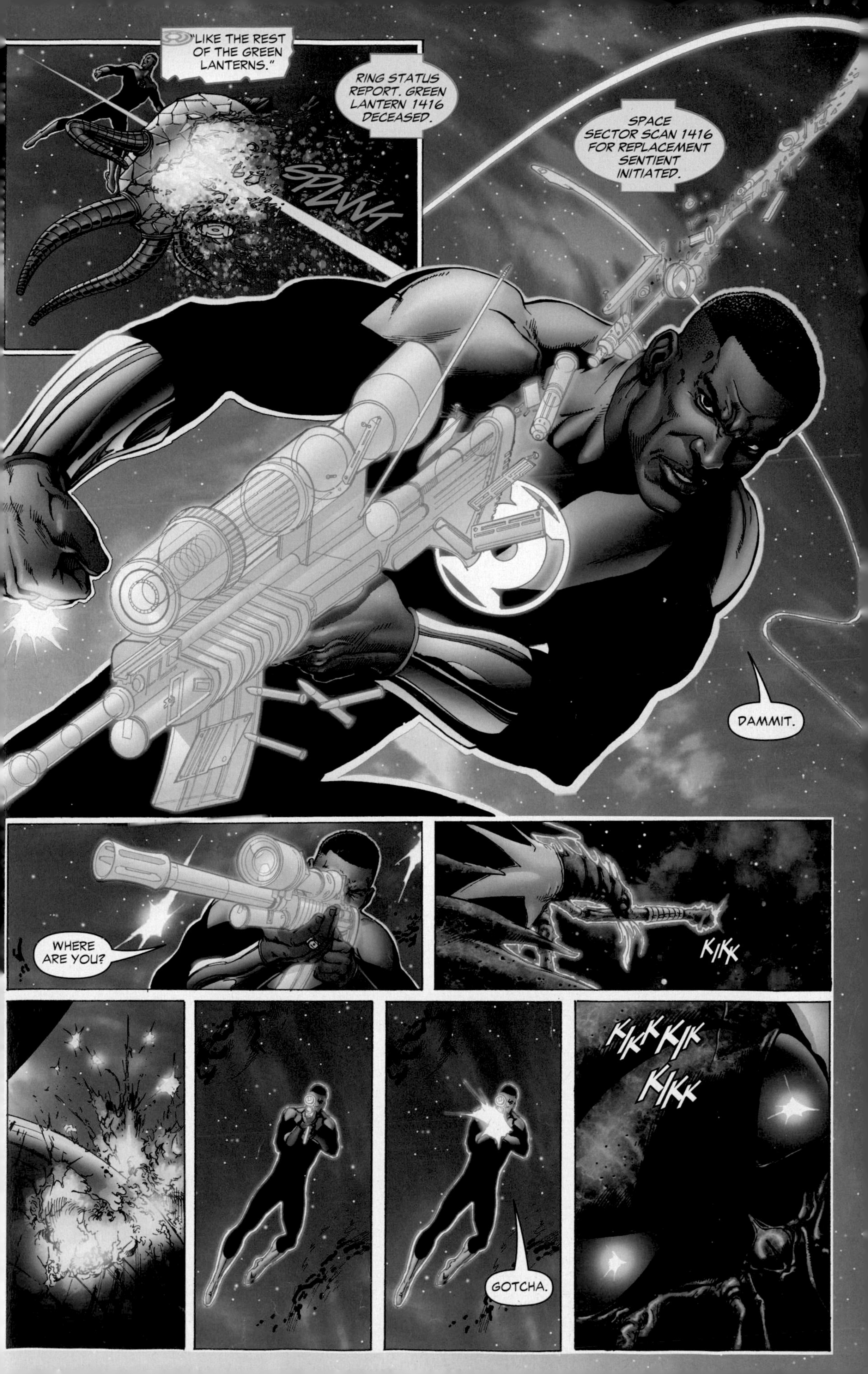
"LIKE THE REST OF THE GREEN LANTERNS."
RING STATUS REPORT. GREEN LANTERN 1416 DECEASED.
SPACE SECTOR SCAN 1416 FOR REPLACEMENT SENTIENT INITIATED.
SPLVVK
DAMMIT.
WHERE ARE YOU?
KIKK
GOTCHA.
KIKKKIK
KIKK

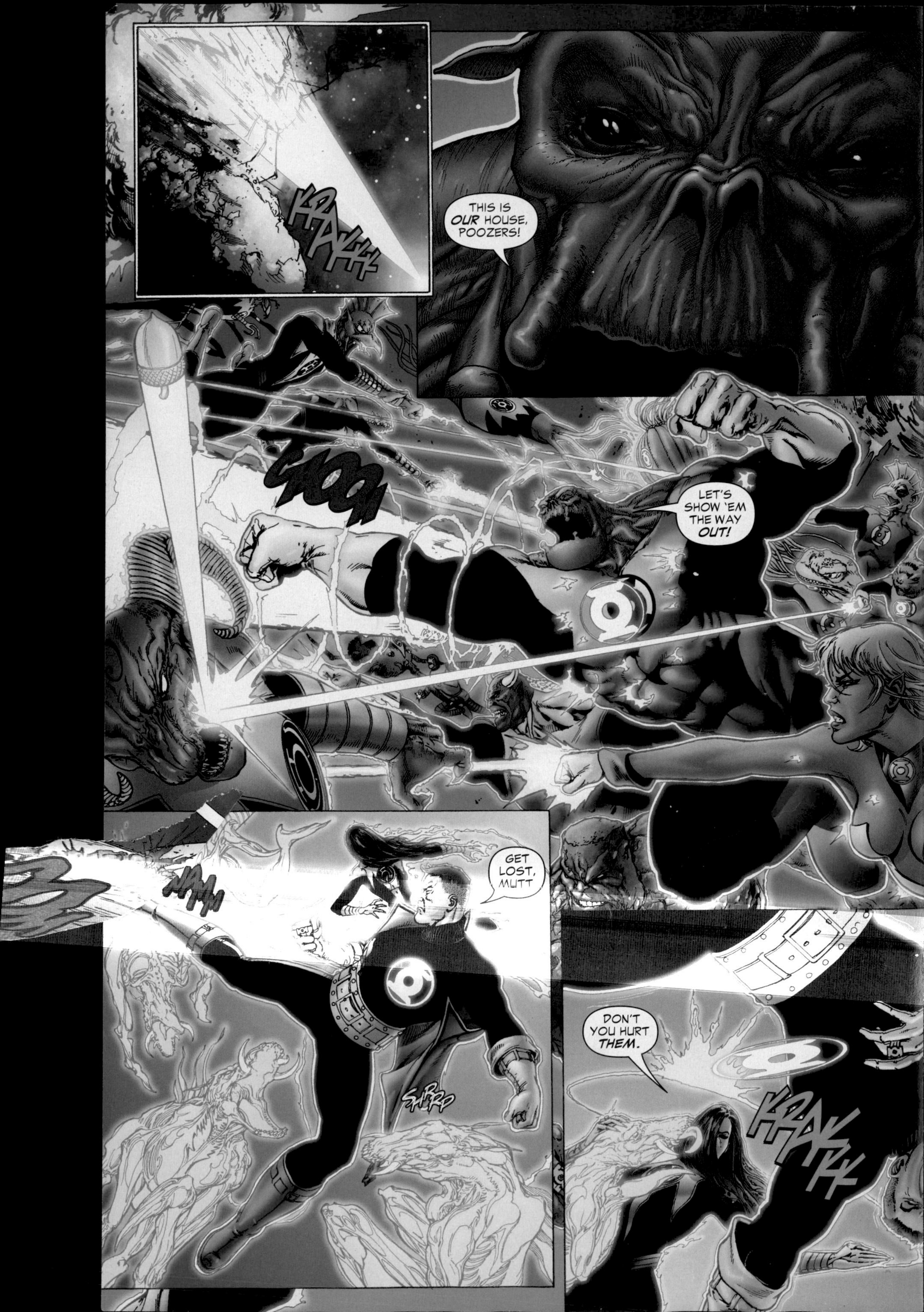
KRAKKK
THIS IS OUR HOUSE, POOZERS!
CHOOM
LET'S SHOW 'EM THE WAY OUT!
GET LOST, MUTT
SHRRP
DON'T YOU HURT THEM.
KRAKKK

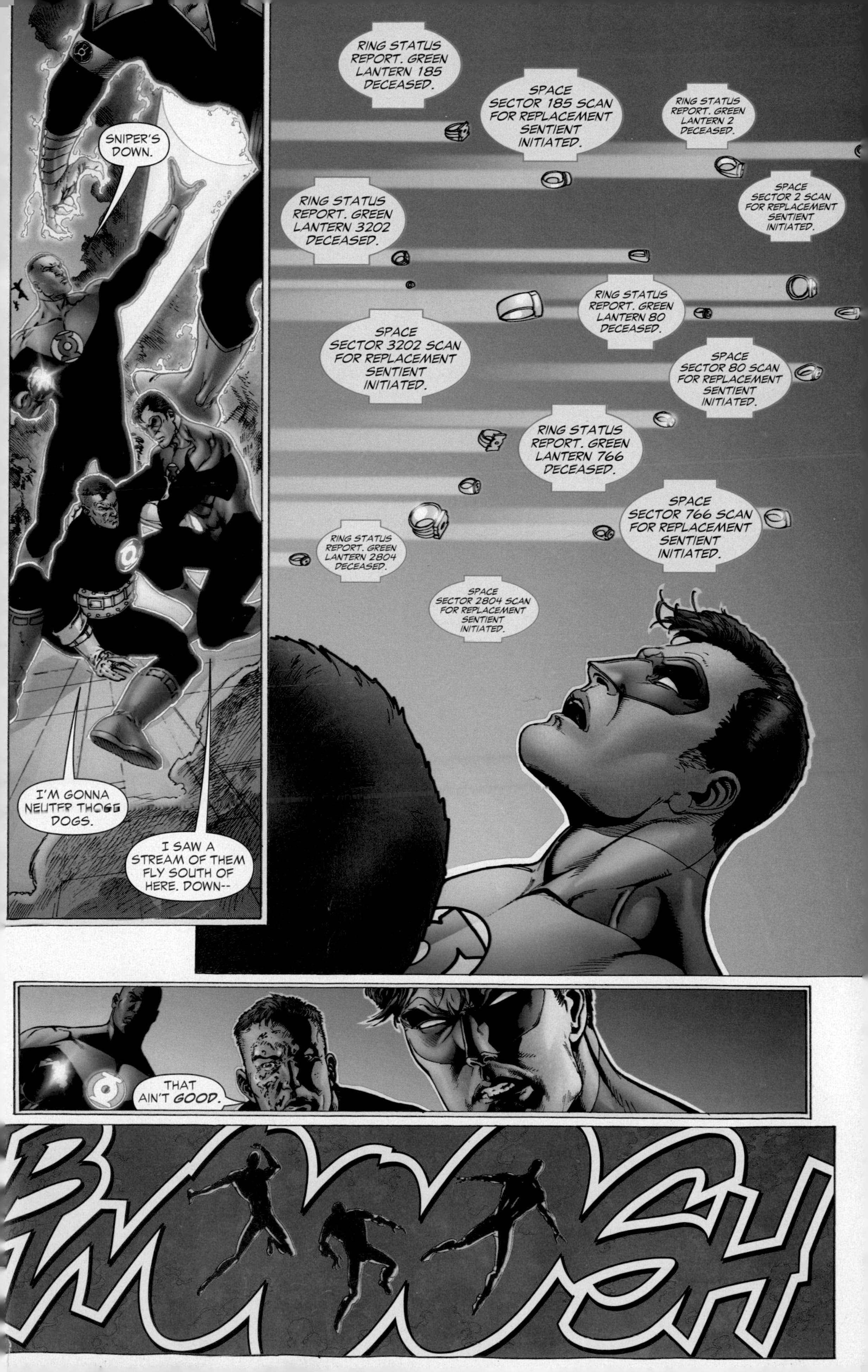

SNIPER'S DOWN.
I'M GONNA NEUTER THOSE DOGS.
I SAW A STREAM OF THEM FLY SOUTH OF HERE. DOWN--
RING STATUS REPORT. GREEN LANTERN 185 DECEASED.
SPACE SECTOR 185 SCAN FOR REPLACEMENT SENTIENT INITIATED.
RING STATUS REPORT. GREEN LANTERN 2 DECEASED.
SPACE SECTOR 2 SCAN FOR REPLACEMENT SENTIENT INITIATED.
RING STATUS REPORT. GREEN LANTERN 3202 DECEASED.
RING STATUS REPORT. GREEN LANTERN 80 DECEASED.
SPACE SECTOR 3202 SCAN FOR REPLACEMENT SENTIENT INITIATED.
SPACE SECTOR 80 SCAN FOR REPLACEMENT SENTIENT INITIATED.
RING STATUS REPORT. GREEN LANTERN 766 DECEASED.
SPACE SECTOR 766 SCAN FOR REPLACEMENT SENTIENT INITIATED.
RING STATUS REPORT. GREEN LANTERN 2804 DECEASED.
SPACE SECTOR 2804 SCAN FOR REPLACEMENT SENTIENT INITIATED.
THAT AIN'T GOOD.

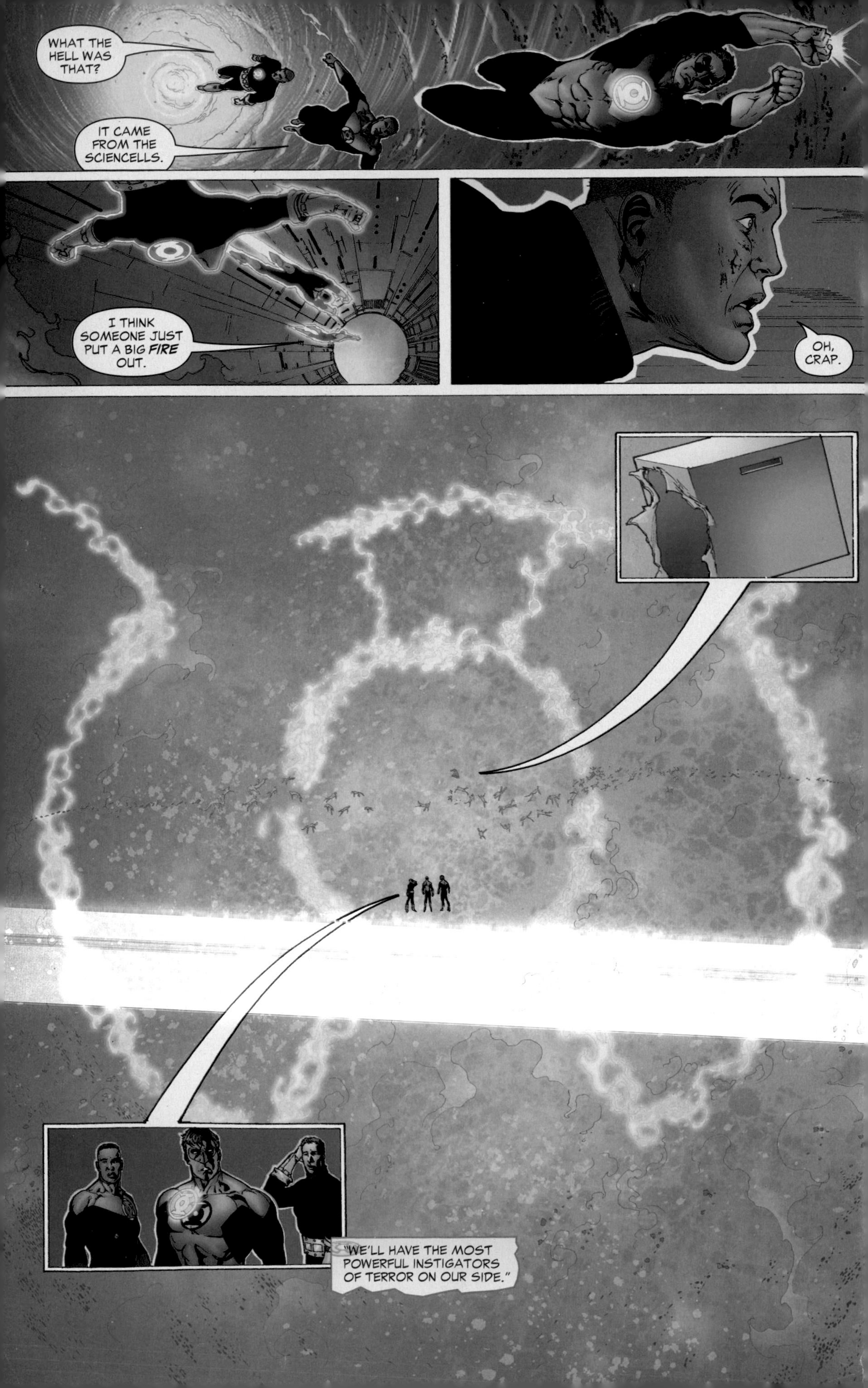
WHAT THE HELL WAS THAT?
IT CAME FROM THE SCIENCELLS.
I THINK SOMEONE JUST PUT A BIG FIRE OUT.
OH, CRAP.
"WE'LL HAVE THE MOST POWERFUL INSTIGATORS OF TERROR ON OUR SIDE."

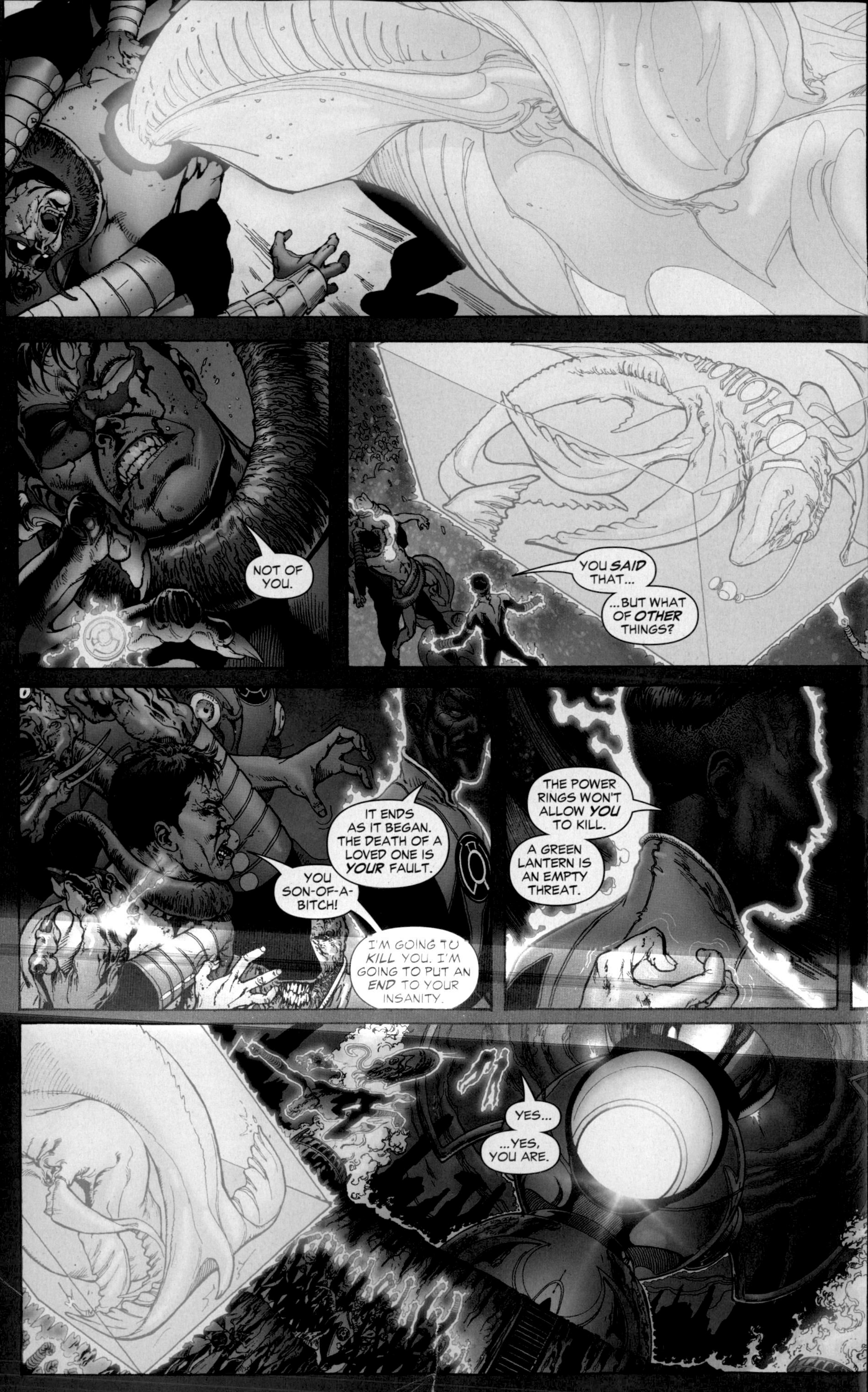
NOT OF YOU.
YOU SAID THAT...
...BUT WHAT OF OTHER THINGS?
IT ENDS AS IT BEGAN. THE DEATH OF A LOVED ONE IS YOUR FAULT.
YOU SON-OF-A-BITCH!
I'M GOING TO KILL YOU. I'M GOING TO PUT AN END TO YOUR INSANITY.
THE POWER RINGS WON'T ALLOW YOU TO KILL.
A GREEN LANTERN IS AN EMPTY THREAT.
YES...
...YES, YOU ARE.

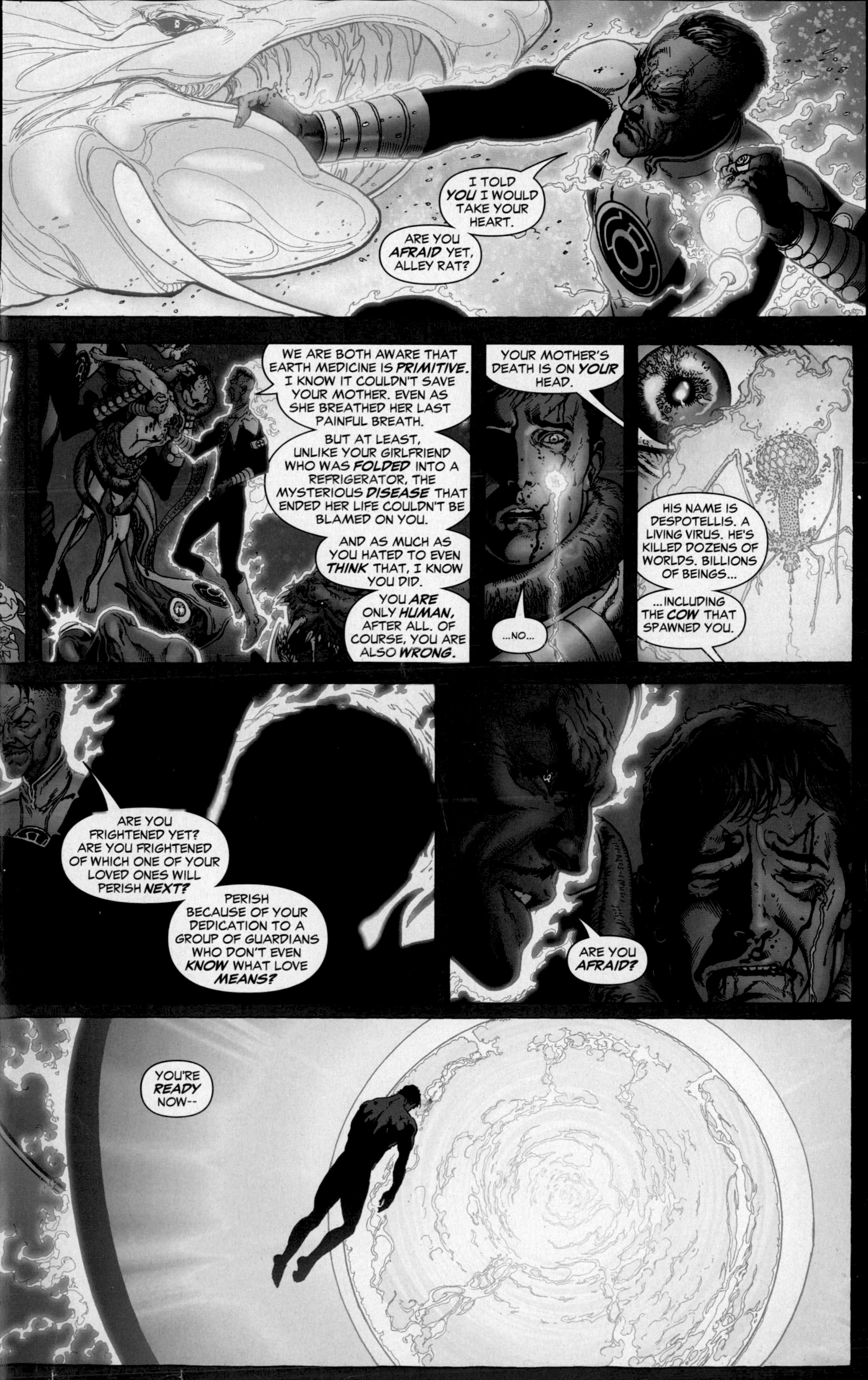
I TOLD YOU I WOULD TAKE YOUR HEART.
ARE YOU AFRAID YET, ALLEY RAT?
WE ARE BOTH AWARE THAT EARTH MEDICINE IS PRIMITIVE. I KNOW IT COULDN'T SAVE YOUR MOTHER. EVEN AS SHE BREATHED HER LAST PAINFUL BREATH.
BUT AT LEAST, UNLIKE YOUR GIRLFRIEND WHO WAS FOLDED INTO A REFRIGERATOR, THE MYSTERIOUS DISEASE THAT ENDED HER LIFE COULDN'T BE BLAMED ON YOU.
AND AS MUCH AS YOU HATED TO EVEN THINK THAT, I KNOW YOU DID.
YOU ARE ONLY HUMAN, AFTER ALL. OF COURSE, YOU ARE ALSO WRONG.
YOUR MOTHER'S DEATH IS ON YOUR HEAD.
...NO...
HIS NAME IS DESPOTELLIS. A LIVING VIRUS. HE'S KILLED DOZENS OF WORLDS. BILLIONS OF BEINGS...
...INCLUDING THE COW THAT SPAWNED YOU.
ARE YOU FRIGHTENED YET? ARE YOU FRIGHTENED OF WHICH ONE OF YOUR LOVED ONES WILL PERISH NEXT?
PERISH BECAUSE OF YOUR DEDICATION TO A GROUP OF GUARDIANS WHO DON'T EVEN KNOW WHAT LOVE MEANS?
ARE YOU AFRAID?
YOU'RE READY NOW--

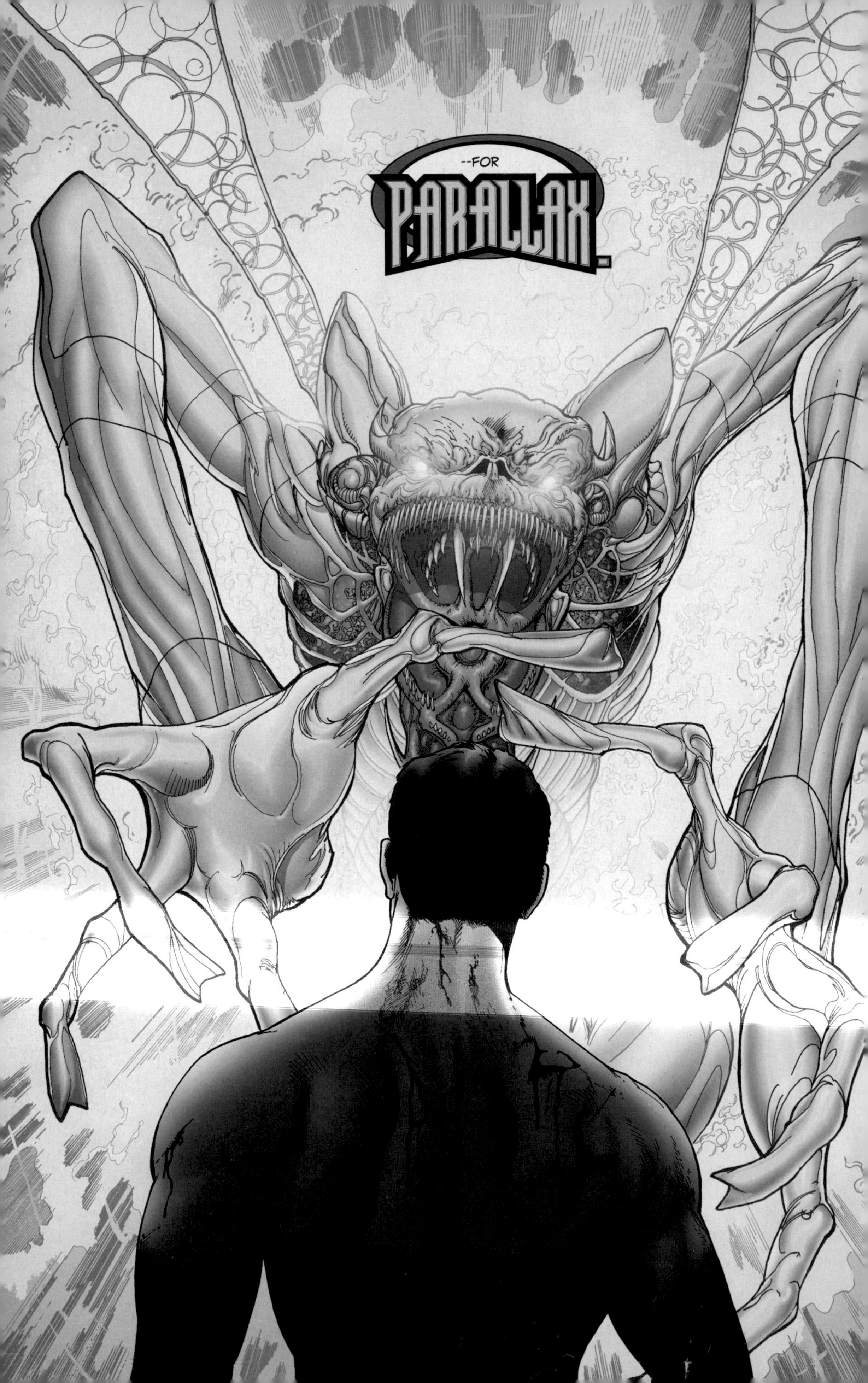
--FOR
PARALLAX.

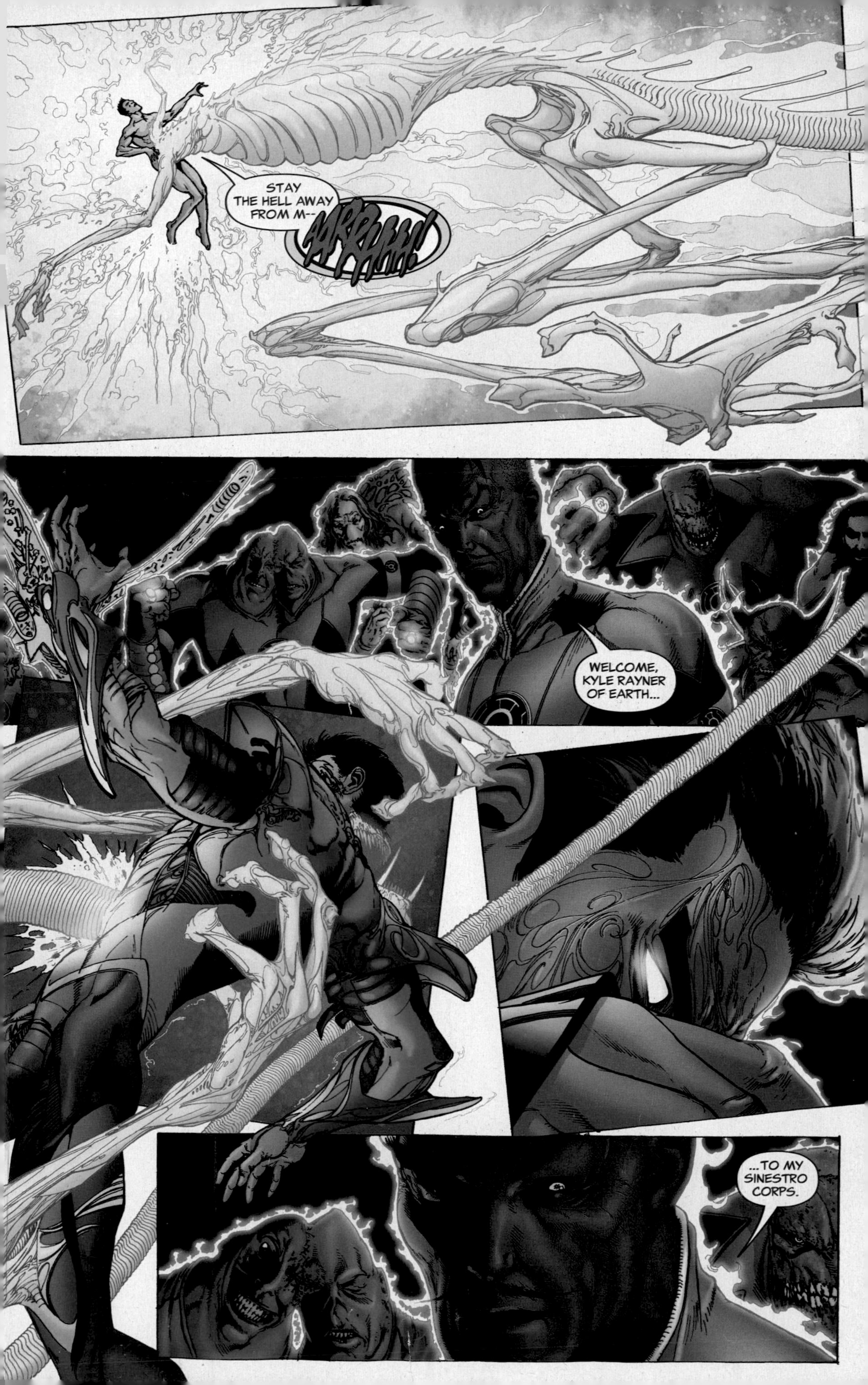
STAY THE HELL AWAY FROM M--
AARRGHHH!
WELCOME, KYLE RAYNER OF EARTH...
...TO MY SINESTRO CORPS.

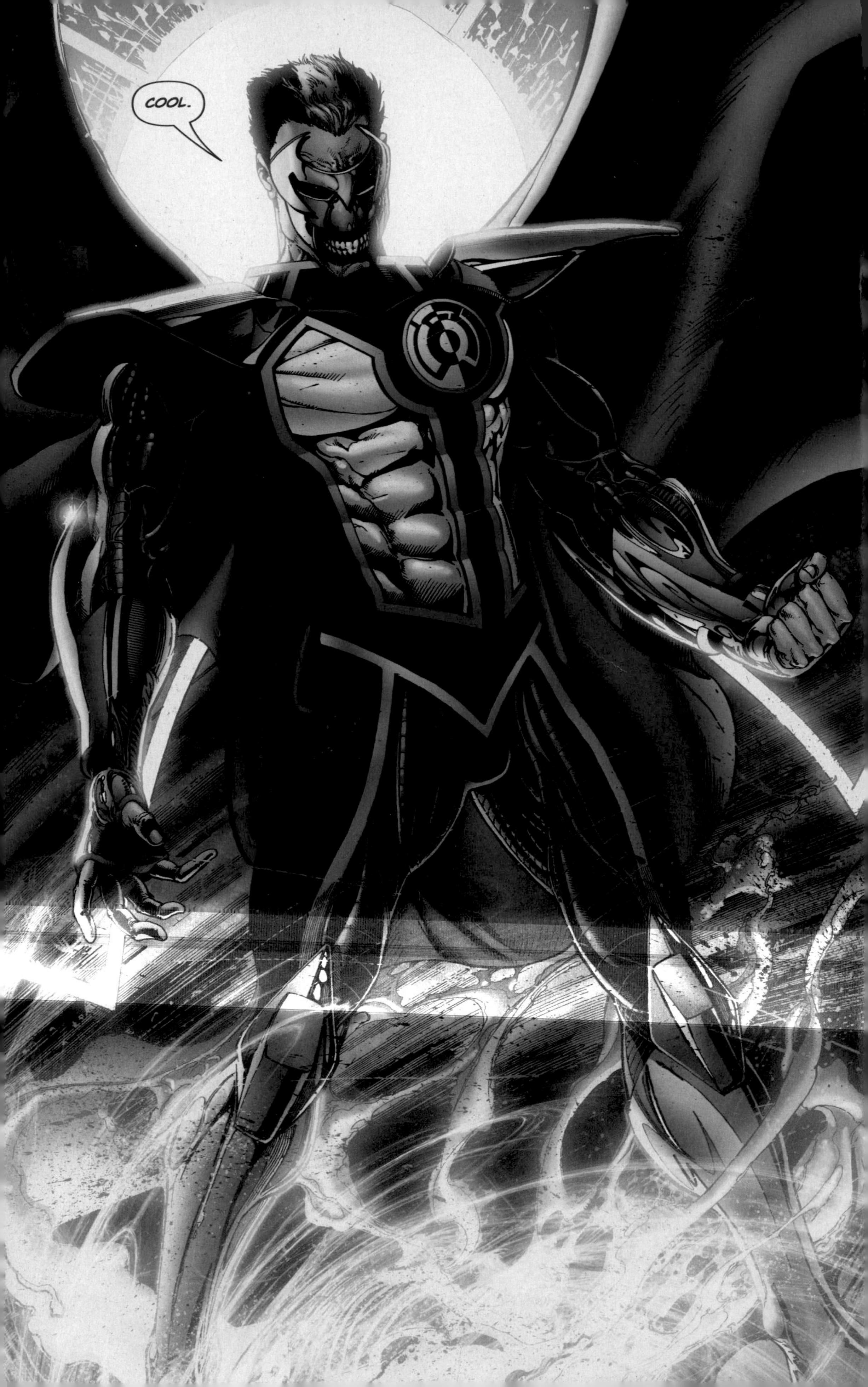
COOL.

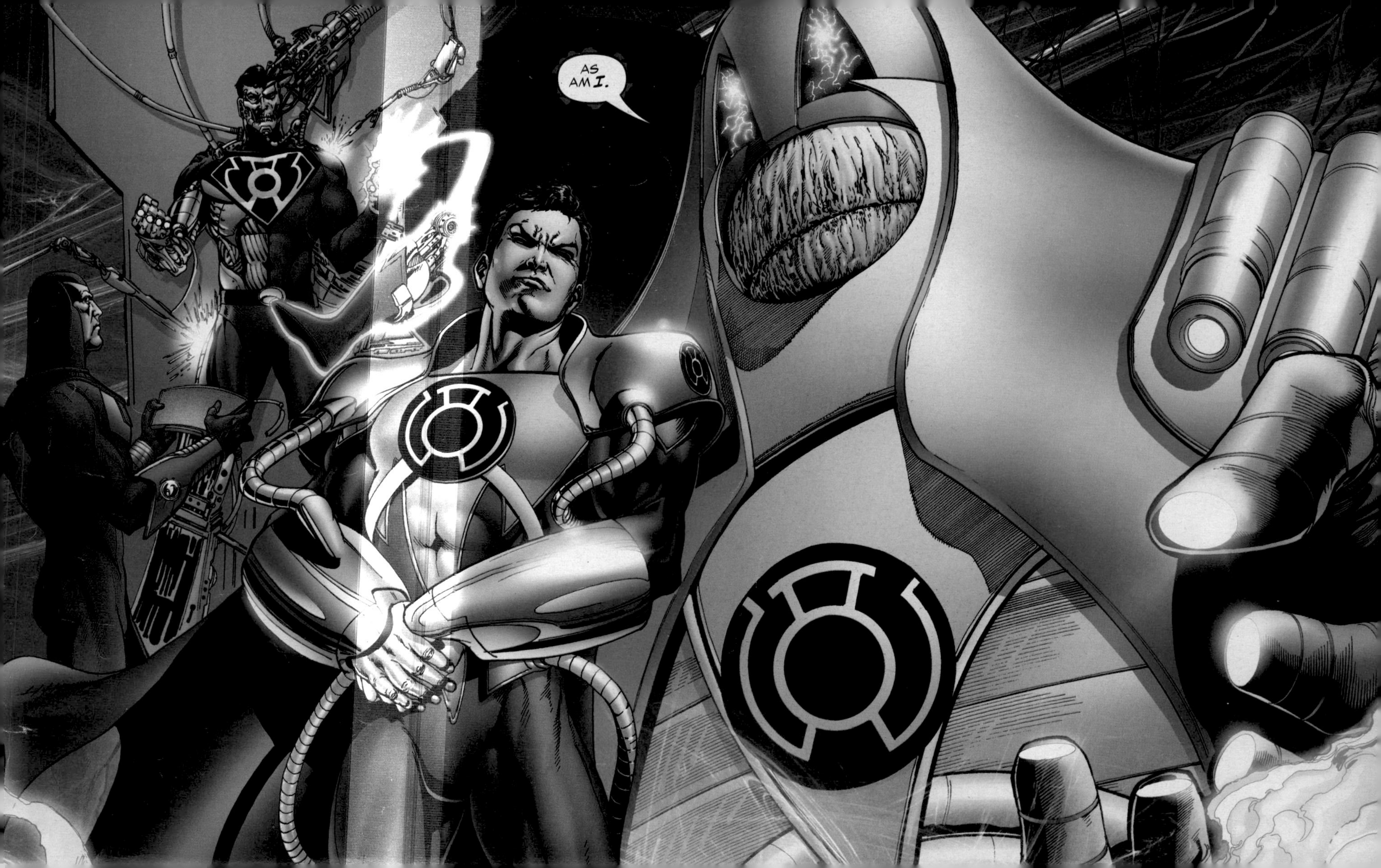
AS AM I.

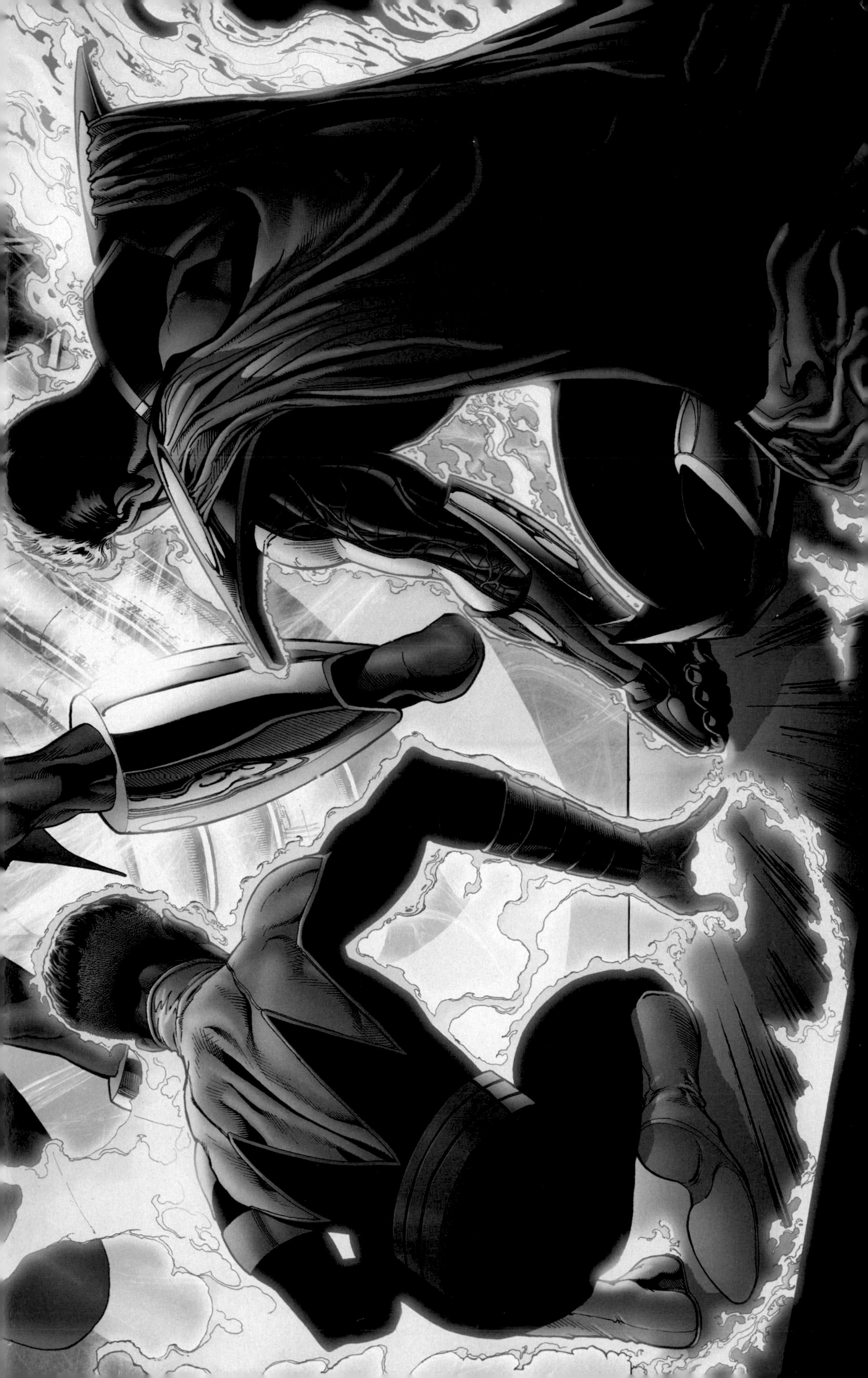

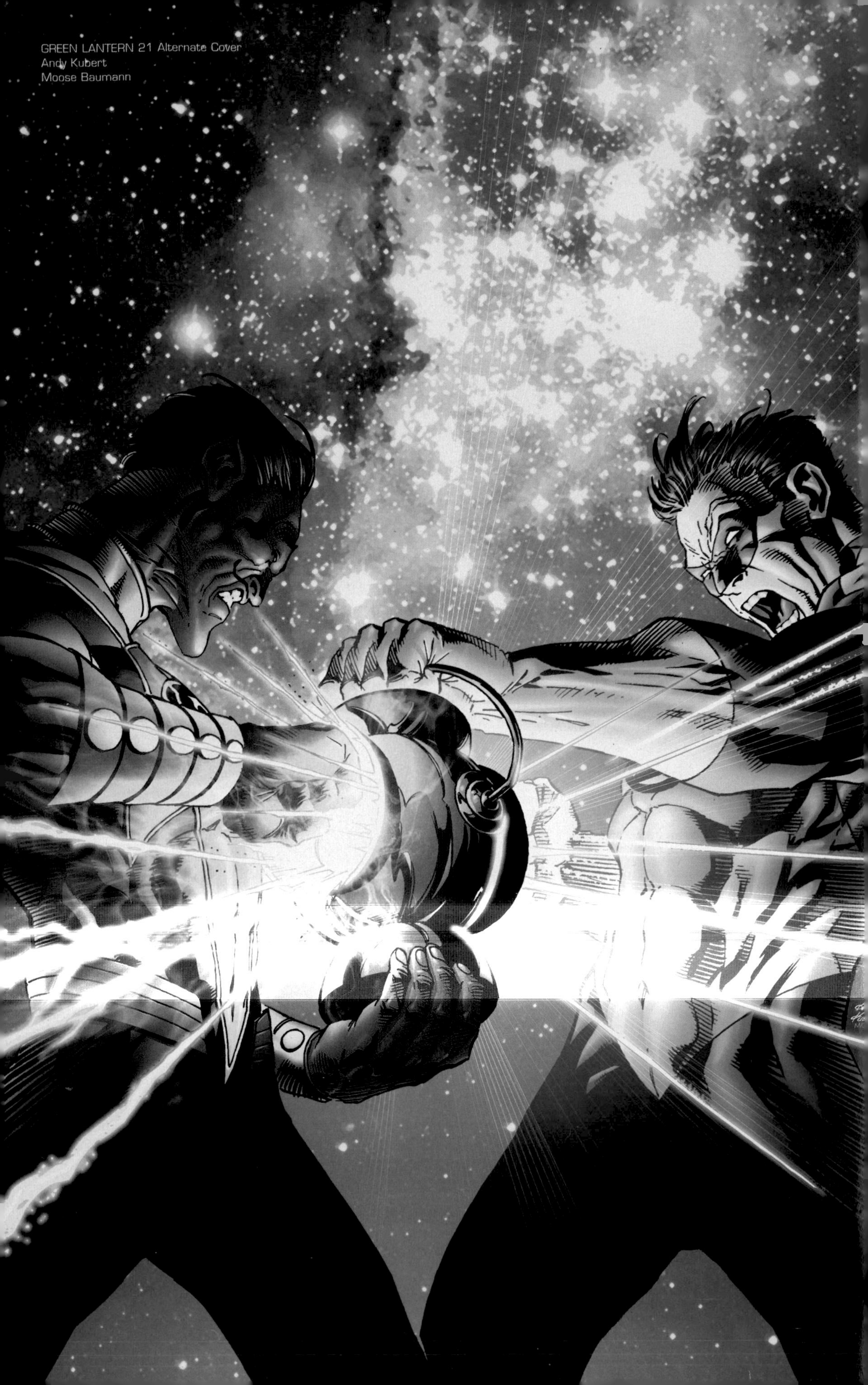

GREEN LANTERN 21 Alternate Cover
Andy Kubert
Moose Baumann

GREEN LANTERN 21
Ivan Reis
Oclair Albert
Moose Baumann

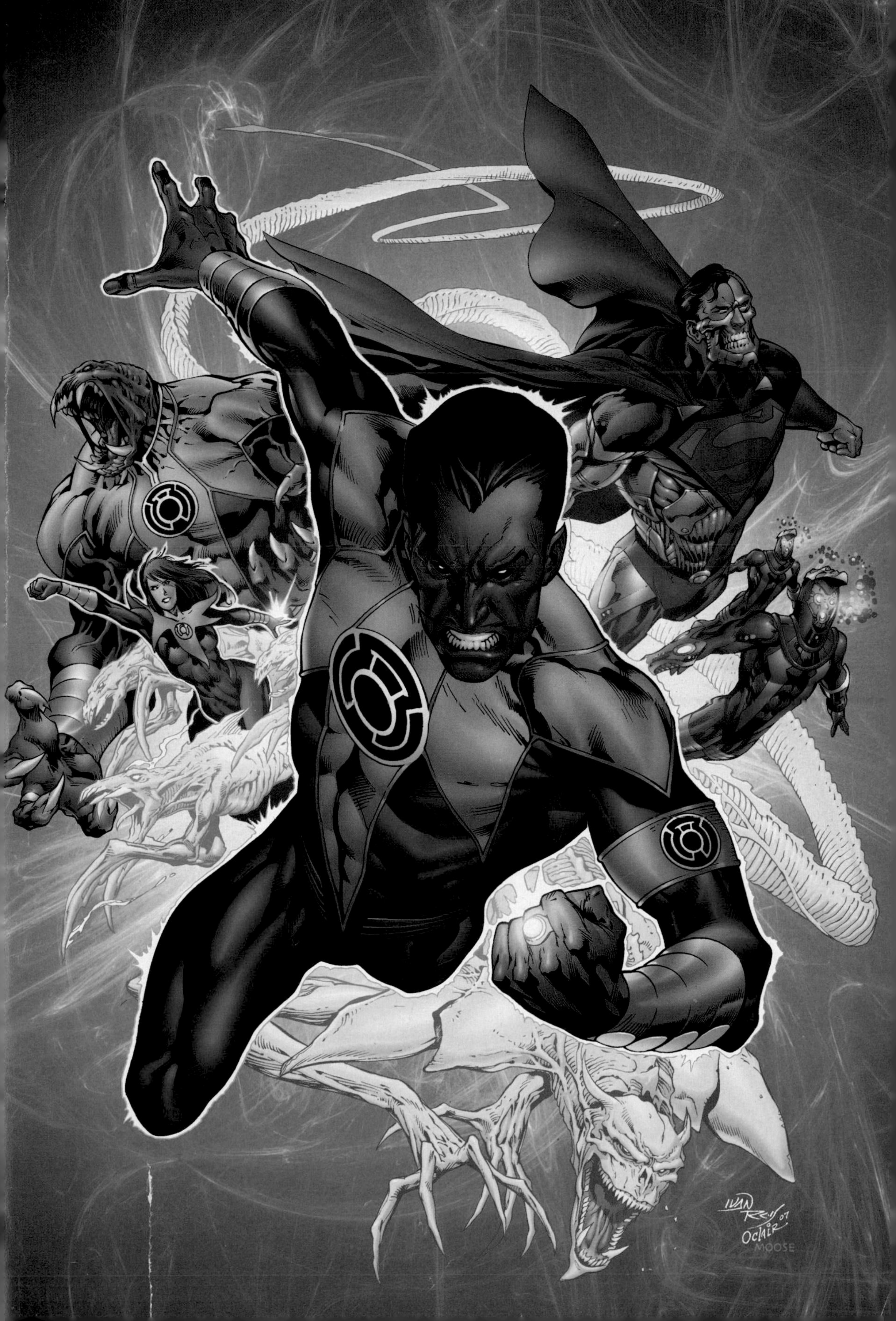
MOOSE

THE SINESTRO CORPS WAR
Chapter One
FEAR & LOATHING
Writer: **Geoff Johns**
Penciller: **Ivan Reis**
Inker: **Oclair Albert**
Colorist: **Moose Baumann**
Letterer: **Rob Leigh**

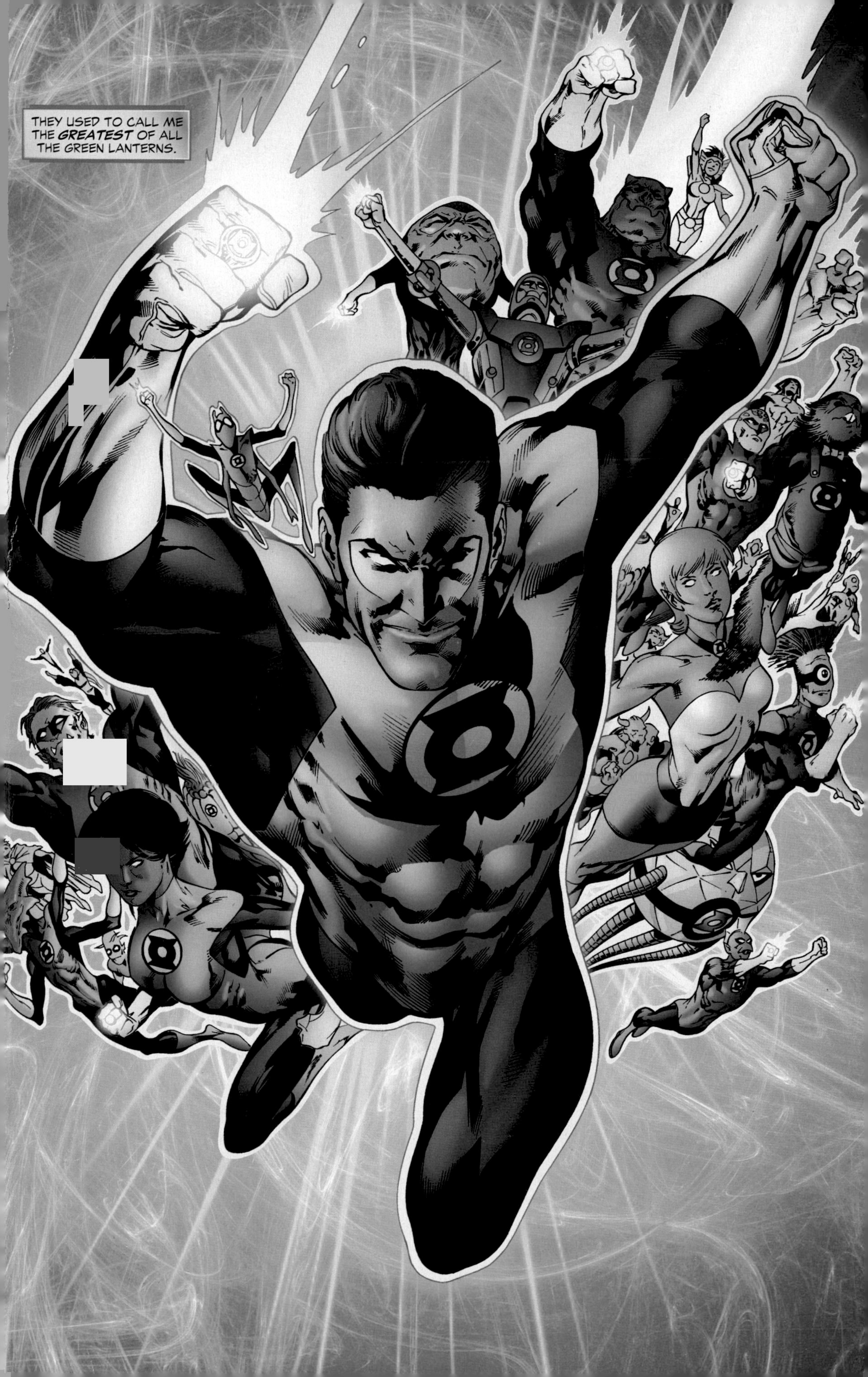
THEY USED TO CALL ME THE GREATEST OF ALL THE GREEN LANTERNS.

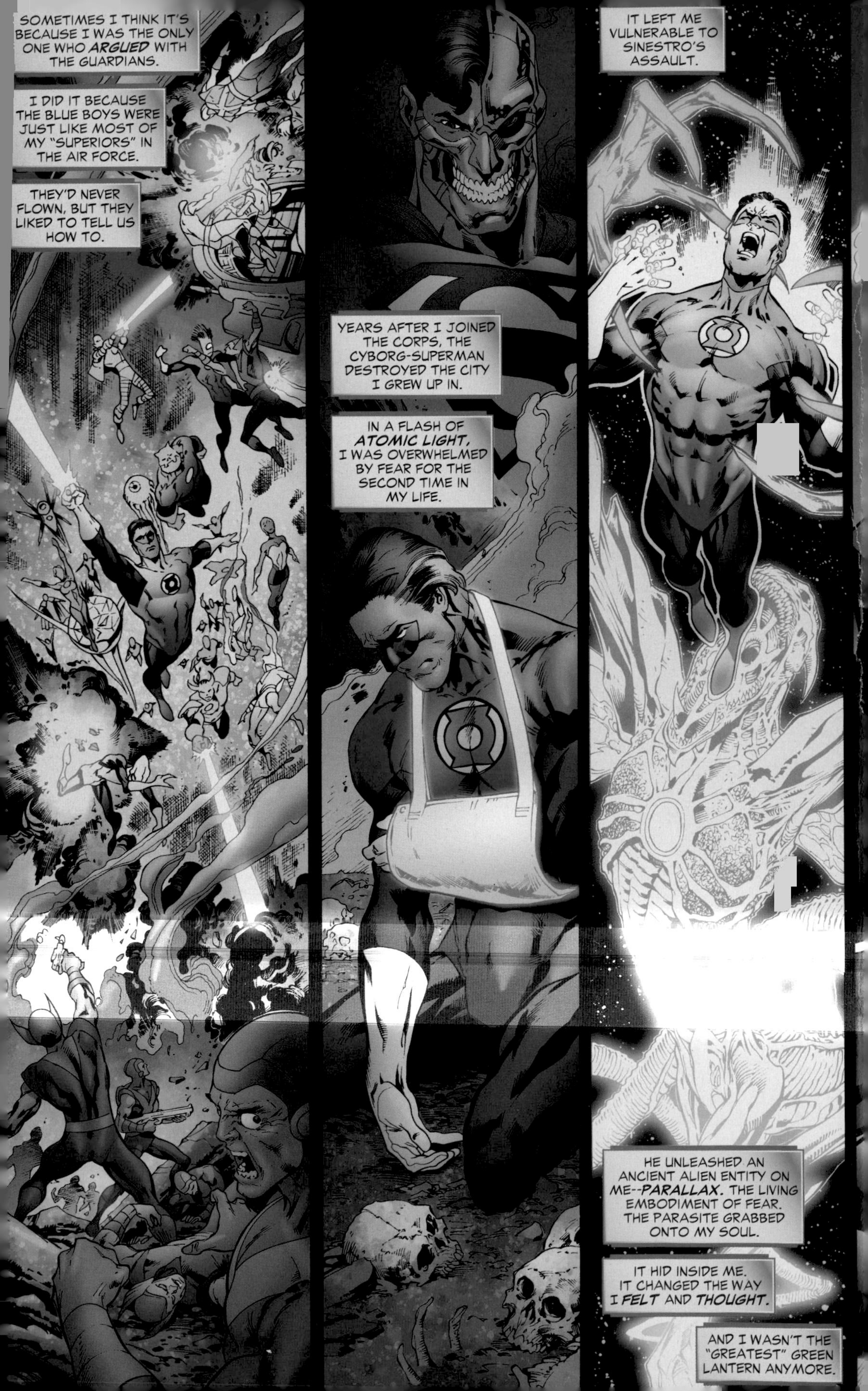
SOMETIMES I THINK IT'S BECAUSE I WAS THE ONLY ONE WHO ARGUED WITH THE GUARDIANS.
I DID IT BECAUSE THE BLUE BOYS WERE JUST LIKE MOST OF MY "SUPERIORS" IN THE AIR FORCE.
THEY'D NEVER FLOWN, BUT THEY LIKED TO TELL US HOW TO.
YEARS AFTER I JOINED THE CORPS, THE CYBORG-SUPERMAN DESTROYED THE CITY I GREW UP IN.
IN A FLASH OF ATOMIC LIGHT, I WAS OVERWHELMED BY FEAR FOR THE SECOND TIME IN MY LIFE.
IT LEFT ME VULNERABLE TO SINESTRO'S ASSAULT.
HE UNLEASHED AN ANCIENT ALIEN ENTITY ON ME--PARALLAX. THE LIVING EMBODIMENT OF FEAR. THE PARASITE GRABBED ONTO MY SOUL.
IT HID INSIDE ME. IT CHANGED THE WAY I FELT AND THOUGHT.
AND I WASN'T THE "GREATEST" GREEN LANTERN ANYMORE.

POSSESSED BY PARALLAX, I WAS THE MOST DANGEROUS.

SINCE THEN, I'VE WATCHED THE GREEN LANTERN CORPS REBUILD.

7200 STRONG. TWO OFFICERS FOR EACH OF THE 3600 SPACE SECTORS THE GUARDIANS DIVIDED THE UNIVERSE INTO.

I WAS FREED FROM PARALLAX BY THE LAST REMAINING LANTERNS.

JOHN STEWART. GUY GARDNER. KYLE RAYNER.

AND OUR DRILL SERGEANT, KILOWOG.

THERE'S NOT A MORE DIVERSE GROUP IN EXISTENCE.

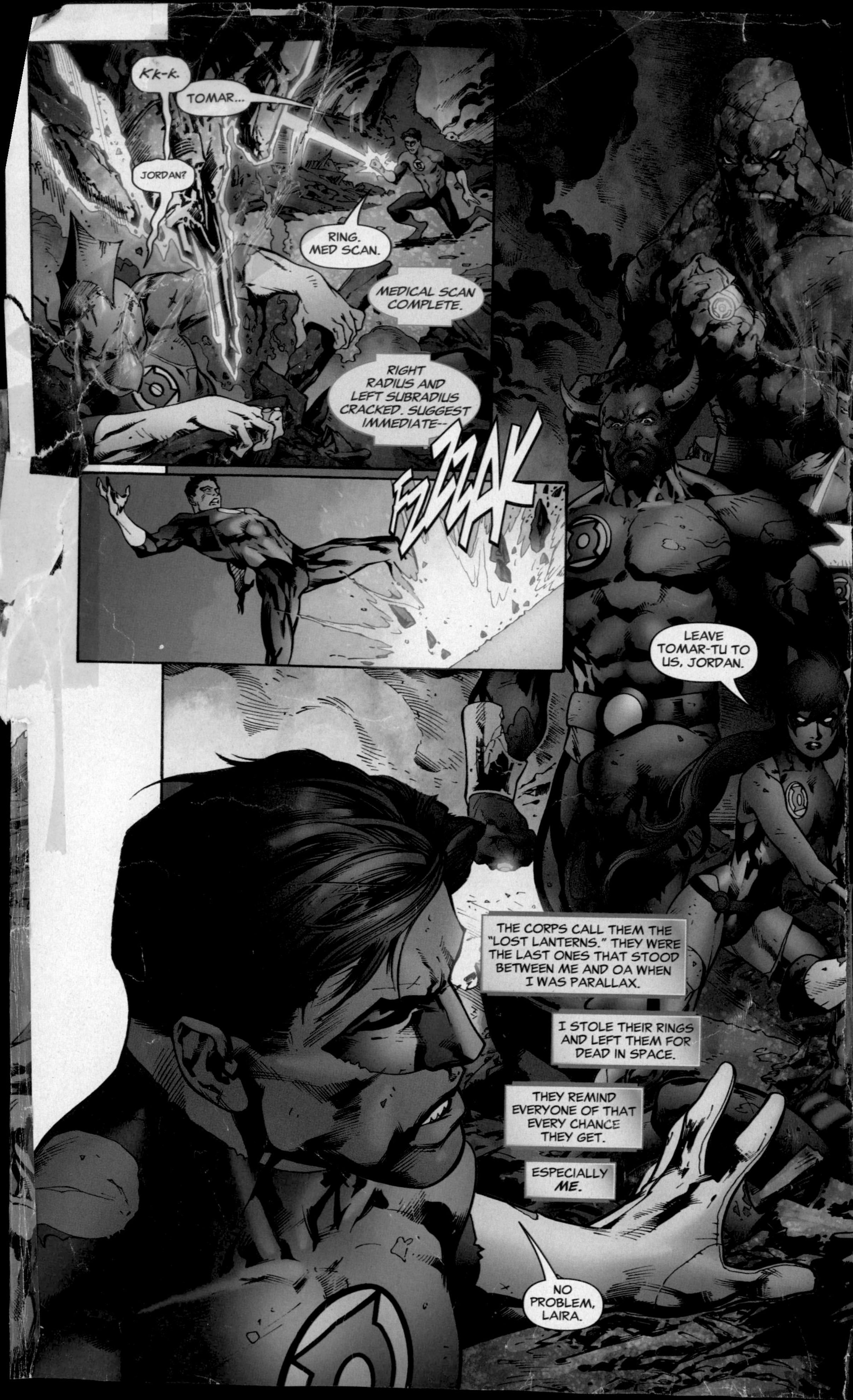
Kk-k.
TOMAR...
JORDAN?
RING. MED SCAN.
MEDICAL SCAN COMPLETE.
RIGHT RADIUS AND LEFT SUBRADIUS CRACKED. SUGGEST IMMEDIATE--
FZZZAK
LEAVE TOMAR-TU TO US, JORDAN.
THE CORPS CALL THEM THE "LOST LANTERNS." THEY WERE THE LAST ONES THAT STOOD BETWEEN ME AND OA WHEN I WAS PARALLAX.
I STOLE THEIR RINGS AND LEFT THEM FOR DEAD IN SPACE.
THEY REMIND EVERYONE OF THAT EVERY CHANCE THEY GET.
ESPECIALLY ME.
NO PROBLEM, LAIRA.

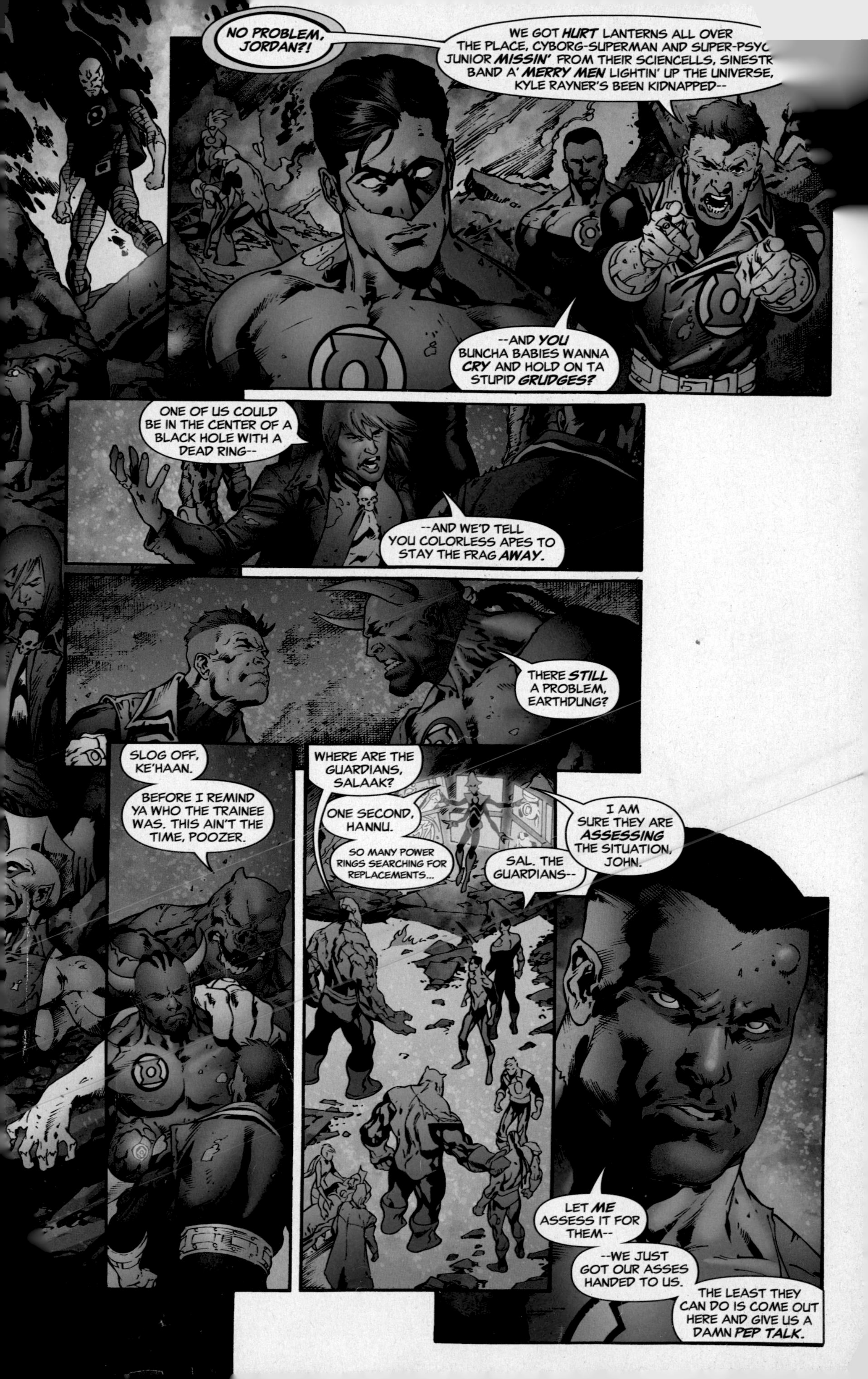
NO PROBLEM, JORDAN?!
WE GOT HURT LANTERNS ALL OVER THE PLACE, CYBORG-SUPERMAN AND SUPER-PSYC JUNIOR MISSIN' FROM THEIR SCIENCELLS, SINESTR BAND A' MERRY MEN LIGHTIN' UP THE UNIVERSE, KYLE RAYNER'S BEEN KIDNAPPED--
--AND YOU BUNCHA BABIES WANNA CRY AND HOLD ON TA STUPID GRUDGES?
ONE OF US COULD BE IN THE CENTER OF A BLACK HOLE WITH A DEAD RING--
--AND WE'D TELL YOU COLORLESS APES TO STAY THE FRAG AWAY.
THERE STILL A PROBLEM, EARTHDUNG?
SLOG OFF, KE'HAAN.
BEFORE I REMIND YA WHO THE TRAINEE WAS. THIS AIN'T THE TIME, POOZER.
WHERE ARE THE GUARDIANS, SALAAK?
ONE SECOND, HANNU.
SO MANY POWER RINGS SEARCHING FOR REPLACEMENTS...
I AM SURE THEY ARE ASSESSING THE SITUATION, JOHN.
SAL. THE GUARDIANS--
LET ME ASSESS IT FOR THEM--
--WE JUST GOT OUR ASSES HANDED TO US.
THE LEAST THEY CAN DO IS COME OUT HERE AND GIVE US A DAMN PEP TALK.

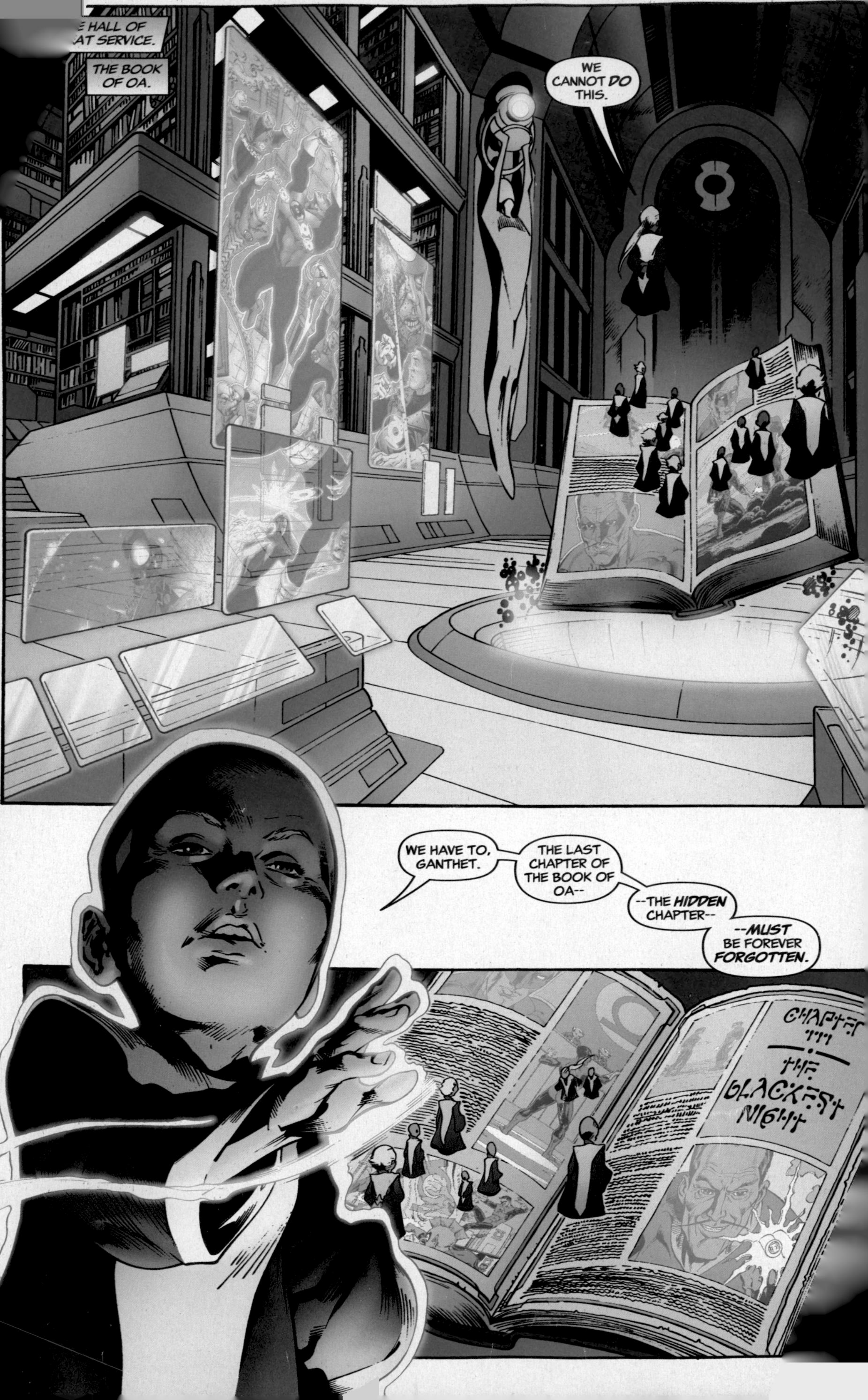

HALL OF
AT SERVICE.
THE BOOK OF OA.
WE CANNOT DO THIS.
WE HAVE TO, GANTHET.
THE LAST CHAPTER OF THE BOOK OF OA--
--THE HIDDEN CHAPTER--
--MUST BE FOREVER FORGOTTEN.
THE BLACKEST NIGHT

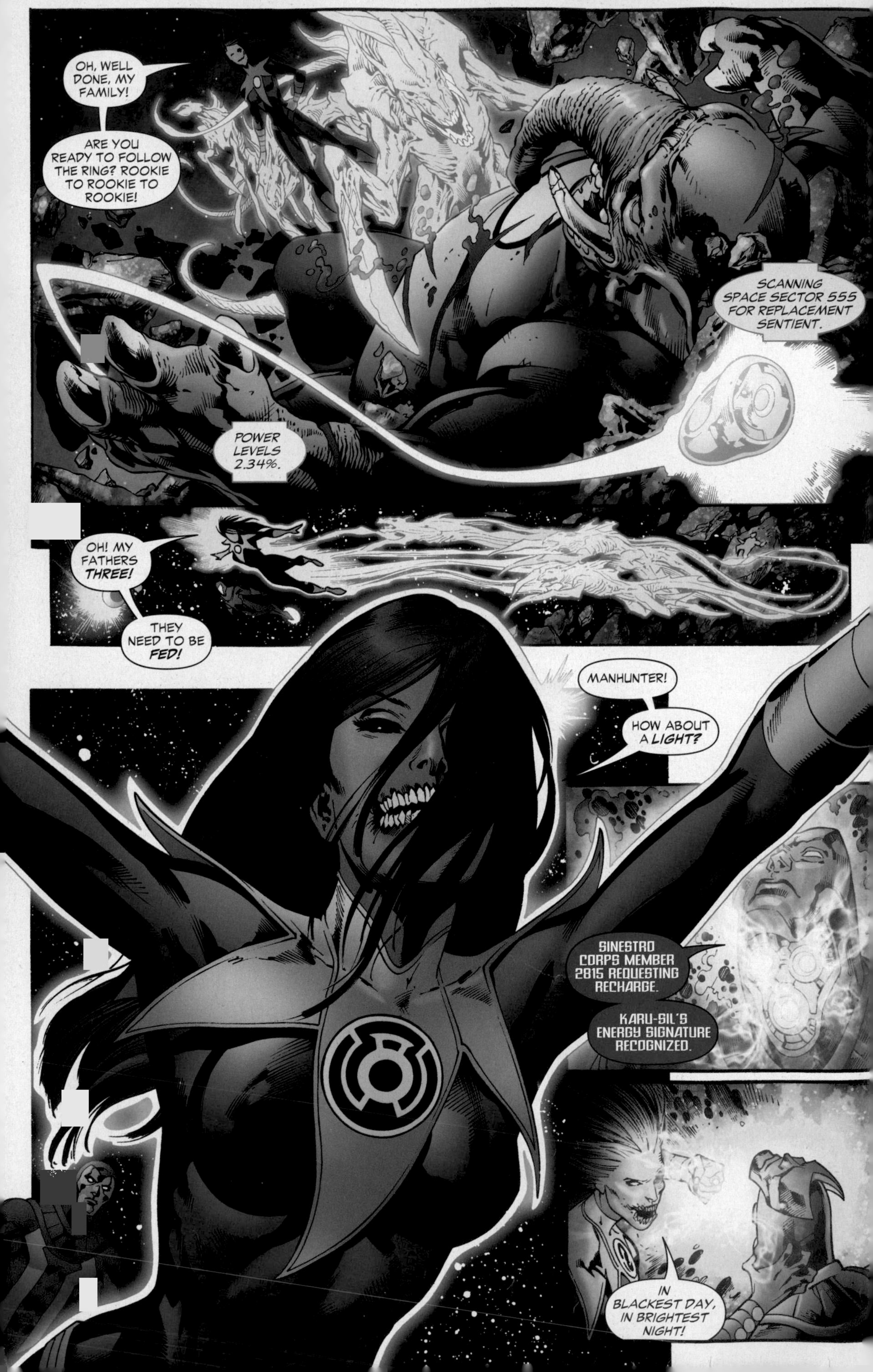
OH, WELL DONE, MY FAMILY!
ARE YOU READY TO FOLLOW THE RING? ROOKIE TO ROOKIE TO ROOKIE!
SCANNING SPACE SECTOR 555 FOR REPLACEMENT SENTIENT.
POWER LEVELS 2.34%.
OH! MY FATHERS THREE!
THEY NEED TO BE FED!
MANHUNTER!
HOW ABOUT A LIGHT?
SINESTRO CORPS MEMBER 2815 REQUESTING RECHARGE.
KARU-SIL'S ENERGY SIGNATURE RECOGNIZED.
IN BLACKEST DAY, IN BRIGHTEST NIGHT!

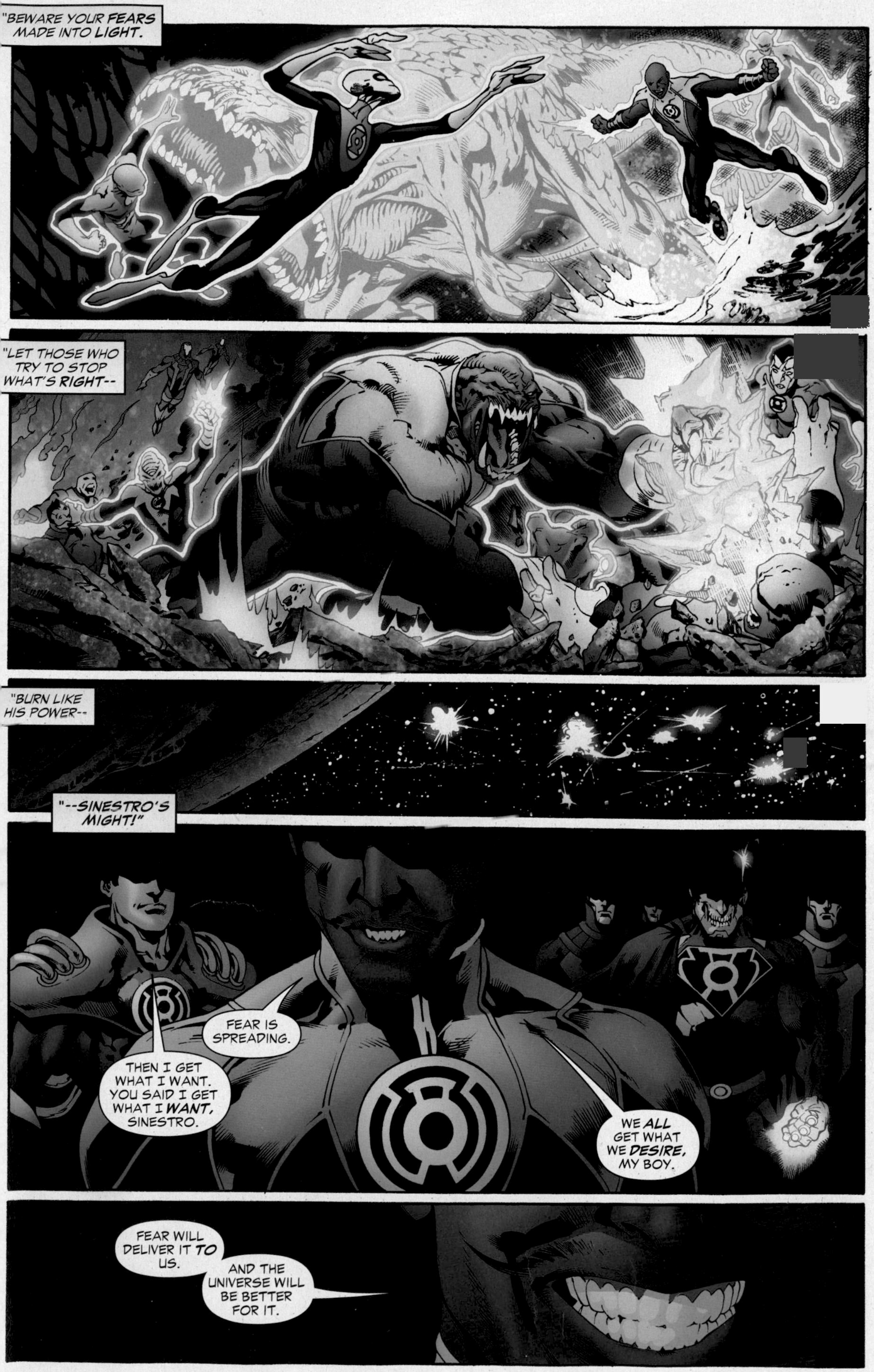

"BEWARE YOUR FEARS MADE INTO LIGHT.
"LET THOSE WHO TRY TO STOP WHAT'S RIGHT--
"BURN LIKE HIS POWER--
"--SINESTRO'S MIGHT!"
FEAR IS SPREADING.
THEN I GET WHAT I WANT. YOU SAID I GET WHAT I WANT, SINESTRO.
WE ALL GET WHAT WE DESIRE, MY BOY.
FEAR WILL DELIVER IT TO US.
AND THE UNIVERSE WILL BE BETTER FOR IT.

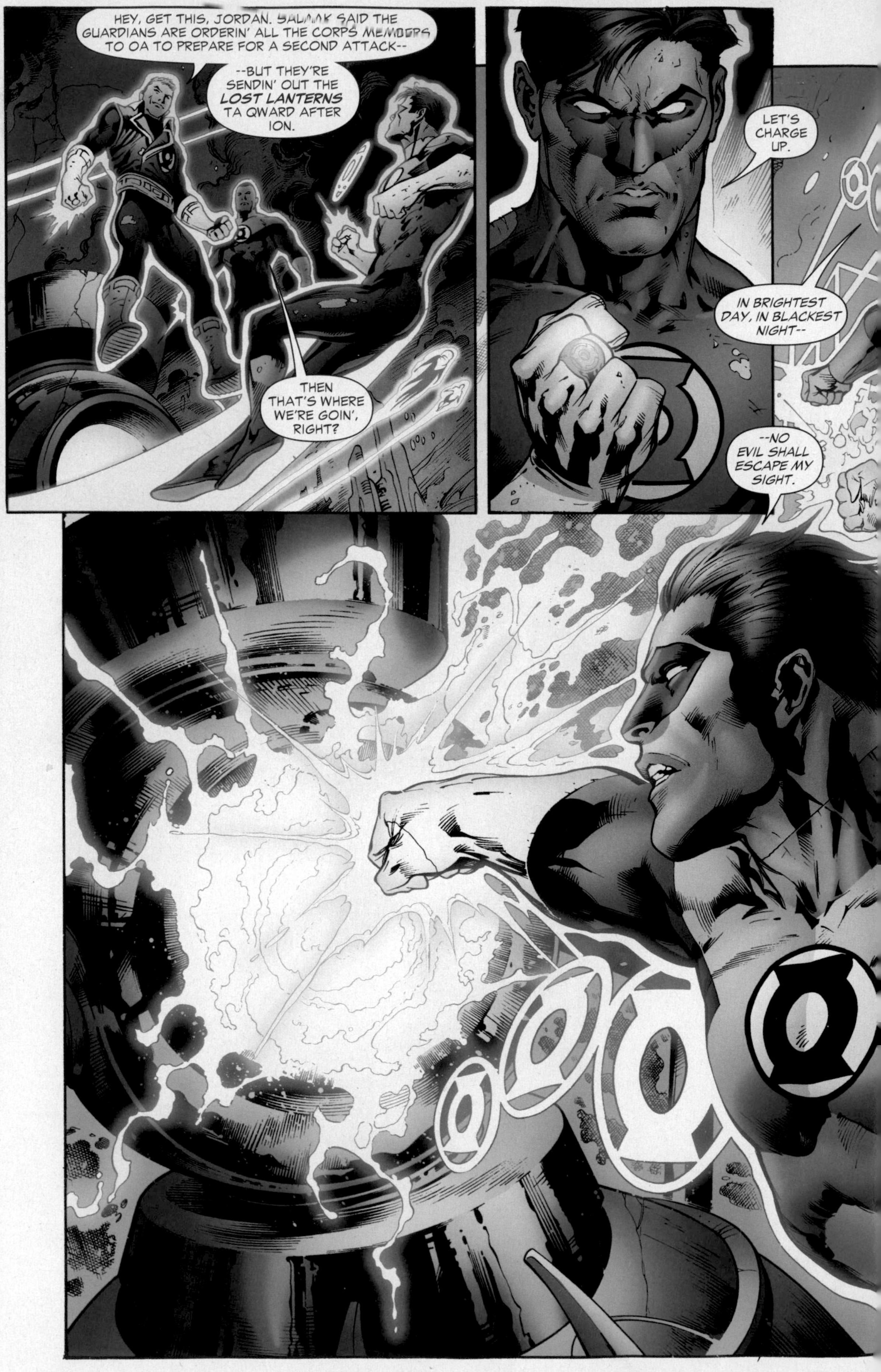
HEY, GET THIS, JORDAN. SALAAK SAID THE GUARDIANS ARE ORDERIN' ALL THE CORPS MEMBERS TO OA TO PREPARE FOR A SECOND ATTACK--
--BUT THEY'RE SENDIN' OUT THE LOST LANTERNS TA QWARD AFTER ION.
THEN THAT'S WHERE WE'RE GOIN', RIGHT?
LET'S CHARGE UP.
IN BRIGHTEST DAY, IN BLACKEST NIGHT--
--NO EVIL SHALL ESCAPE MY SIGHT.

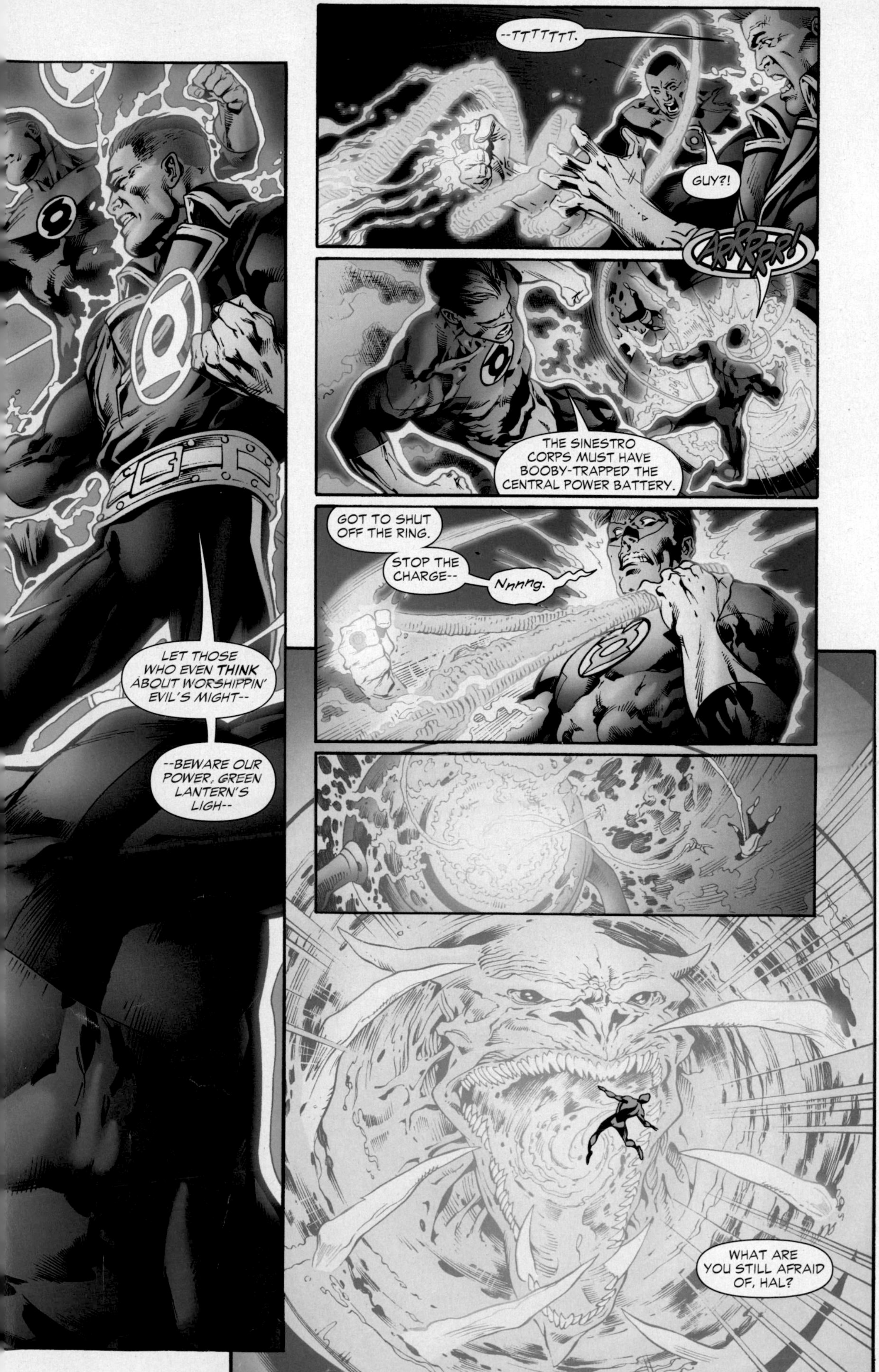
--TTTTTTT.
GUY?!
ARRRRR!
LET THOSE WHO EVEN THINK ABOUT WORSHIPPIN' EVIL'S MIGHT--
--BEWARE OUR POWER, GREEN LANTERN'S LIGH--
THE SINESTRO CORPS MUST HAVE BOOBY-TRAPPED THE CENTRAL POWER BATTERY.
GOT TO SHUT OFF THE RING.
STOP THE CHARGE--
Nnnng.
WHAT ARE YOU STILL AFRAID OF, HAL?

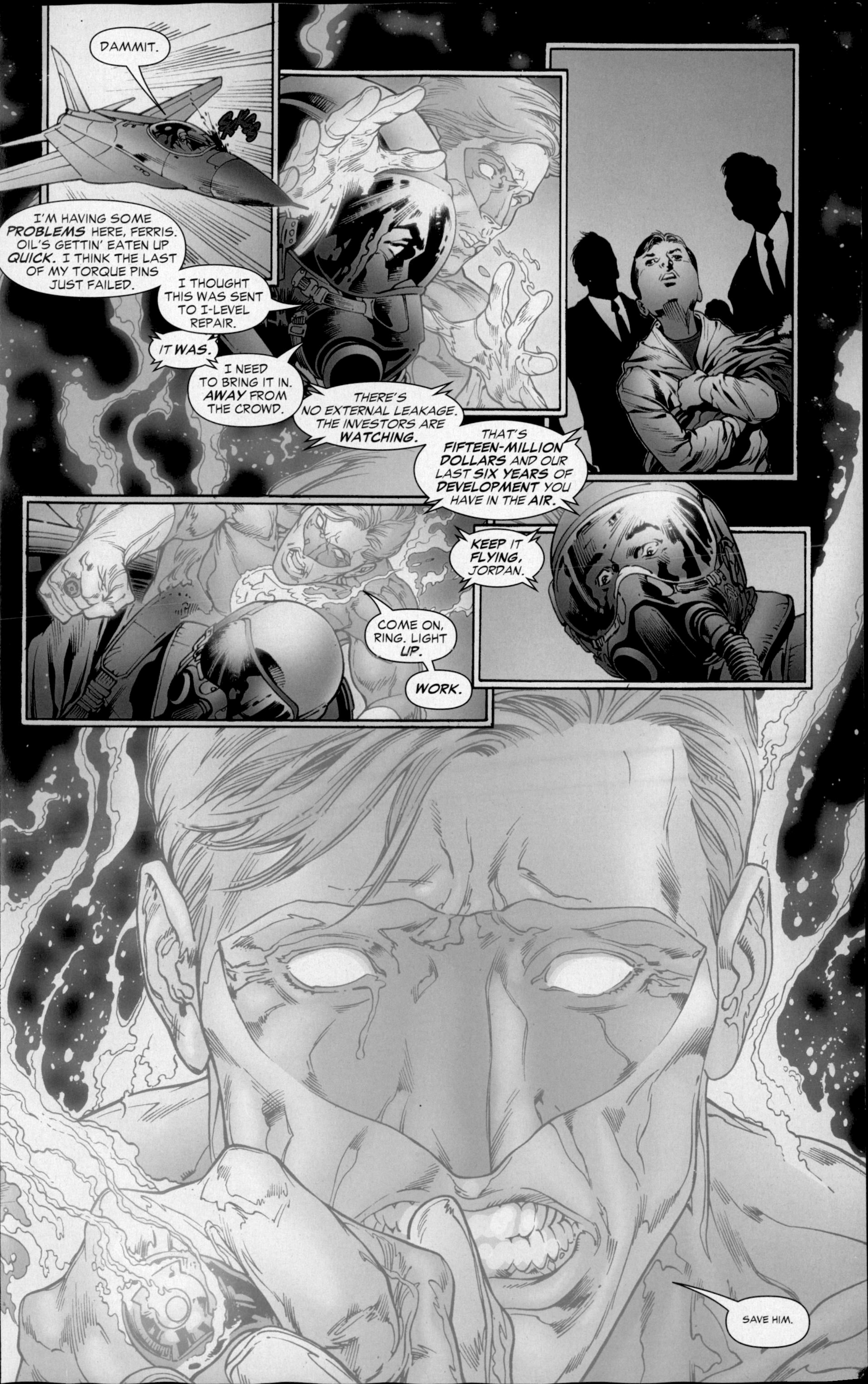
DAMMIT.
I'M HAVING SOME PROBLEMS HERE, FERRIS. OIL'S GETTIN' EATEN UP QUICK. I THINK THE LAST OF MY TORQUE PINS JUST FAILED.
I THOUGHT THIS WAS SENT TO I-LEVEL REPAIR.
IT WAS.
I NEED TO BRING IT IN. AWAY FROM THE CROWD.
THERE'S NO EXTERNAL LEAKAGE. THE INVESTORS ARE WATCHING.
THAT'S FIFTEEN-MILLION DOLLARS AND OUR LAST SIX YEARS OF DEVELOPMENT YOU HAVE IN THE AIR.
KEEP IT FLYING, JORDAN.
COME ON, RING. LIGHT UP.
WORK.
SAVE HIM.

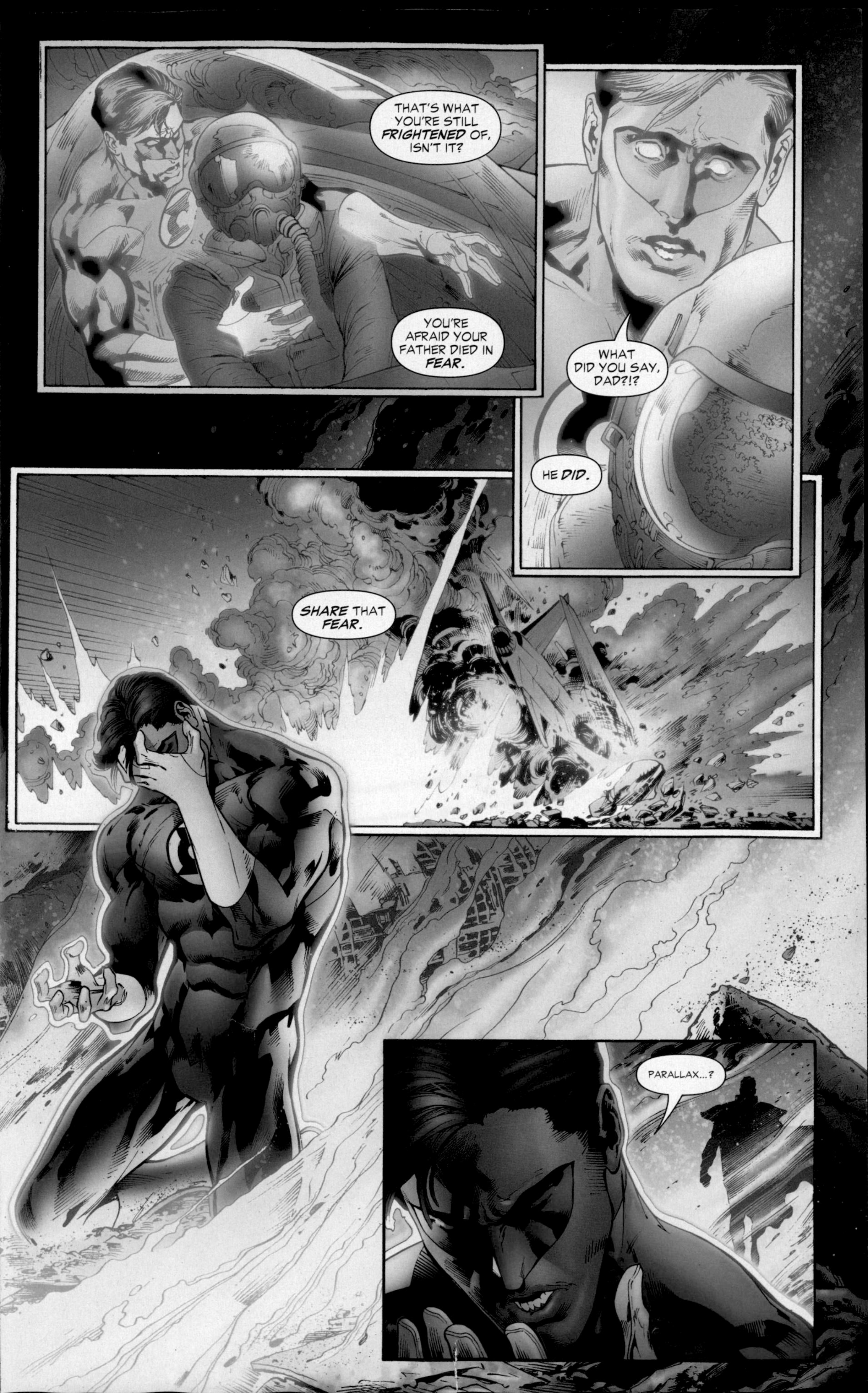
THAT'S WHAT YOU'RE STILL FRIGHTENED OF, ISN'T IT?
YOU'RE AFRAID YOUR FATHER DIED IN FEAR.
WHAT DID YOU SAY, DAD?!?
HE DID.
SHARE THAT FEAR.
PARALLAX...?

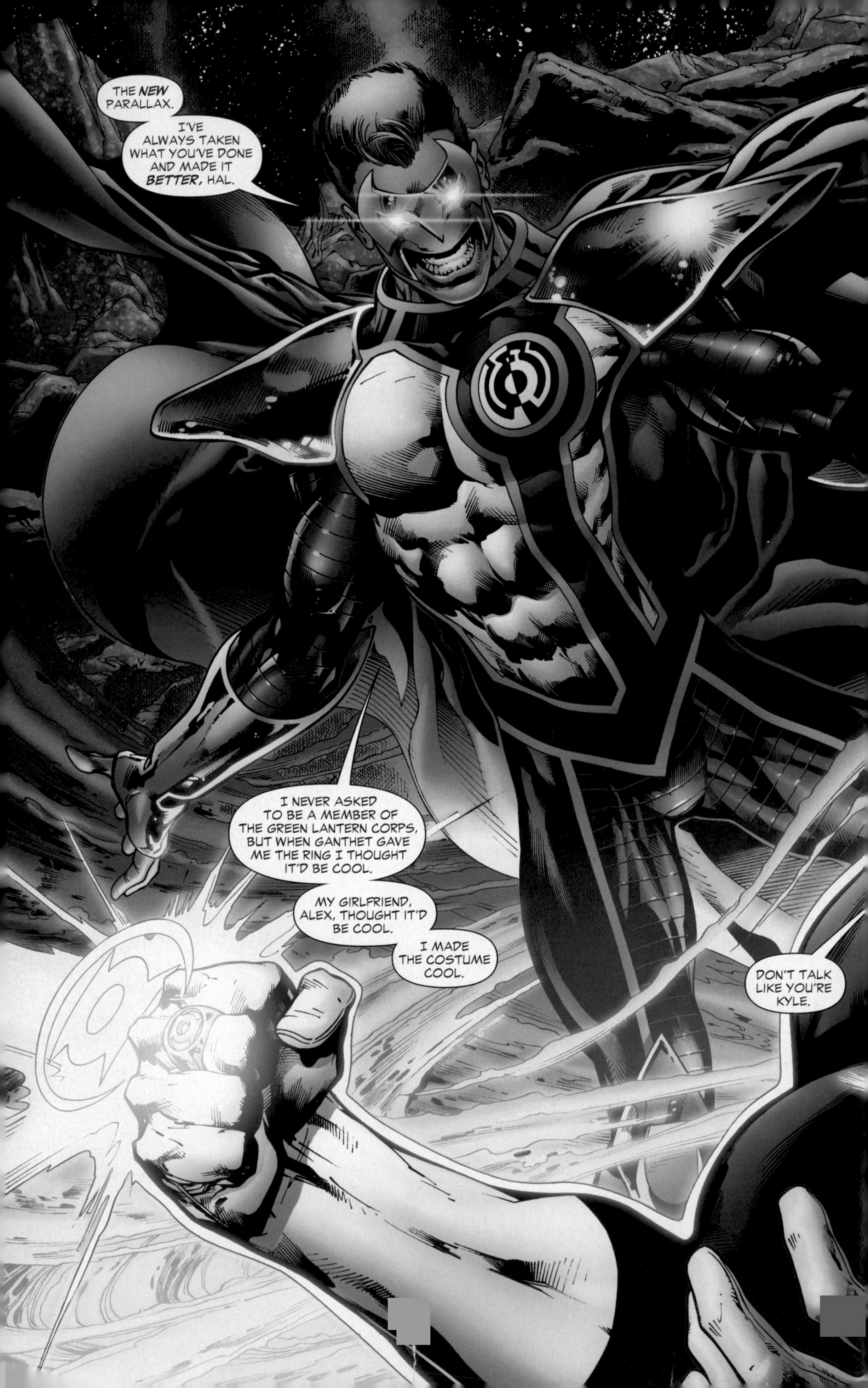
THE NEW PARALLAX.
I'VE ALWAYS TAKEN WHAT YOU'VE DONE AND MADE IT BETTER, HAL.
I NEVER ASKED TO BE A MEMBER OF THE GREEN LANTERN CORPS, BUT WHEN GANTHET GAVE ME THE RING I THOUGHT IT'D BE COOL.
MY GIRLFRIEND, ALEX, THOUGHT IT'D BE COOL.
I MADE THE COSTUME COOL.
DON'T TALK LIKE YOU'RE KYLE.

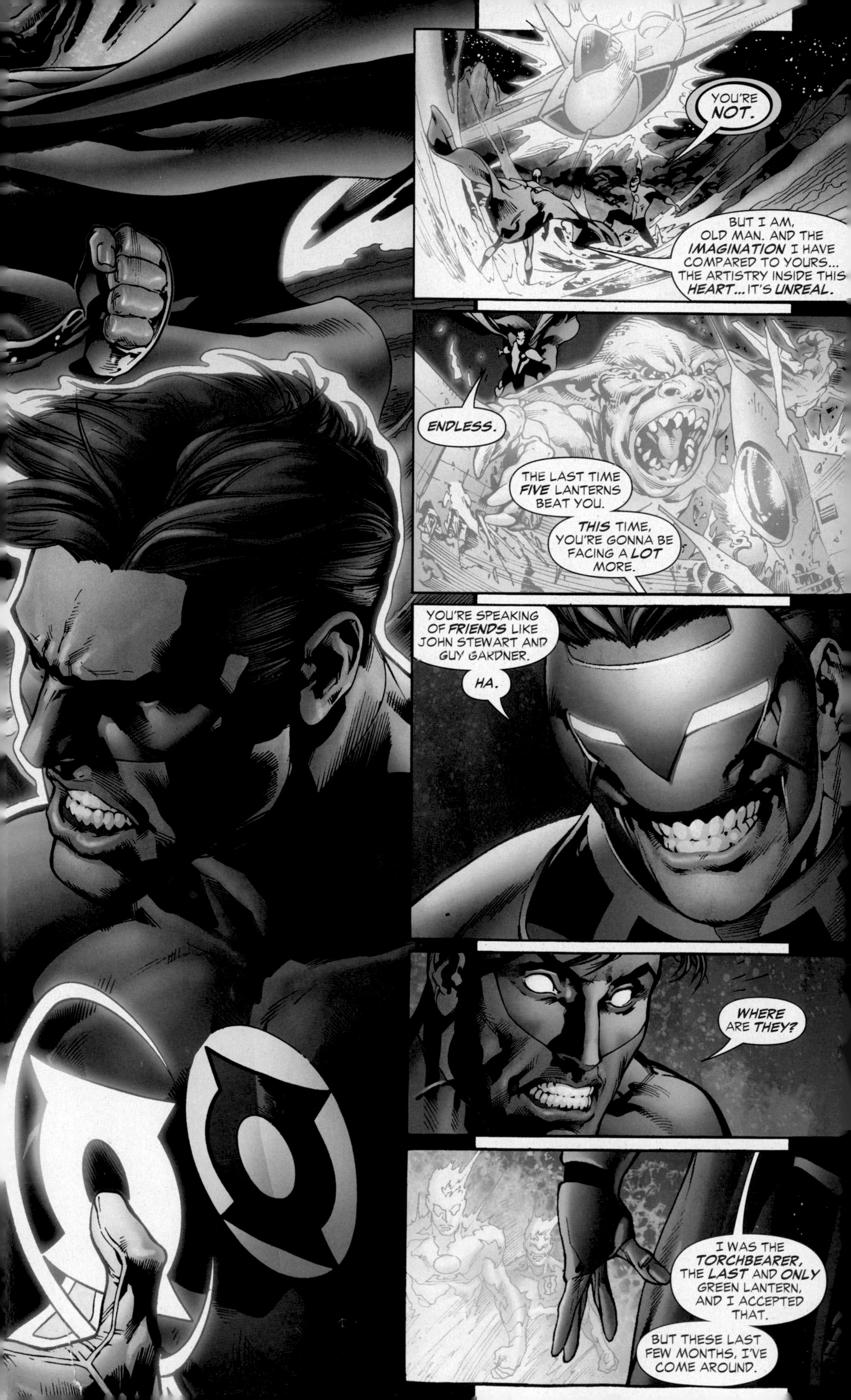

YOU'RE NOT.
BUT I AM, OLD MAN. AND THE IMAGINATION I HAVE COMPARED TO YOURS... THE ARTISTRY INSIDE THIS HEART... IT'S UNREAL.
ENDLESS.
THE LAST TIME FIVE LANTERNS BEAT YOU.
THIS TIME, YOU'RE GONNA BE FACING A LOT MORE.
YOU'RE SPEAKING OF FRIENDS LIKE JOHN STEWART AND GUY GARDNER.
HA.
WHERE ARE THEY?
I WAS THE TORCHBEARER, THE LAST AND ONLY GREEN LANTERN, AND I ACCEPTED THAT.
BUT THESE LAST FEW MONTHS, I'VE COME AROUND.

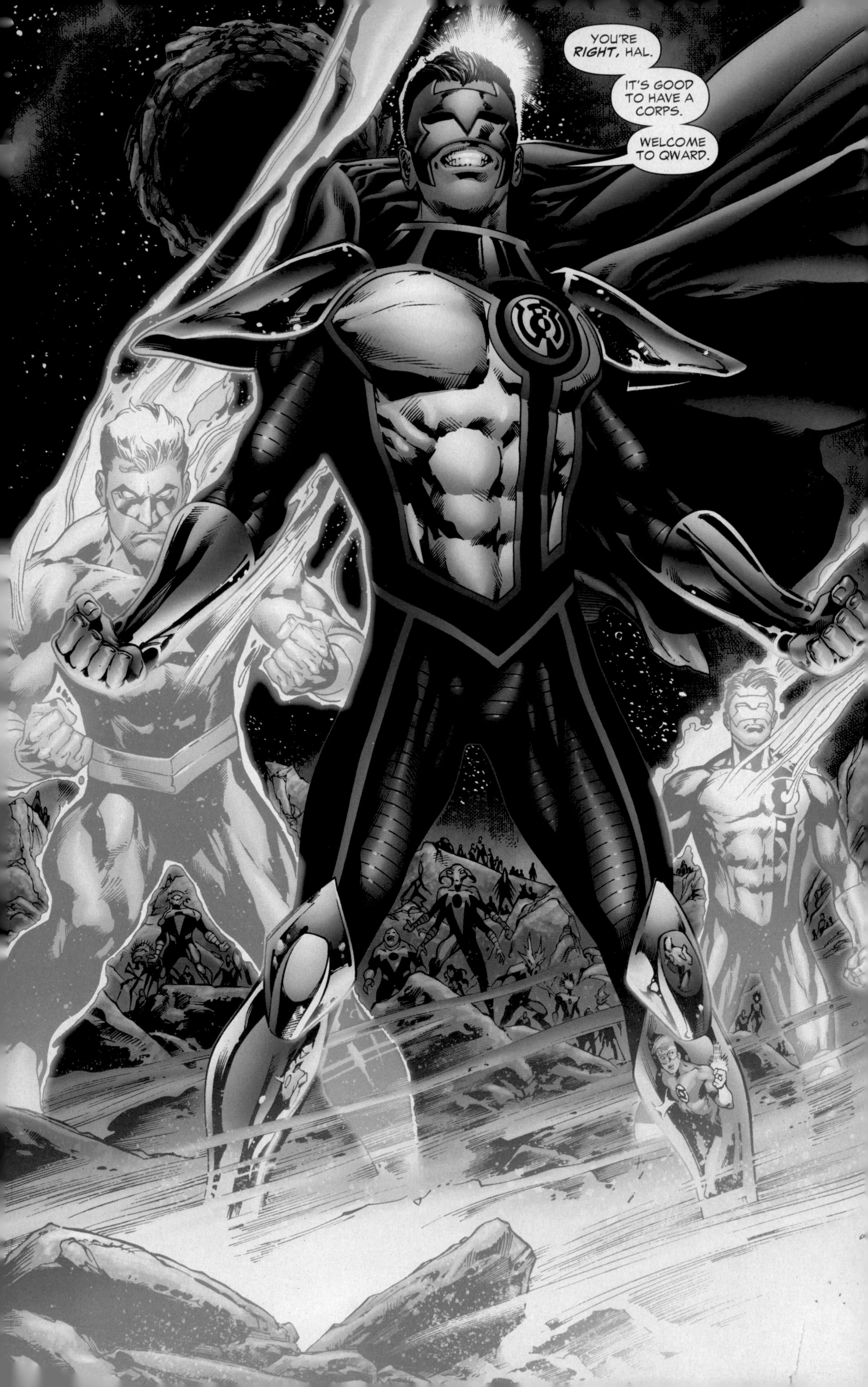
YOU'RE RIGHT, HAL.
IT'S GOOD TO HAVE A CORPS.
WELCOME TO QWARD.

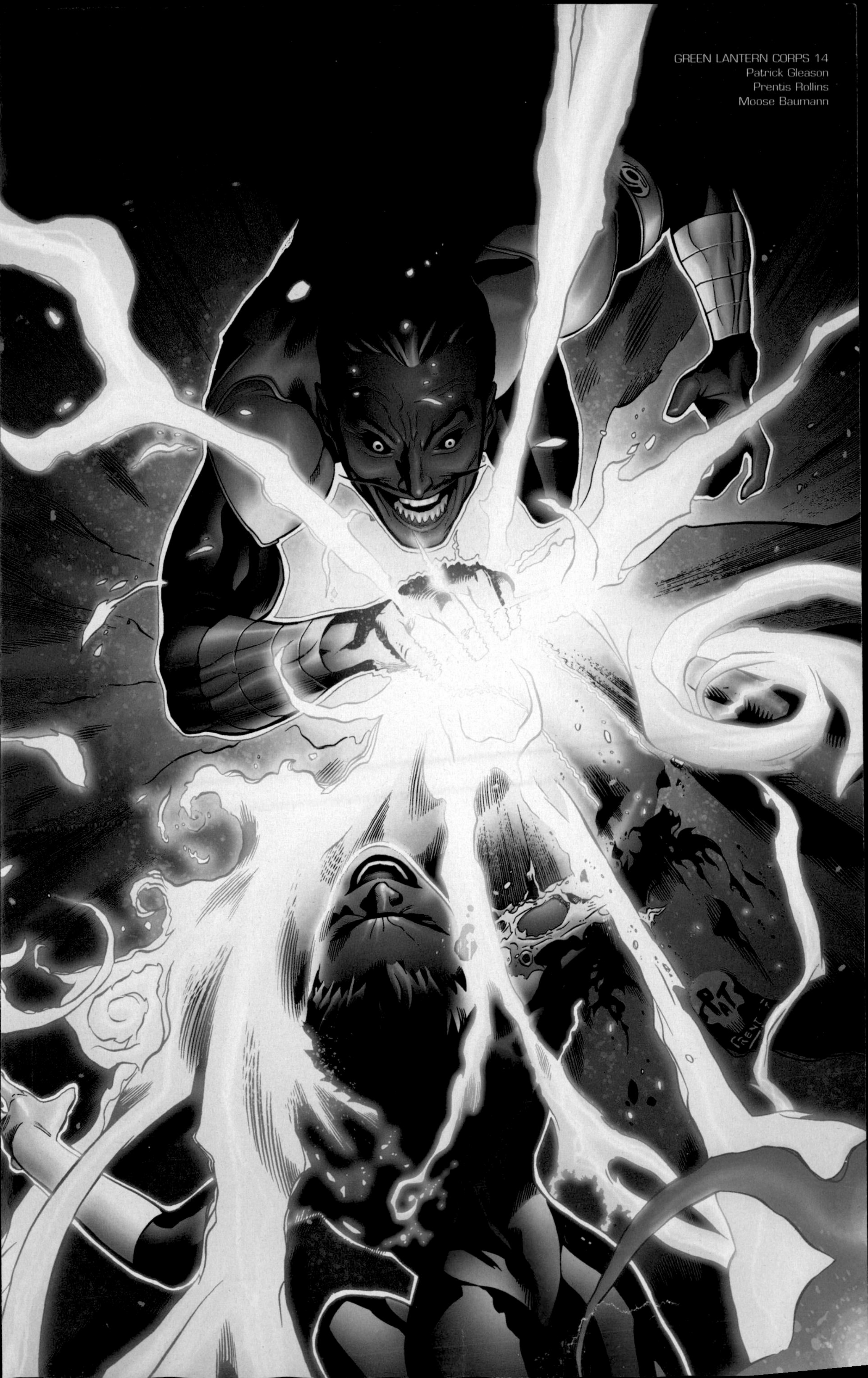

GREEN LANTERN CORPS 14
Patrick Gleason
Prentis Rollins
Moose Baumann

THE SINESTRO CORPS WAR
Chapter Two
THE GATHERING STORM
Penciller: **Patrick Gleason** (pages 81-91, 94-97, 100-102)
Penciller: **Angel Unzueta** (pages 92-93, 98-99)
Inker: **Prentis Rollins**
Colorist: **Guy Major**
Letterer: **Phil Balsman**

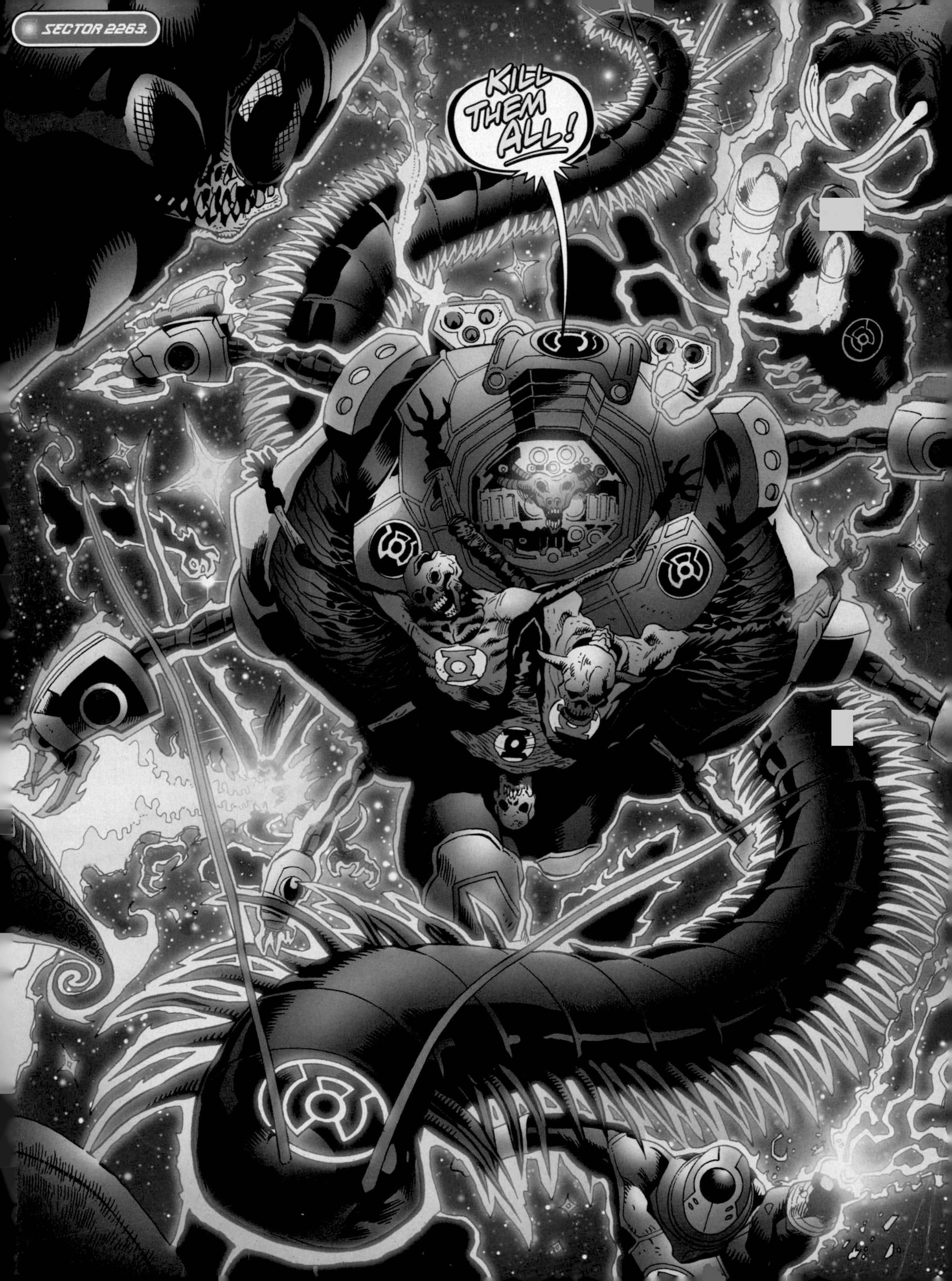
SECTOR 2263.
KILL THEM ALL!

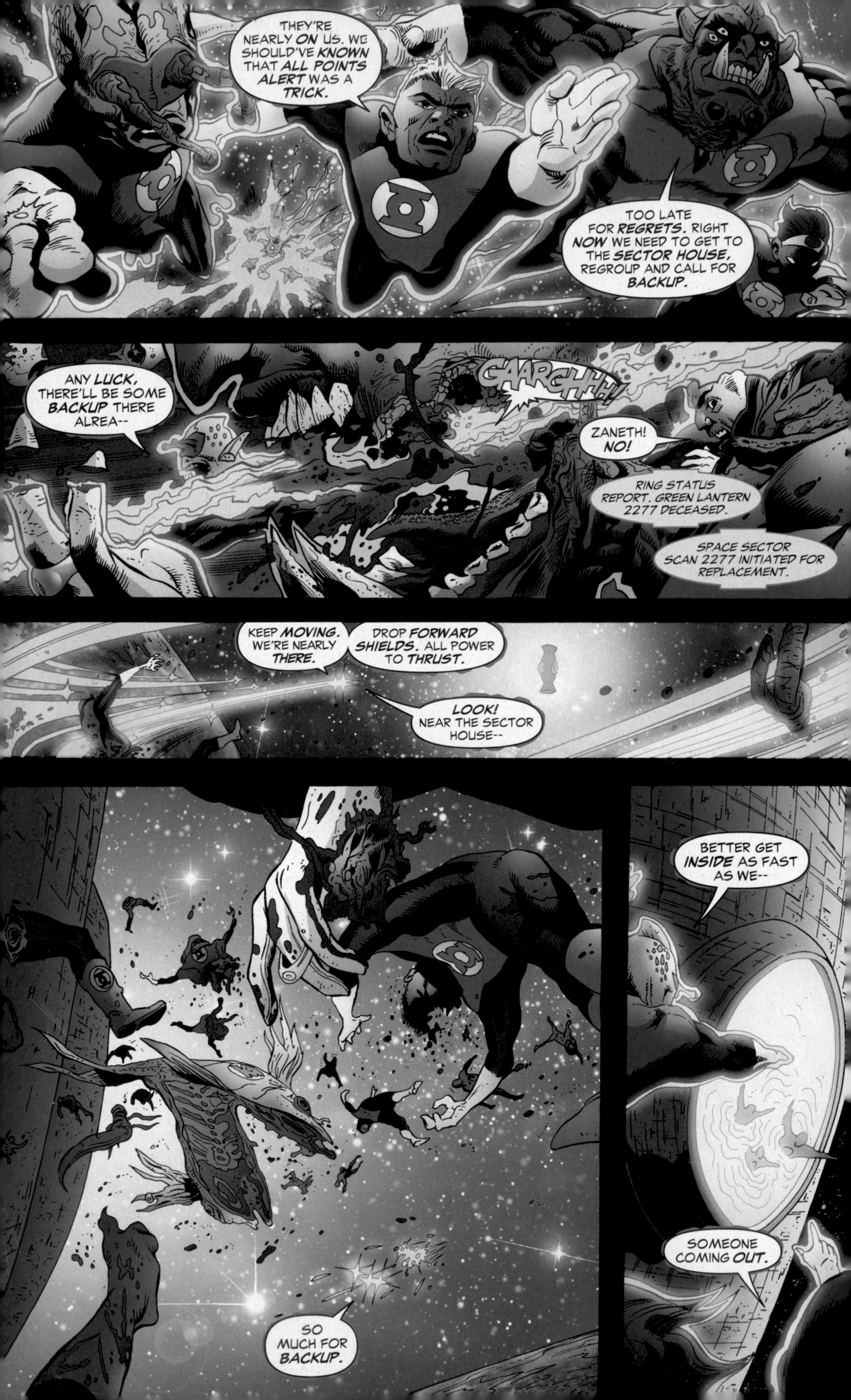
THEY'RE NEARLY ON US. WE SHOULD'VE KNOWN THAT ALL POINTS ALERT WAS A TRICK.
TOO LATE FOR REGRETS. RIGHT NOW WE NEED TO GET TO THE SECTOR HOUSE, REGROUP AND CALL FOR BACKUP.
ANY LUCK, THERE'LL BE SOME BACKUP THERE ALREA--
GAARGHH!
ZANETH! NO!
RING STATUS REPORT. GREEN LANTERN 2277 DECEASED.
SPACE SECTOR SCAN 2277 INITIATED FOR REPLACEMENT.
KEEP MOVING. WE'RE NEARLY THERE.
DROP FORWARD SHIELDS. ALL POWER TO THRUST.
LOOK! NEAR THE SECTOR HOUSE--
SO MUCH FOR BACKUP.
BETTER GET INSIDE AS FAST AS WE--
SOMEONE COMING OUT.

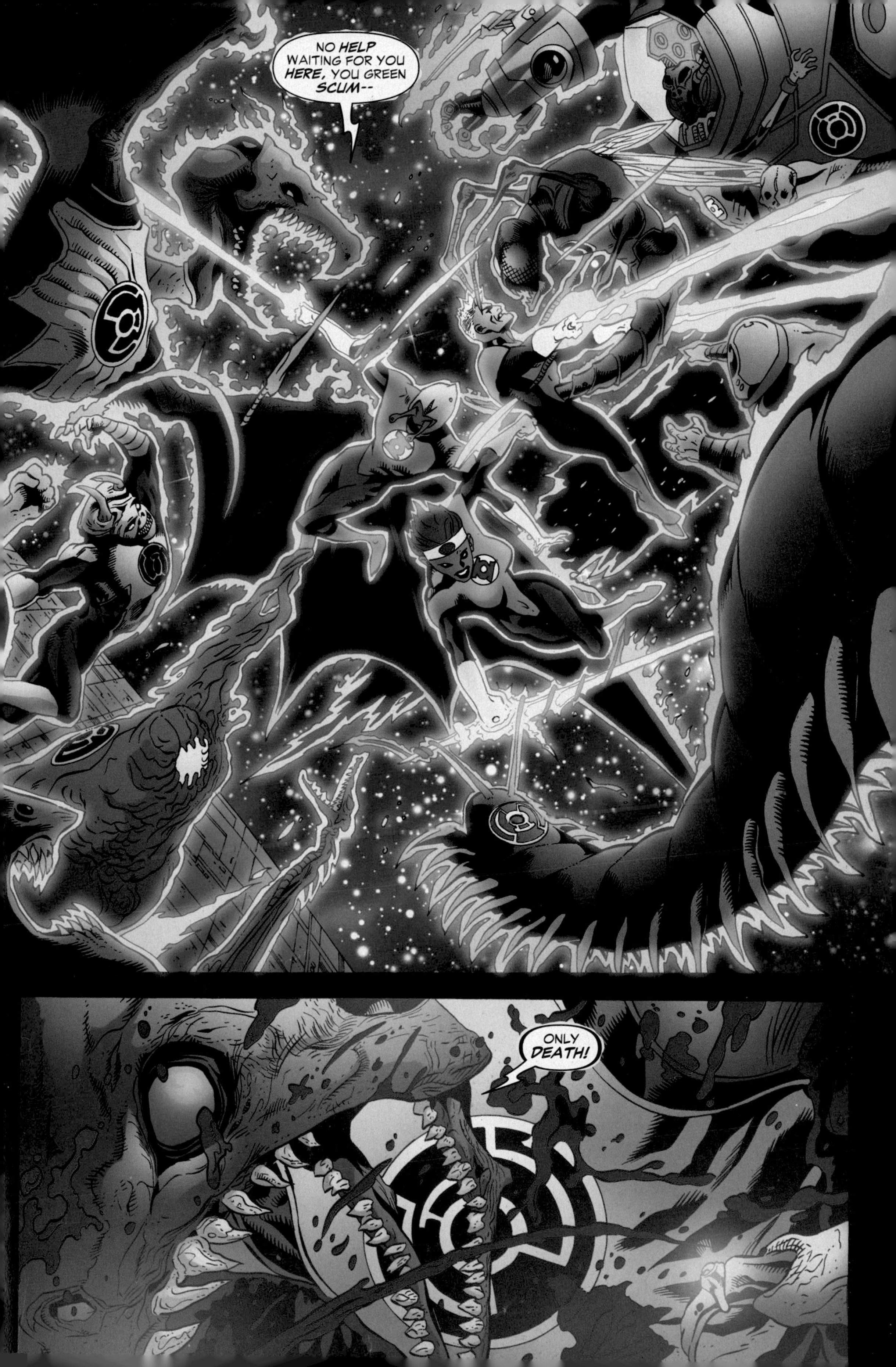
NO HELP WAITING FOR YOU HERE, YOU GREEN SCUM--
ONLY DEATH!

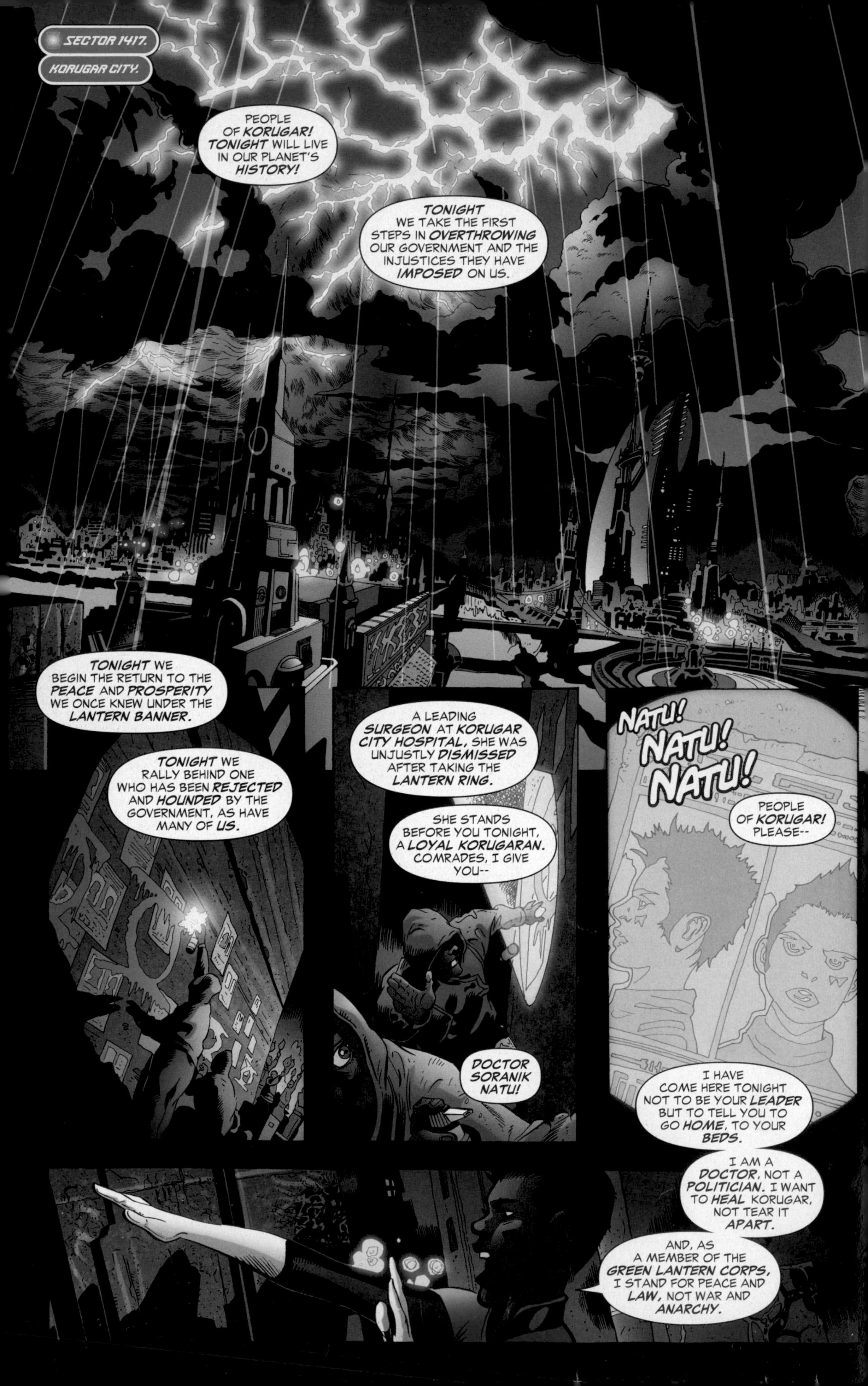
SECTOR 1417.
KORUGAR CITY.
PEOPLE OF KORUGAR! TONIGHT WILL LIVE IN OUR PLANET'S HISTORY!
TONIGHT WE TAKE THE FIRST STEPS IN OVERTHROWING OUR GOVERNMENT AND THE INJUSTICES THEY HAVE IMPOSED ON US.
TONIGHT WE BEGIN THE RETURN TO THE PEACE AND PROSPERITY WE ONCE KNEW UNDER THE LANTERN BANNER.
TONIGHT WE RALLY BEHIND ONE WHO HAS BEEN REJECTED AND HOUNDED BY THE GOVERNMENT, AS HAVE MANY OF US.
A LEADING SURGEON AT KORUGAR CITY HOSPITAL, SHE WAS UNJUSTLY DISMISSED AFTER TAKING THE LANTERN RING.
SHE STANDS BEFORE YOU TONIGHT, A LOYAL KORUGARAN. COMRADES, I GIVE YOU--
DOCTOR SORANIK NATU!
NATU! NATU! NATU!
PEOPLE OF KORUGAR! PLEASE--
I HAVE COME HERE TONIGHT NOT TO BE YOUR LEADER BUT TO TELL YOU TO GO HOME, TO YOUR BEDS.
I AM A DOCTOR, NOT A POLITICIAN. I WANT TO HEAL KORUGAR, NOT TEAR IT APART.
AND, AS A MEMBER OF THE GREEN LANTERN CORPS, I STAND FOR PEACE AND LAW, NOT WAR AND ANARCHY.

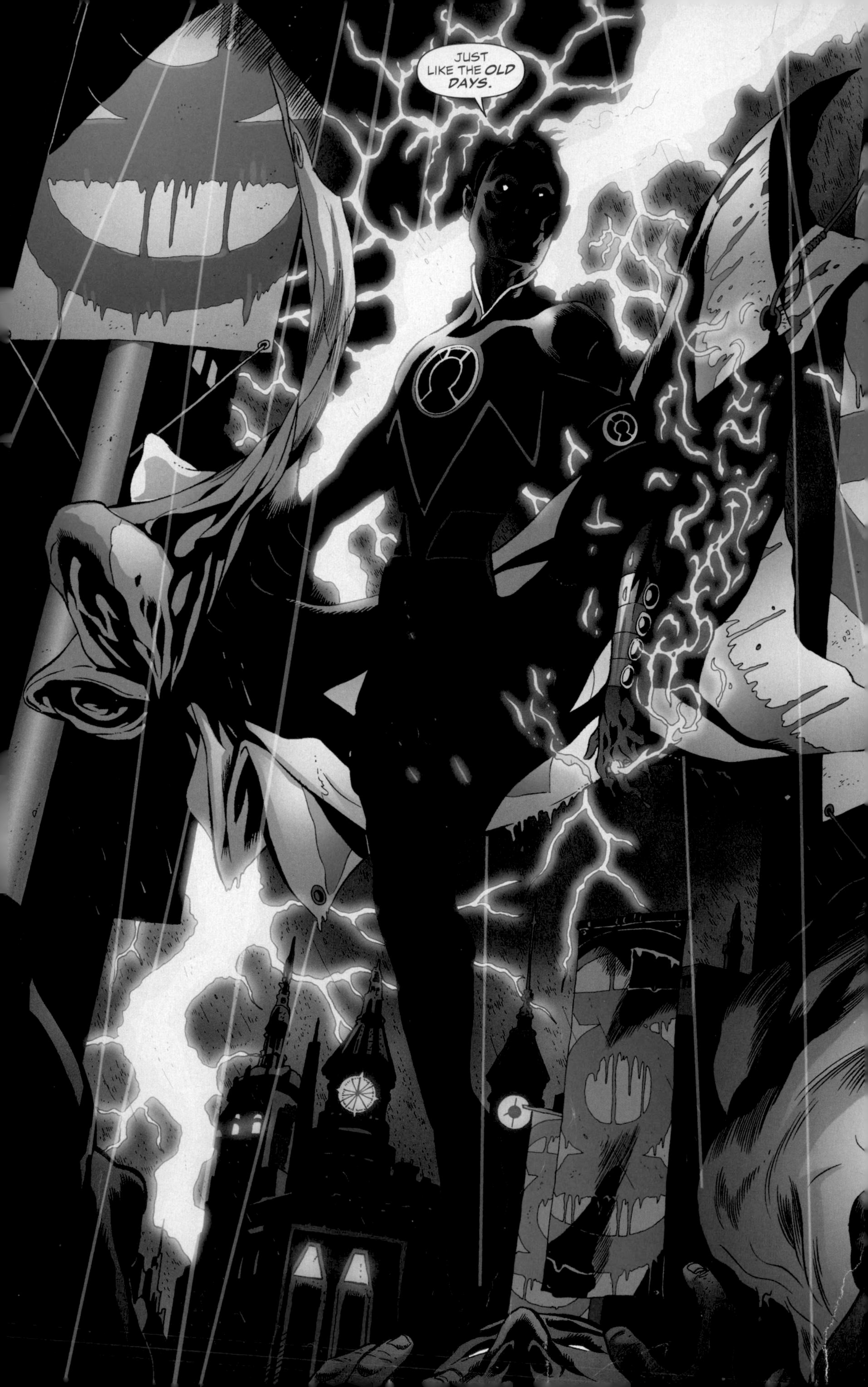
JUST LIKE THE OLD DAYS.

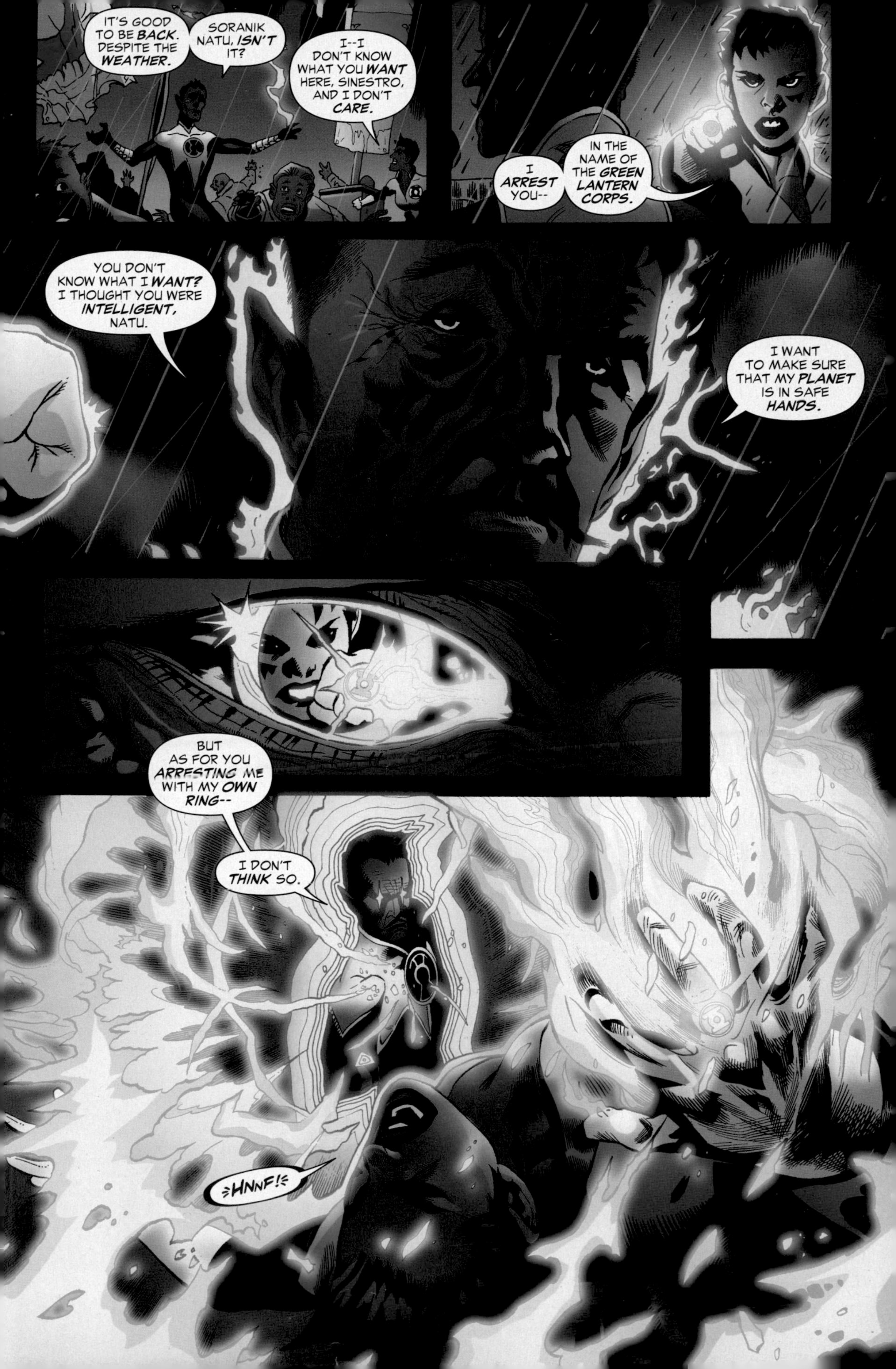
IT'S GOOD TO BE BACK. DESPITE THE WEATHER.
SORANIK NATU, ISN'T IT?
I--I DON'T KNOW WHAT YOU WANT HERE, SINESTRO, AND I DON'T CARE.
I ARREST YOU--
IN THE NAME OF THE GREEN LANTERN CORPS.
YOU DON'T KNOW WHAT I WANT? I THOUGHT YOU WERE INTELLIGENT, NATU.
I WANT TO MAKE SURE THAT MY PLANET IS IN SAFE HANDS.
BUT AS FOR YOU ARRESTING ME WITH MY OWN RING--
I DON'T THINK SO.
HNNF!

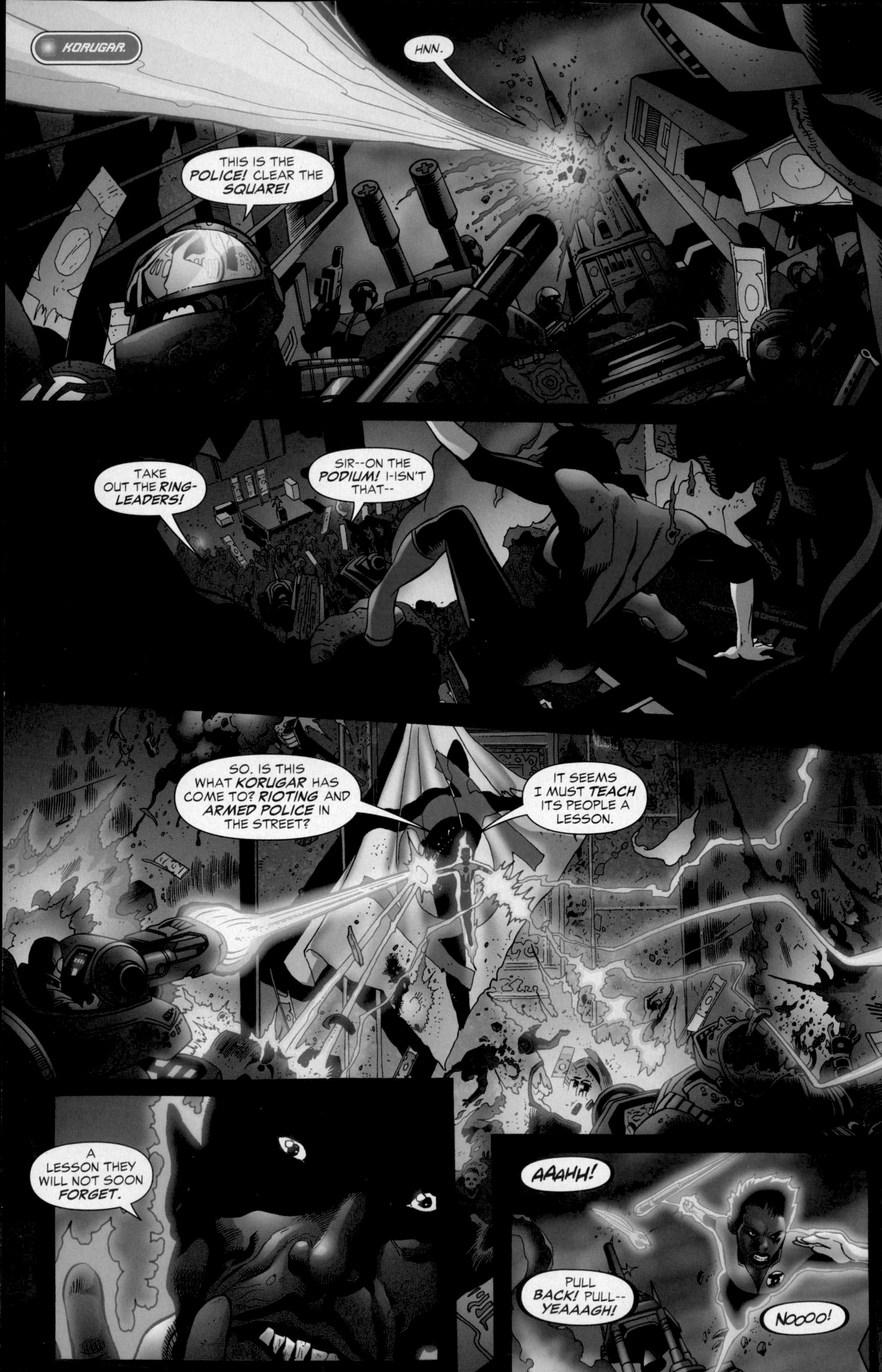
KORUGAR.
HNN.
THIS IS THE POLICE! CLEAR THE SQUARE!
TAKE OUT THE RING-LEADERS!
SIR--ON THE PODIUM! I-ISN'T THAT--
SO. IS THIS WHAT KORUGAR HAS COME TO? RIOTING AND ARMED POLICE IN THE STREET?
IT SEEMS I MUST TEACH ITS PEOPLE A LESSON.
A LESSON THEY WILL NOT SOON FORGET.
AAAHH!
PULL BACK! PULL-- YEAAAGH!
NOOOO!

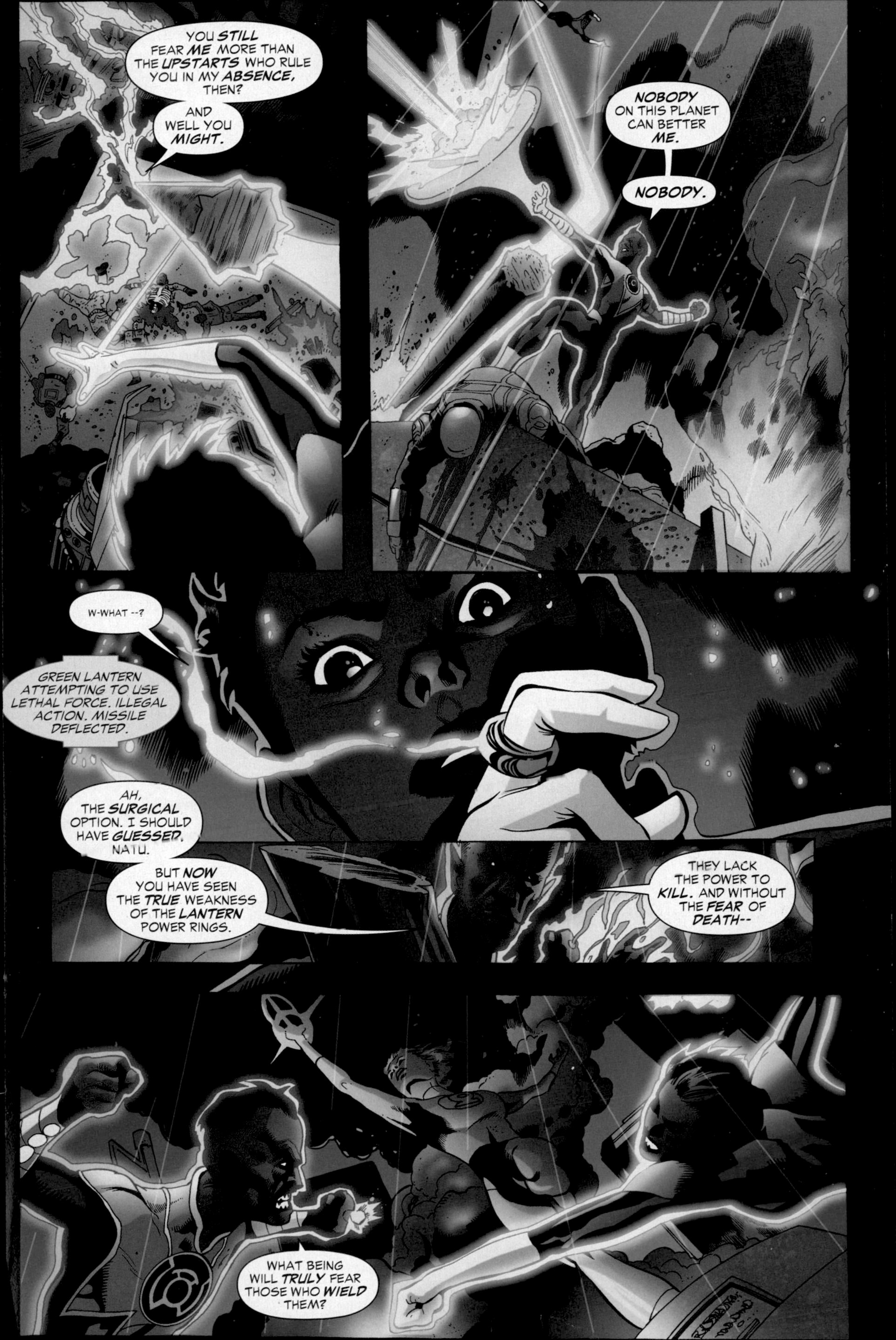
YOU STILL FEAR ME MORE THAN THE UPSTARTS WHO RULE YOU IN MY ABSENCE, THEN?
AND WELL YOU MIGHT.
NOBODY ON THIS PLANET CAN BETTER ME.
NOBODY.
W-WHAT --?
GREEN LANTERN ATTEMPTING TO USE LETHAL FORCE. ILLEGAL ACTION. MISSILE DEFLECTED.
AH, THE SURGICAL OPTION. I SHOULD HAVE GUESSED, NATU.
BUT NOW YOU HAVE SEEN THE TRUE WEAKNESS OF THE LANTERN POWER RINGS.
THEY LACK THE POWER TO KILL. AND WITHOUT THE FEAR OF DEATH--
WHAT BEING WILL TRULY FEAR THOSE WHO WIELD THEM?

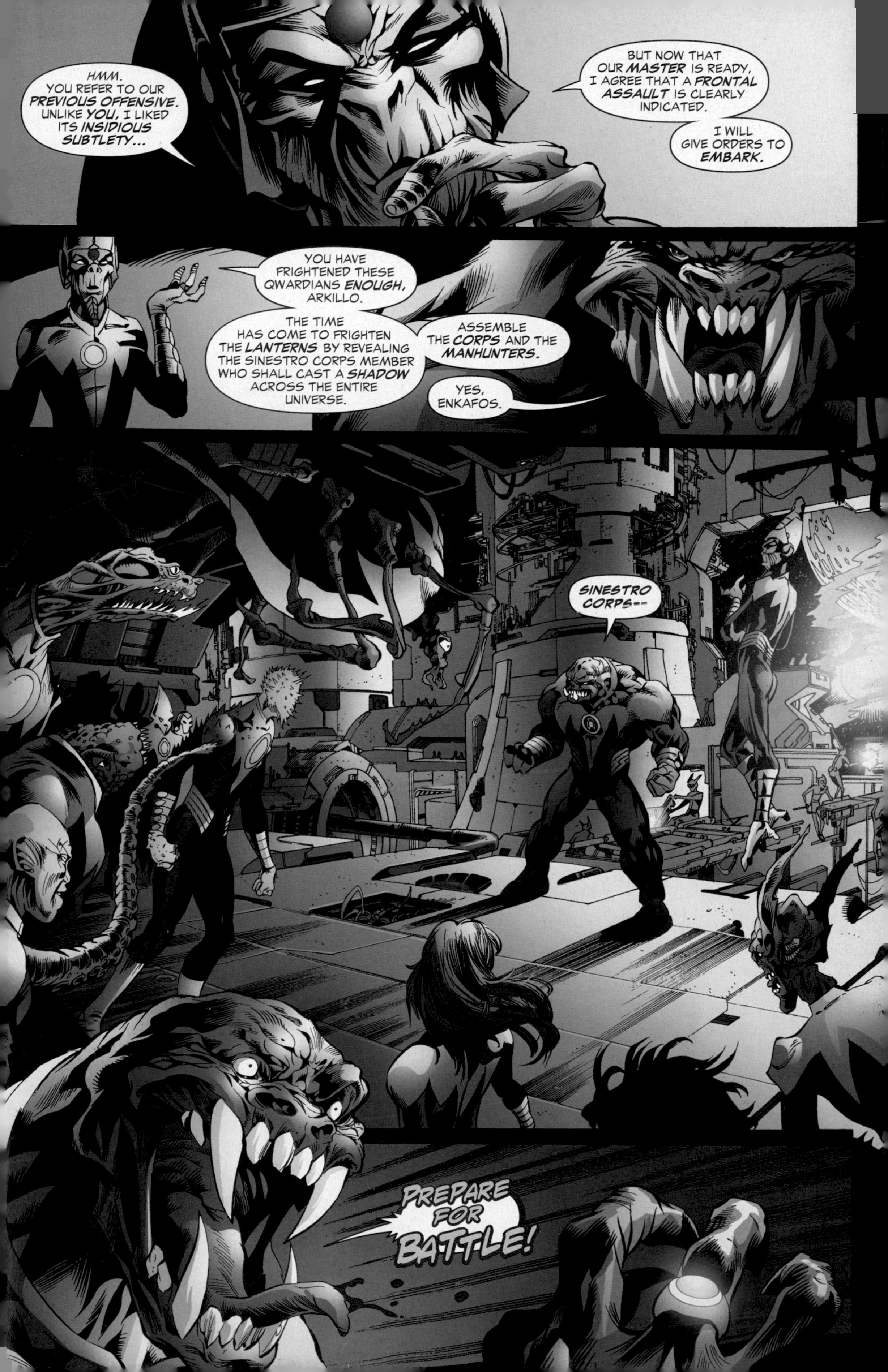
HMM. YOU REFER TO OUR PREVIOUS OFFENSIVE. UNLIKE YOU, I LIKED ITS INSIDIOUS SUBTLETY...
BUT NOW THAT OUR MASTER IS READY, I AGREE THAT A FRONTAL ASSAULT IS CLEARLY INDICATED.
I WILL GIVE ORDERS TO EMBARK.
YOU HAVE FRIGHTENED THESE QWARDIANS ENOUGH, ARKILLO.
THE TIME HAS COME TO FRIGHTEN THE LANTERNS BY REVEALING THE SINESTRO CORPS MEMBER WHO SHALL CAST A SHADOW ACROSS THE ENTIRE UNIVERSE.
ASSEMBLE THE CORPS AND THE MANHUNTERS.
YES, ENKAFOS.
SINESTRO CORPS--
PREPARE FOR BATTLE!

LISTEN UP, POOZERS.

THE SINESTRO CORPS ARE MASSIN' IN THE TWO-TWENTY-SIXES. THEY ALREADY TOOK OUT A SECTOR HOUSE AND MANY OF OUR BROTHERS.

THIS IS WAR.

THE GREEN LINE IS SPREAD THIN, AND THINGS ARE LOOKIN' BAD--WHICH GIVES YOU ROOKIES, JUST GRADUATED, THE CHANCE TO SHINE.

OA'S BEEN HIT BAD, AND A BUNCH O' YER BROTHERS FROM EARTH ARE TAKIN' THE FIGHT TO QWARD.

YOU READY, SODAM?

WE'RE LEAVIN' RIGHT NOW.

SO CHARGE YOUR RINGS AND GET READY TA BE TESTED TA THE LIMIT.

I--I BETTER BE. WE ALL HAD.

LANTERN ARISIA.

I HAVE ORDERS FOR YOU.

WHAT'S UP, SALAAK? ASIDE FROM THE UNIVERSE FALLING APART, THAT IS...

LANTERN YAT. YOU WILL STAY CLOSE TO HIM. WATCH HIS BACK.

ER, SURE.

"SODAM YAT'S A GOOD KID. THEY ALL ARE.

"DOES SOMETHING MAKE HIM SPECIAL?"

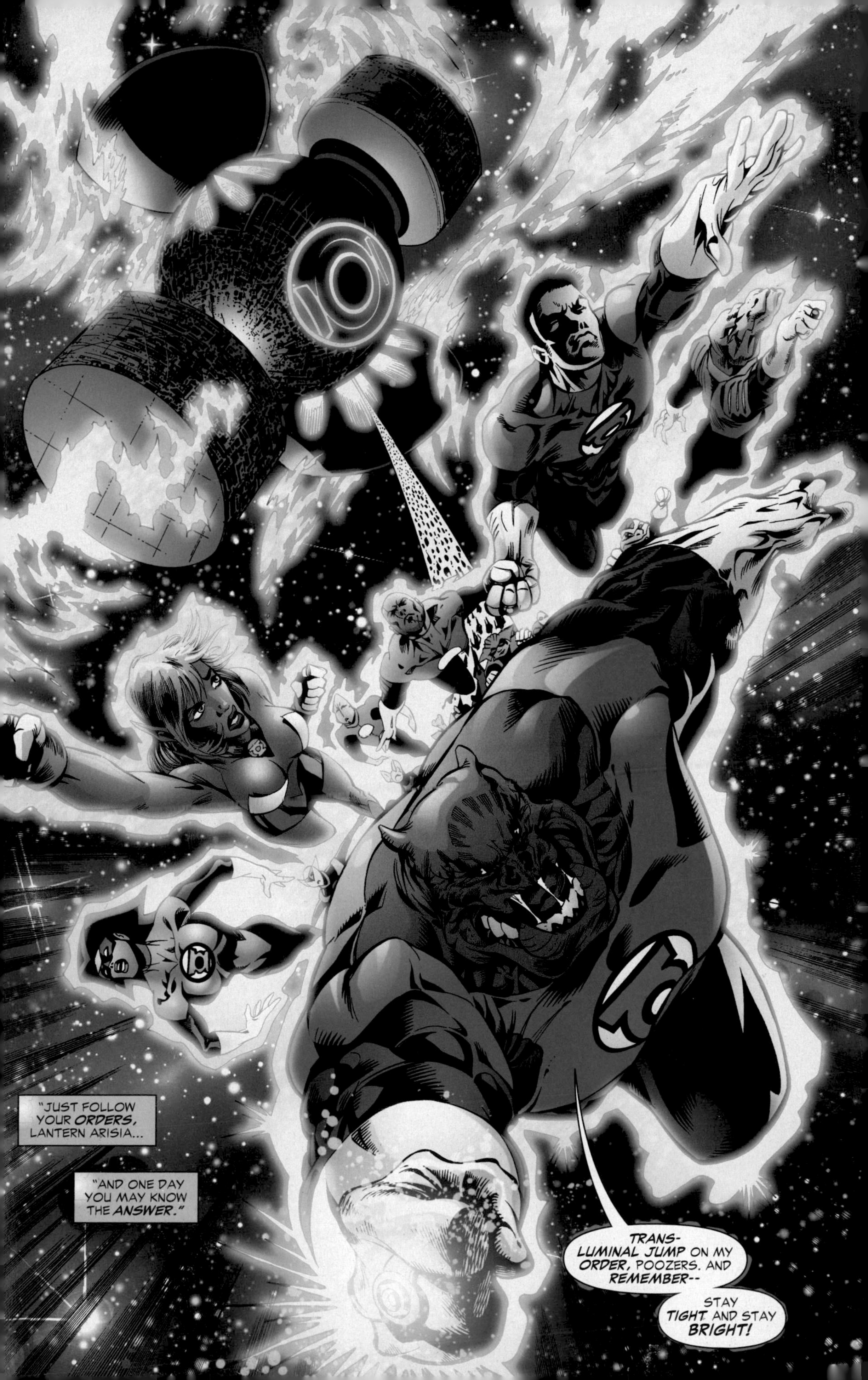
"JUST FOLLOW YOUR ORDERS, LANTERN ARISIA...
"AND ONE DAY YOU MAY KNOW THE ANSWER."
TRANS-LUMINAL JUMP ON MY ORDER, POOZERS. AND REMEMBER--
STAY TIGHT AND STAY BRIGHT!

REPORT. HOW GOES THE WAR?

MASTER. QWARD IS UNDER ATTACK BY THE GREEN LANTERN CORPS.

THE GUARDIANS' PUPPETS ARE HERE? AND HOW MANY HAVE THEY SENT TO THE SLAUGHTER?

A MERE HANDFUL, MASTER.

BUT THERE IS ONE THING YOU WOULD WANT TO KNOW--

HAL JORDAN IS AMONG THEM.

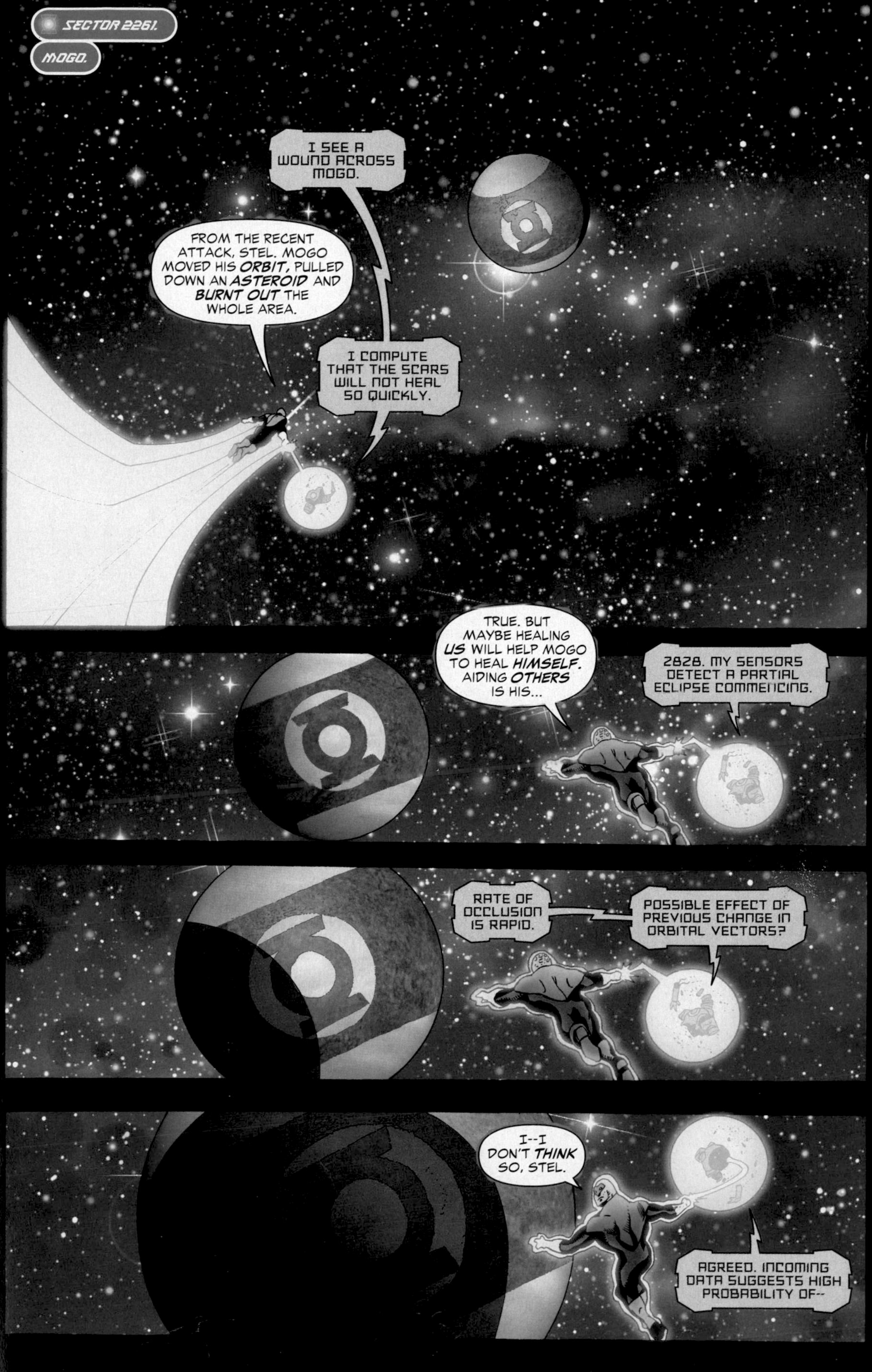
SECTOR 2261.
MOGO.
I SEE A WOUND ACROSS MOGO.
FROM THE RECENT ATTACK, STEL. MOGO MOVED HIS ORBIT, PULLED DOWN AN ASTEROID AND BURNT OUT THE WHOLE AREA.
I COMPUTE THAT THE SCARS WILL NOT HEAL SO QUICKLY.
TRUE. BUT MAYBE HEALING US WILL HELP MOGO TO HEAL HIMSELF. AIDING OTHERS IS HIS...
2828. MY SENSORS DETECT A PARTIAL ECLIPSE COMMENCING.
RATE OF OCCLUSION IS RAPID.
POSSIBLE EFFECT OF PREVIOUS CHANGE IN ORBITAL VECTORS?
I--I DON'T THINK SO, STEL.
AGREED. INCOMING DATA SUGGESTS HIGH PROBABILITY OF--

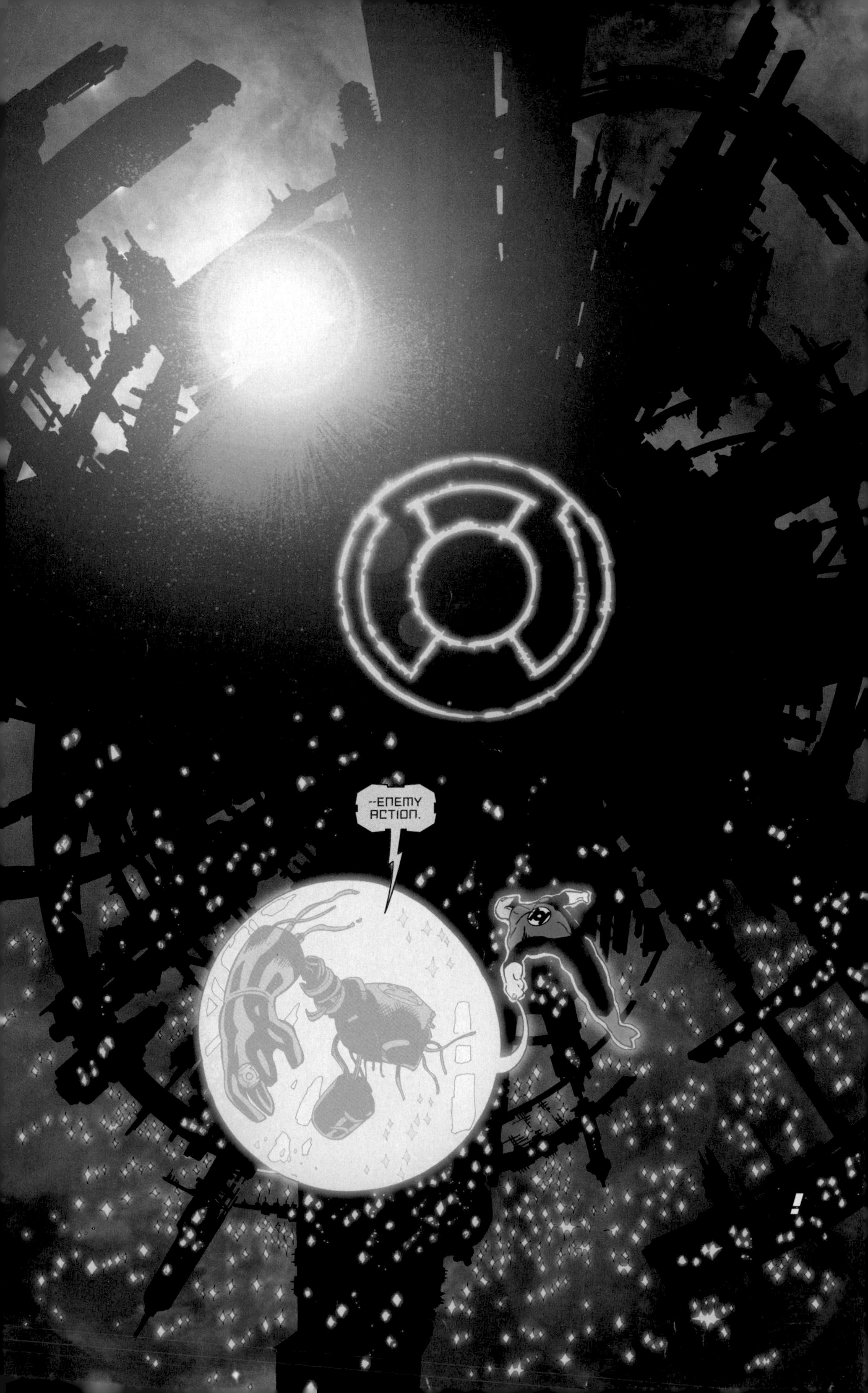
--ENEMY ACTION.
!

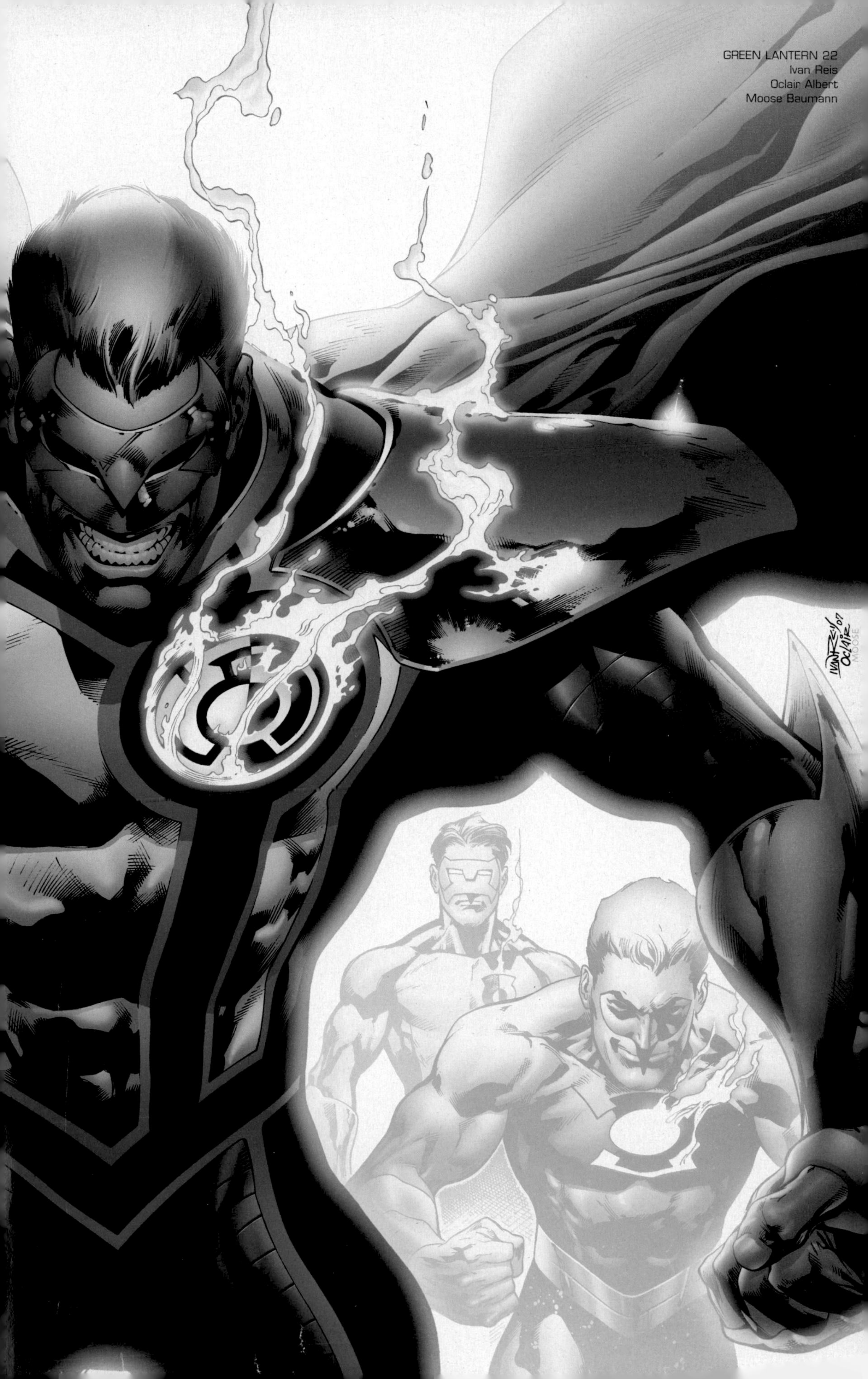

GREEN LANTERN 22
Ivan Reis
Oclair Albert
Moose Baumann

THE SINESTRO CORPS WAR
Chapter Three
RUNNING SCARED
Writer: **Geoff Johns**
Penciller: **Ivan Reis**
Inker: **Oclair Albert**
Colorist: **Moose Baumann**
Letterer: **Rob Leigh**

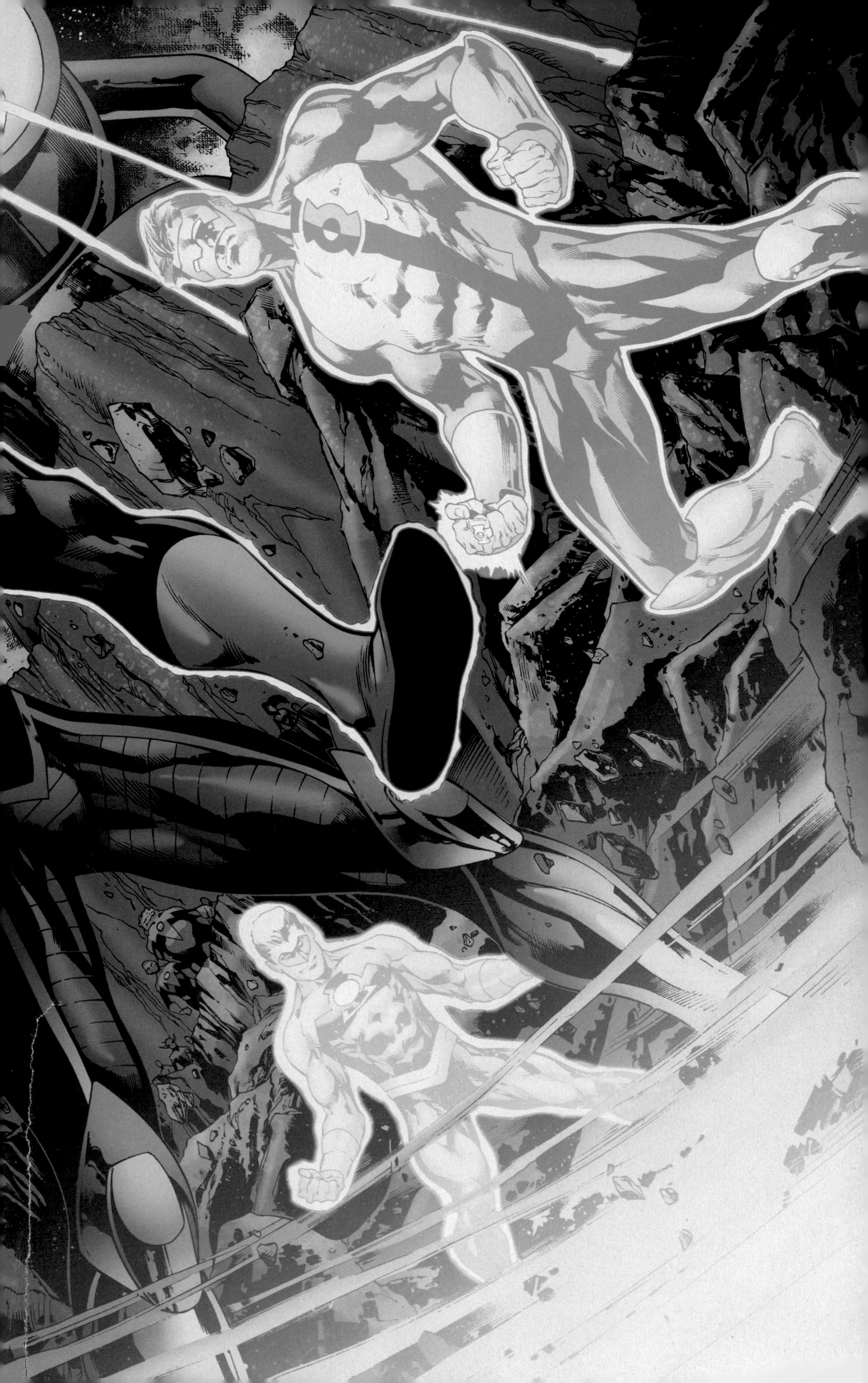

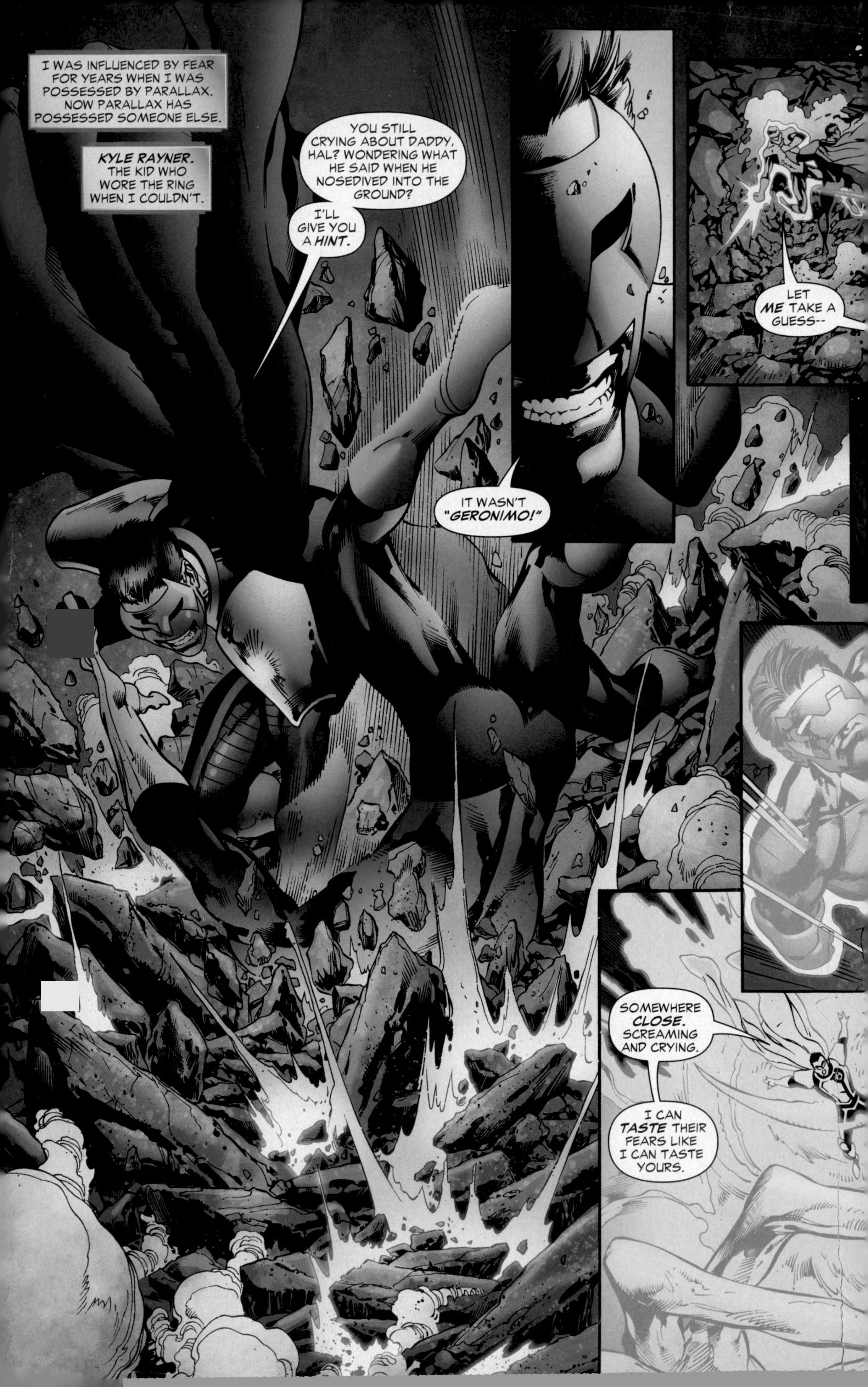
I WAS INFLUENCED BY FEAR FOR YEARS WHEN I WAS POSSESSED BY PARALLAX. NOW PARALLAX HAS POSSESSED SOMEONE ELSE.
KYLE RAYNER. THE KID WHO WORE THE RING WHEN I COULDN'T.
YOU STILL CRYING ABOUT DADDY, HAL? WONDERING WHAT HE SAID WHEN HE NOSEDIVED INTO THE GROUND?
I'LL GIVE YOU A HINT.
IT WASN'T "GERONIMO!"
LET ME TAKE A GUESS--
SOMEWHERE CLOSE. SCREAMING AND CRYING.
I CAN TASTE THEIR FEARS LIKE I CAN TASTE YOURS.

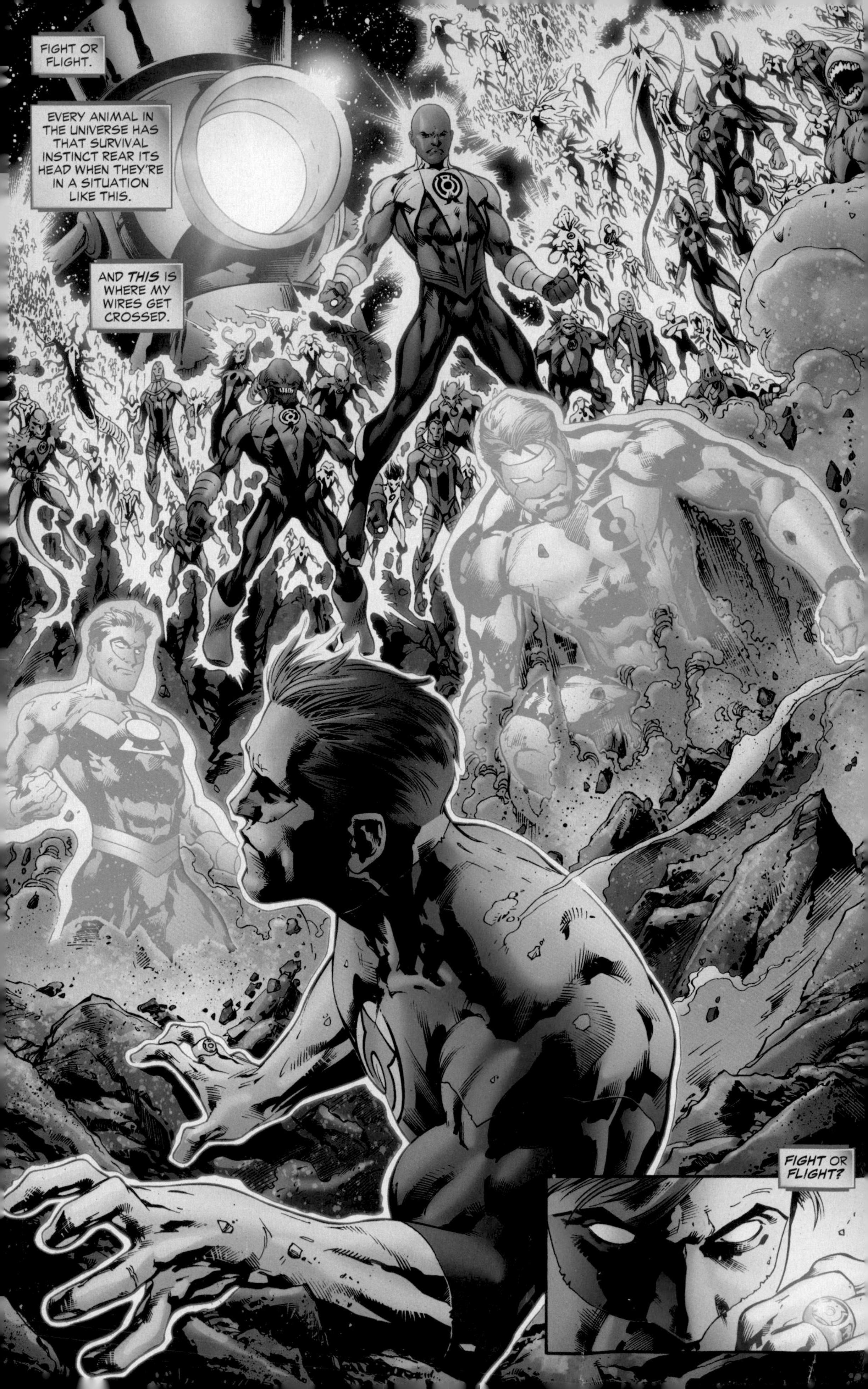
FIGHT OR FLIGHT.
EVERY ANIMAL IN THE UNIVERSE HAS THAT SURVIVAL INSTINCT REAR ITS HEAD WHEN THEY'RE IN A SITUATION LIKE THIS.
AND *THIS* IS WHERE MY WIRES GET CROSSED.
FIGHT OR *FLIGHT?*

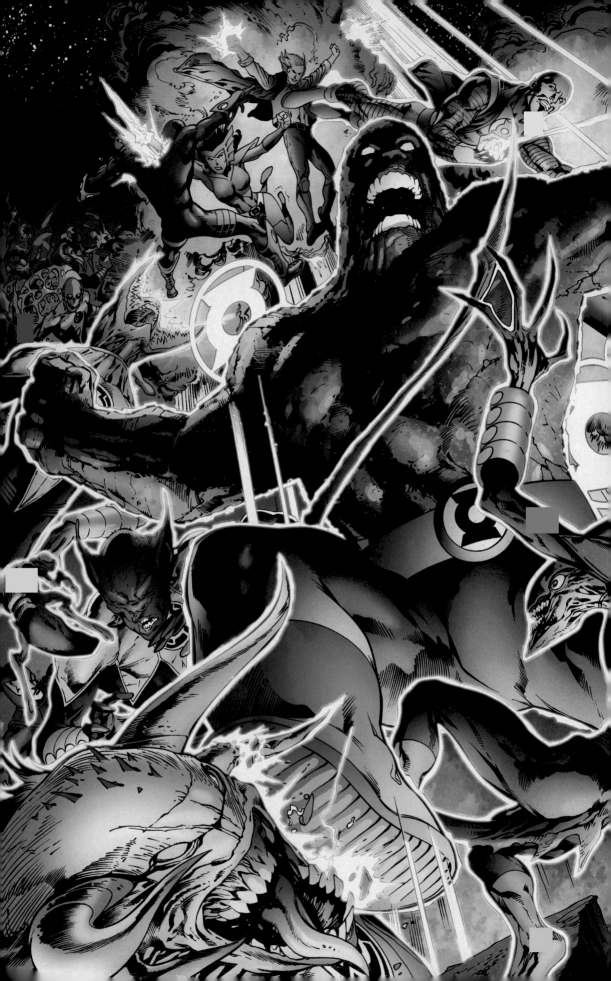

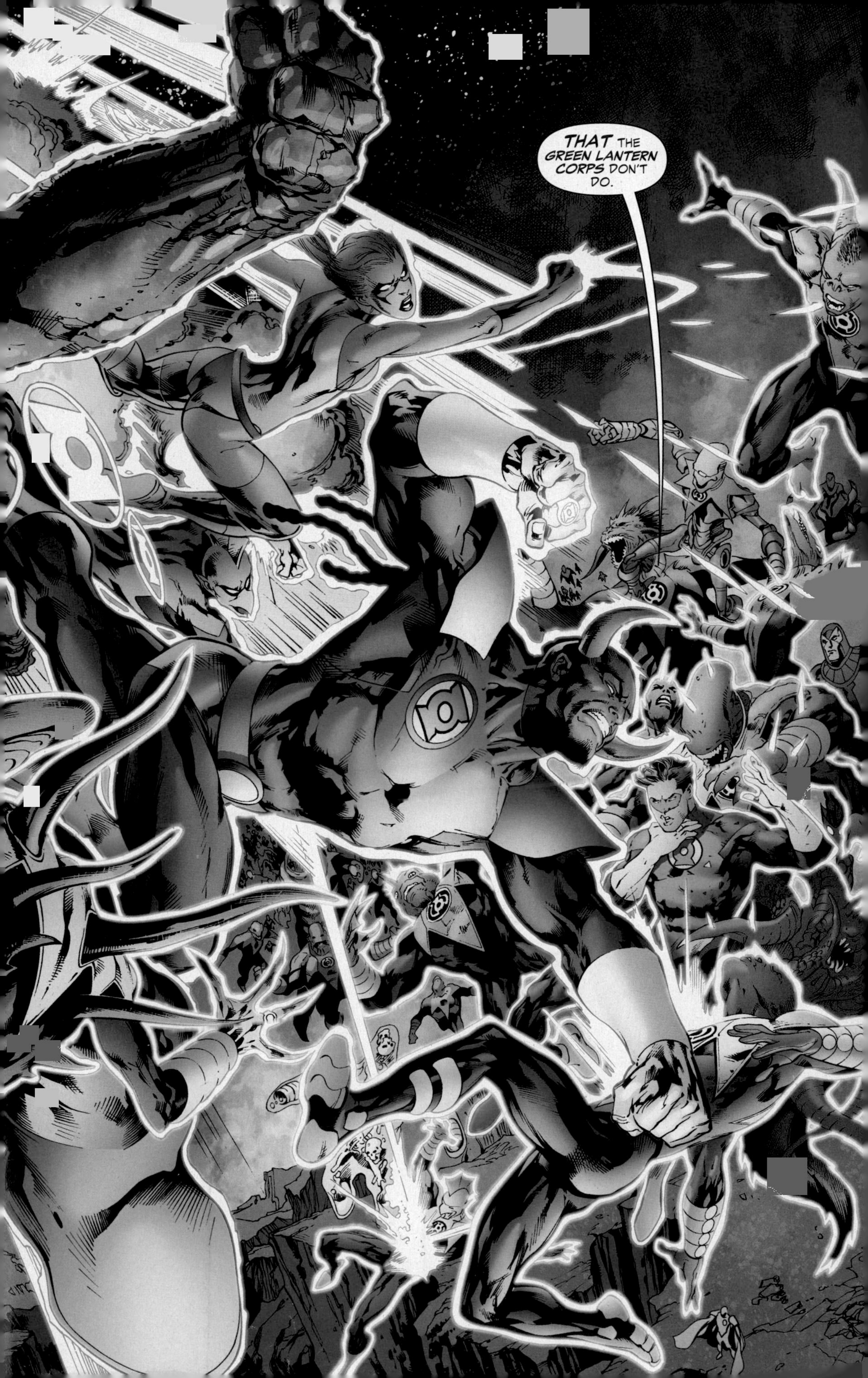
THAT THE GREEN LANTERN CORPS DON'T DO.

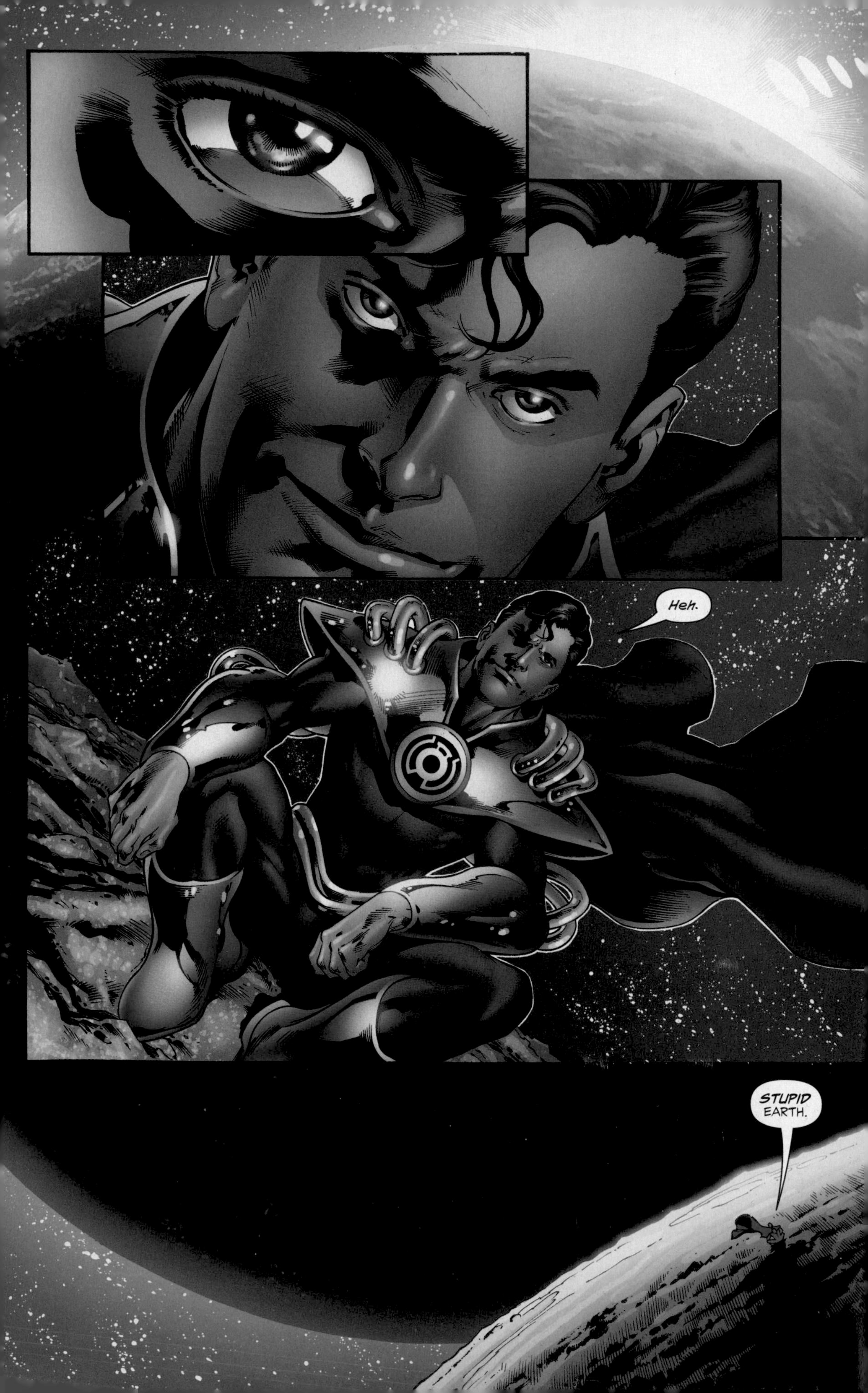
Heh.
STUPID EARTH.

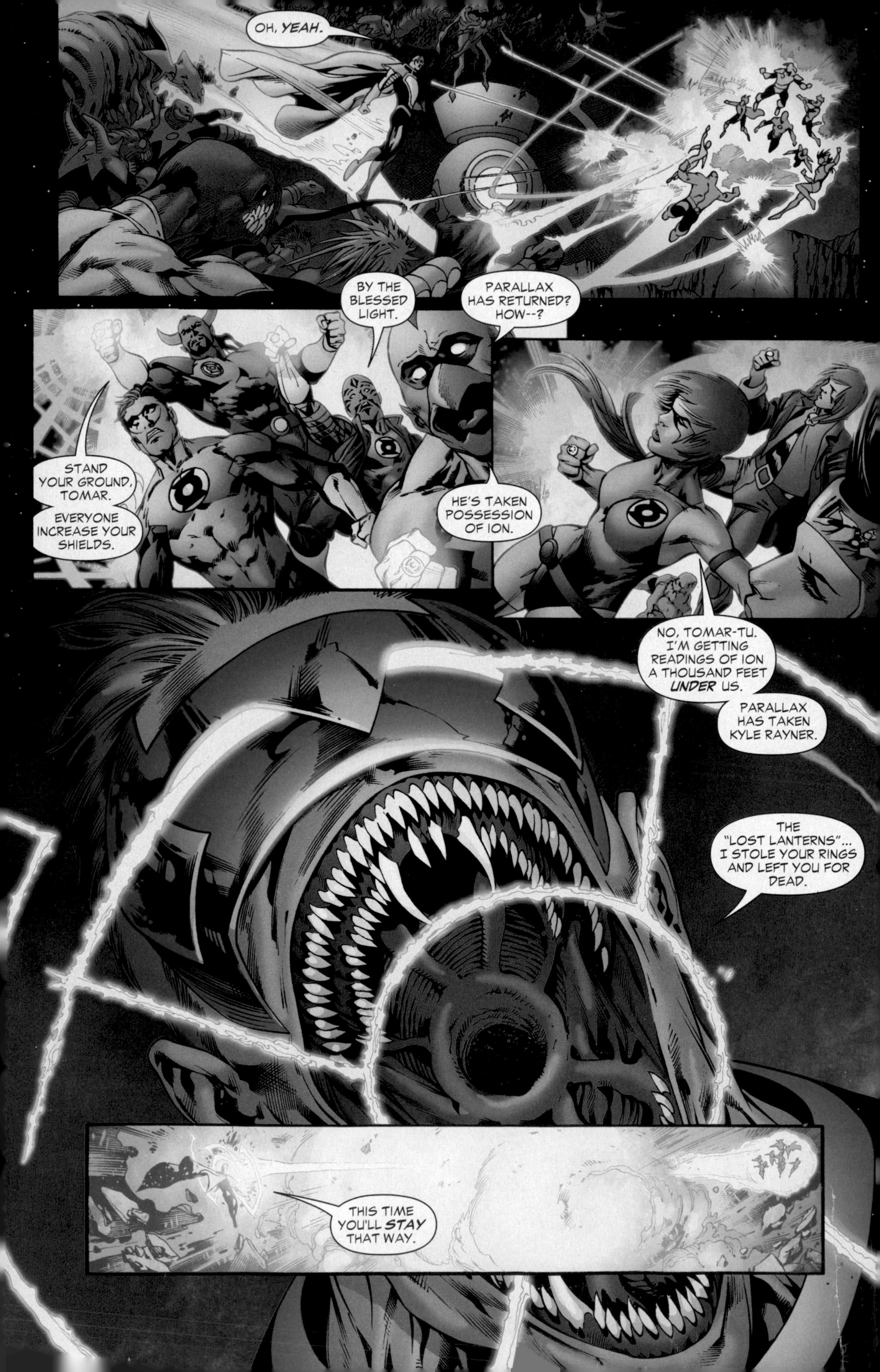
OH, YEAH.
BY THE BLESSED LIGHT.
PARALLAX HAS RETURNED? HOW--?
STAND YOUR GROUND, TOMAR.
EVERYONE INCREASE YOUR SHIELDS.
HE'S TAKEN POSSESSION OF ION.
NO, TOMAR-TU. I'M GETTING READINGS OF ION A THOUSAND FEET UNDER US.
PARALLAX HAS TAKEN KYLE RAYNER.
THE "LOST LANTERNS"... I STOLE YOUR RINGS AND LEFT YOU FOR DEAD.
THIS TIME YOU'LL STAY THAT WAY.

VZZP

VZZP

VZZP

VZZP

VZZP

AARGHHH!

RING STATUS REPORT. GREEN LANTERN 17 DECEASED.

SPACE SECTOR SCAN 17 INITIATED FOR REPLACEMENT--

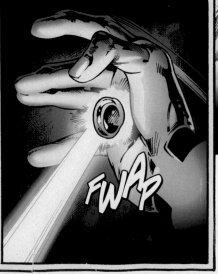

FWAP

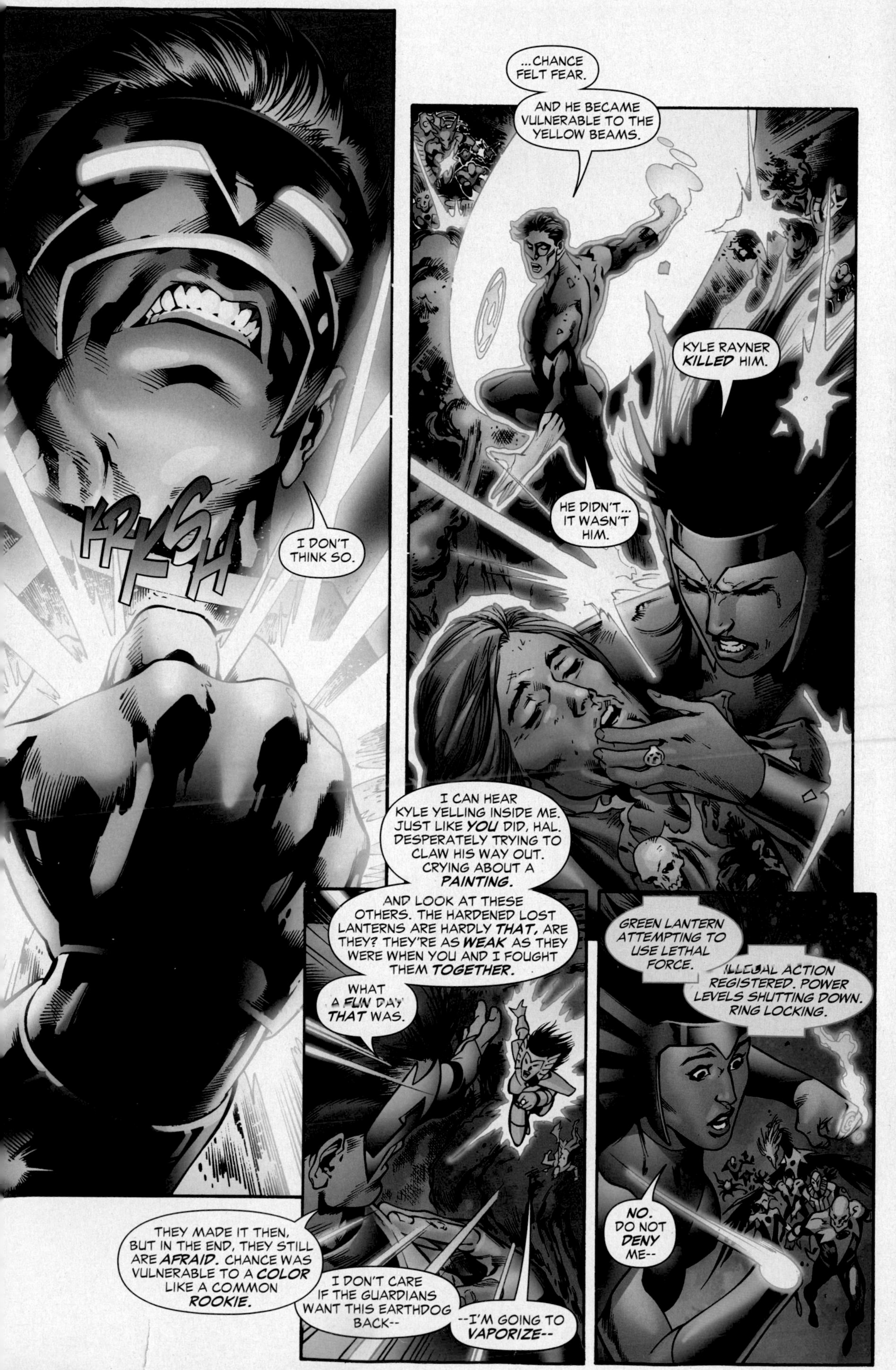
KRKSH
I DON'T THINK SO.
...CHANCE FELT FEAR.
AND HE BECAME VULNERABLE TO THE YELLOW BEAMS.
KYLE RAYNER *KILLED* HIM.
HE DIDN'T... IT WASN'T HIM.
I CAN HEAR KYLE YELLING INSIDE ME. JUST LIKE *YOU* DID, HAL. DESPERATELY TRYING TO CLAW HIS WAY OUT. CRYING ABOUT A *PAINTING.*
AND LOOK AT THESE OTHERS. THE HARDENED LOST LANTERNS ARE HARDLY *THAT,* ARE THEY? THEY'RE AS *WEAK* AS THEY WERE WHEN YOU AND I FOUGHT THEM *TOGETHER.*
WHAT A *FUN* DAY *THAT* WAS.
THEY MADE IT THEN, BUT IN THE END, THEY STILL ARE *AFRAID.* CHANCE WAS VULNERABLE TO A *COLOR* LIKE A COMMON *ROOKIE.*
I DON'T CARE IF THE GUARDIANS WANT THIS EARTHDOG BACK--
--I'M GOING TO *VAPORIZE*--
GREEN LANTERN ATTEMPTING TO USE LETHAL FORCE.
ILLEGAL ACTION REGISTERED. POWER LEVELS SHUTTING DOWN. RING LOCKING.
NO. DO NOT *DENY* ME--

POWER LEVEL CHECK.
SPX
POWER LEVELS 14.9%
POWER LEVELS 55.5%
DAMN RING.
POWER LEVELS 13.6%
POWER LEVELS 25.1%
POWER LEVELS 18%
POWER LEVELS 98.5%
THAT RUBBLE ISN'T GOING TO KEEP THEM OUT FOR LONG.
WHERE ARE WE?
THEIR CITADEL'S CATACOMBS.
THIS IS MORE THAN THAT, LAIRA.
THIS IS THEIR TEMPLE.
THE WALLS ARE CARVED WITH SCRIPTURES. WRITTEN IN AN ANCIENT LIGHT MONK DIALECT FROM THE PAGALUSIAN SYSTEM.
FWOOSH
WHAT'S IT SAY?
"FEAR INFECTS."
OVER AND OVER AND OVER.
ENOUGH SIGHTSEEING. RING. LOCATE ION.
RING. LOCATE JOHN STEWART AND GUY GARDNER.

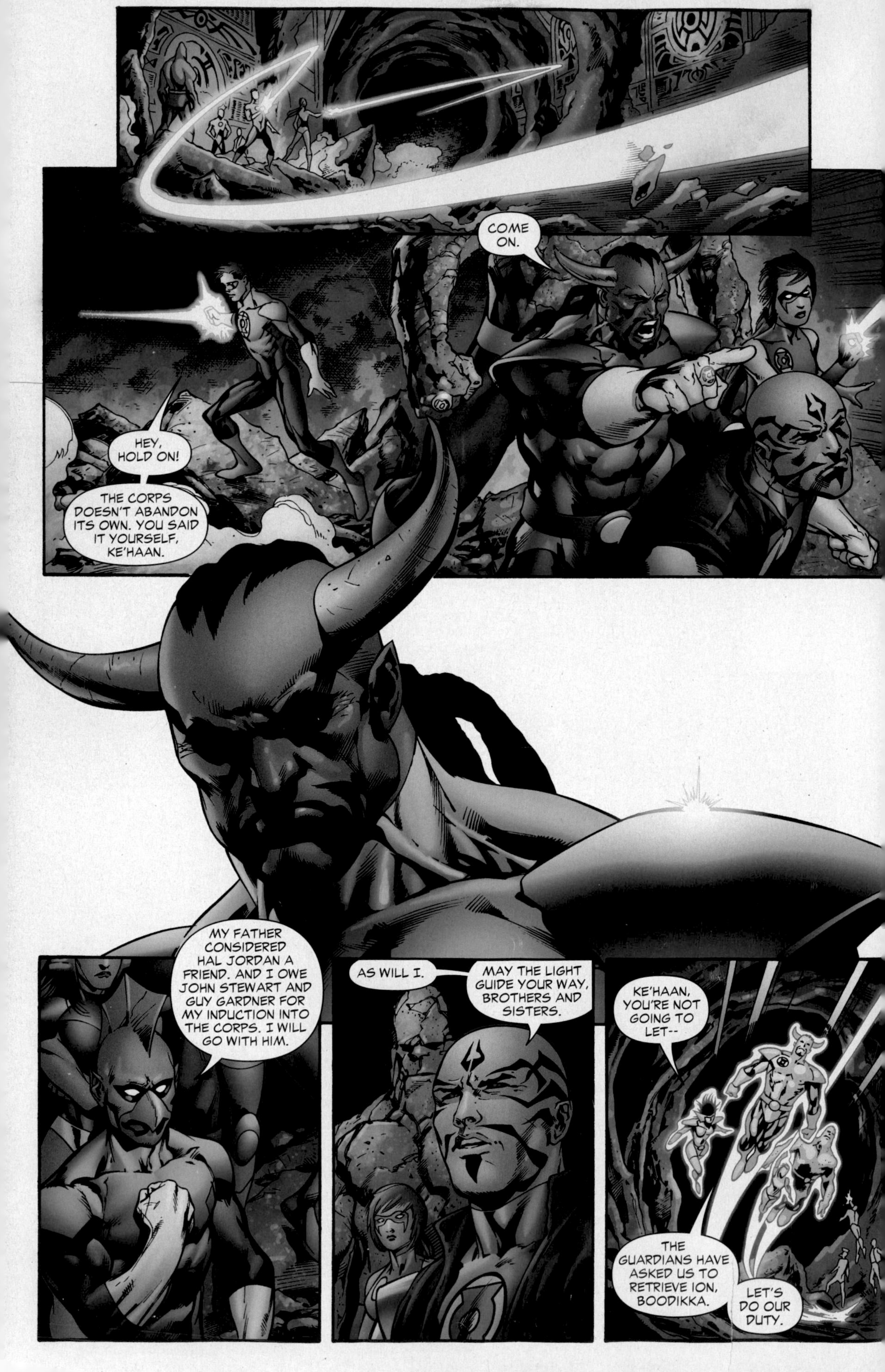
COME ON.
HEY, HOLD ON!
THE CORPS DOESN'T ABANDON ITS OWN. YOU SAID IT YOURSELF, KE'HAAN.
MY FATHER CONSIDERED HAL JORDAN A FRIEND. AND I OWE JOHN STEWART AND GUY GARDNER FOR MY INDUCTION INTO THE CORPS. I WILL GO WITH HIM.
AS WILL I.
MAY THE LIGHT GUIDE YOUR WAY, BROTHERS AND SISTERS.
KE'HAAN, YOU'RE NOT GOING TO LET--
THE GUARDIANS HAVE ASKED US TO RETRIEVE ION, BOODIKKA.
LET'S DO OUR DUTY.

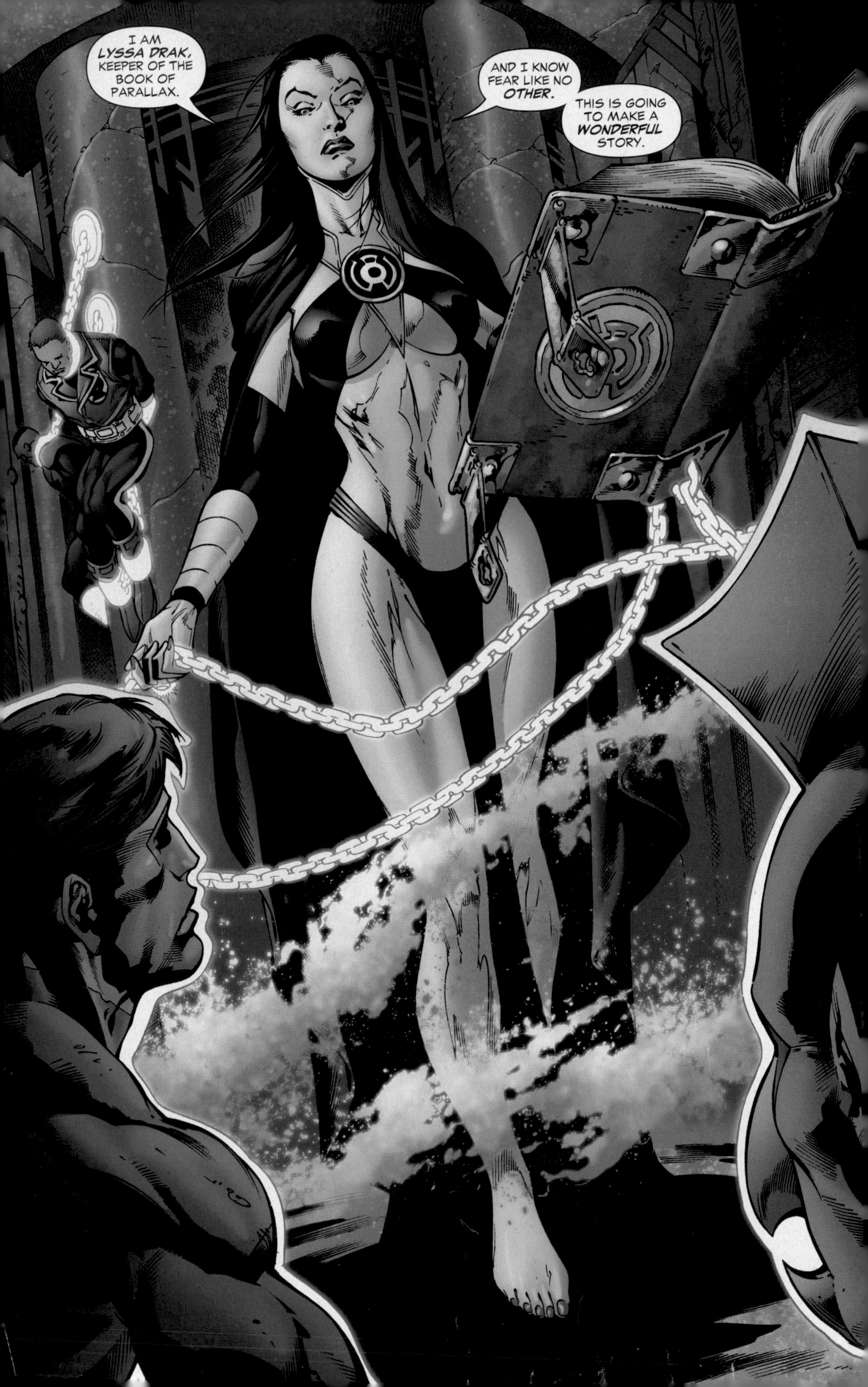
I AM *LYSSA DRAK,* KEEPER OF THE BOOK OF PARALLAX.
AND I KNOW FEAR LIKE NO *OTHER.*
THIS IS GOING TO MAKE A *WONDERFUL* STORY.

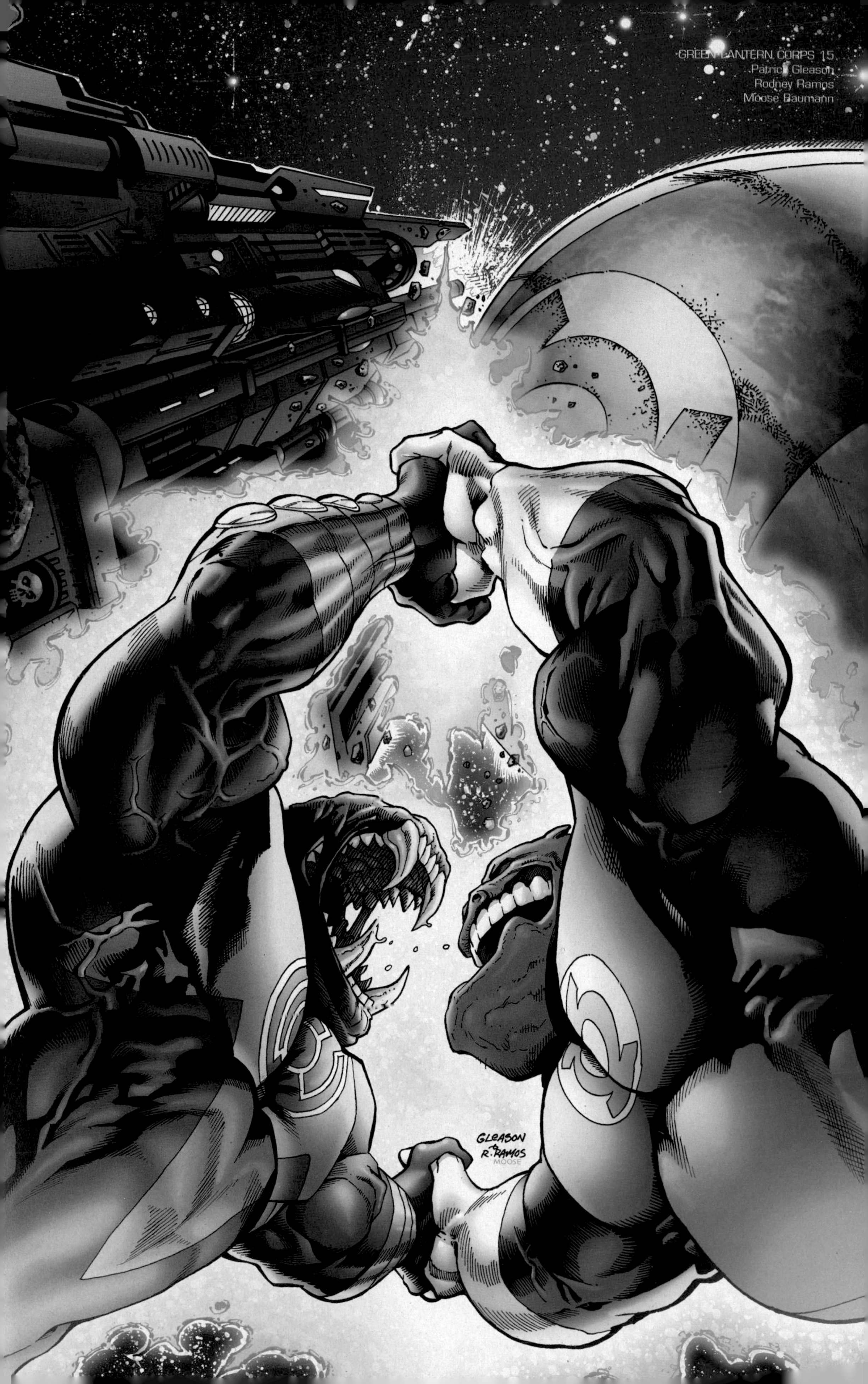
GLEASON
R. RAMOS
MOOSE

GREEN LANTERN CORPS 15
Patrick Gleason
Rodney Ramos
Moose Baumann

THE SINESTRO CORPS WAR
Chapter Four
THE BATTLE OF MOGO

Penciller: **Patrick Gleason** (pages 129-135, 142-147)
Penciller: **Angel Unzueta** (pages 136-141, 148-150)
Inker: **Prentis Rollins** (pages 129-136, 140-150)
Inker: **Drew Geraci** (pages 137-139)
Colorist: **Guy Major**
Letterer: **Phil Balsman**

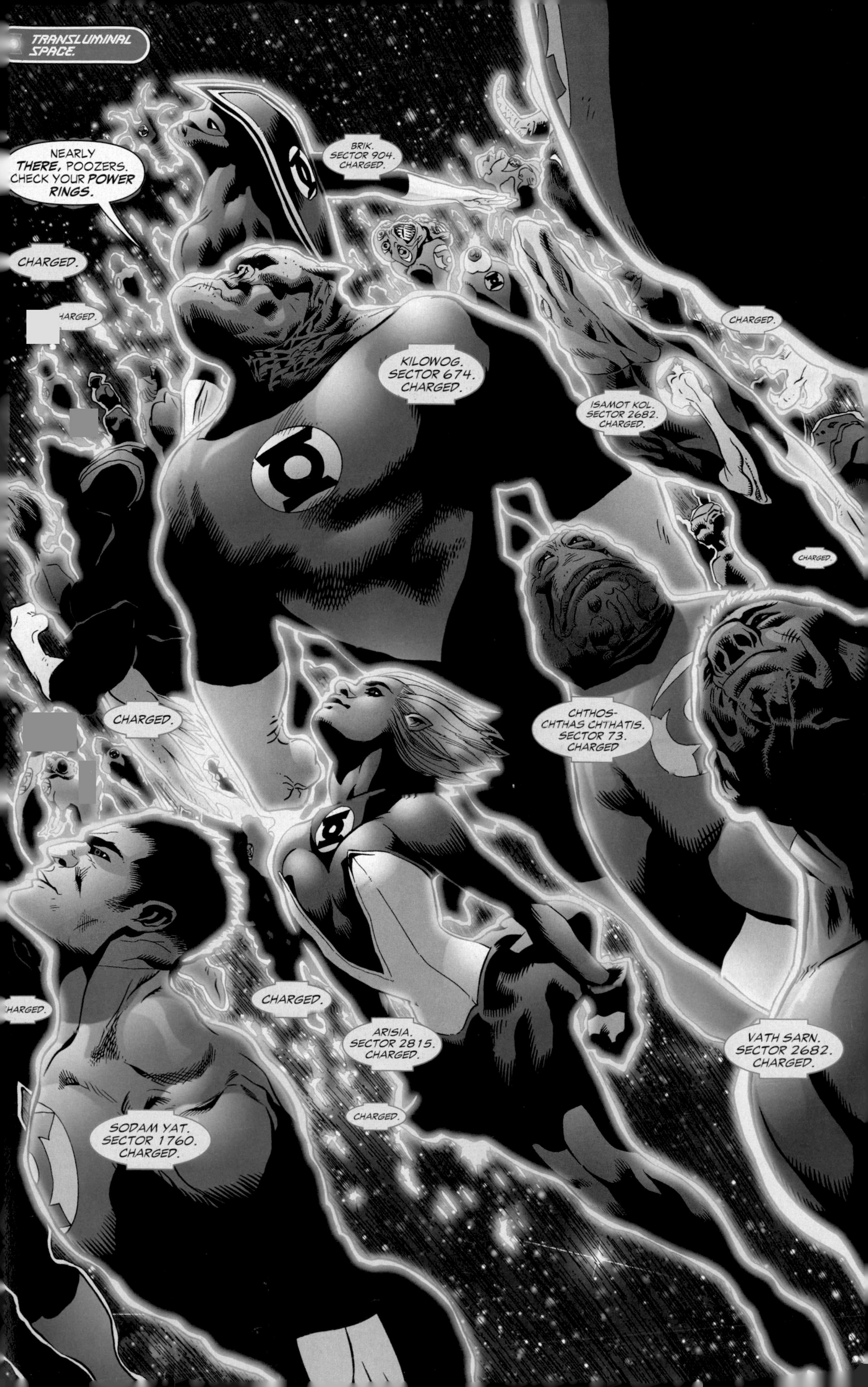
TRANSLUMINAL SPACE.
NEARLY THERE, POOZERS. CHECK YOUR POWER RINGS.
BRIK. SECTOR 904. CHARGED.
CHARGED.
HARGED.
KILOWOG. SECTOR 674. CHARGED.
CHARGED.
ISAMOT KOL. SECTOR 2682. CHARGED.
CHARGED.
CHARGED.
CHTHOS-CHTHAS CHTHATIS. SECTOR 73. CHARGED
HARGED.
CHARGED.
ARISIA. SECTOR 2815. CHARGED.
VATH SARN. SECTOR 2682. CHARGED.
CHARGED.
SODAM YAT. SECTOR 1760. CHARGED.

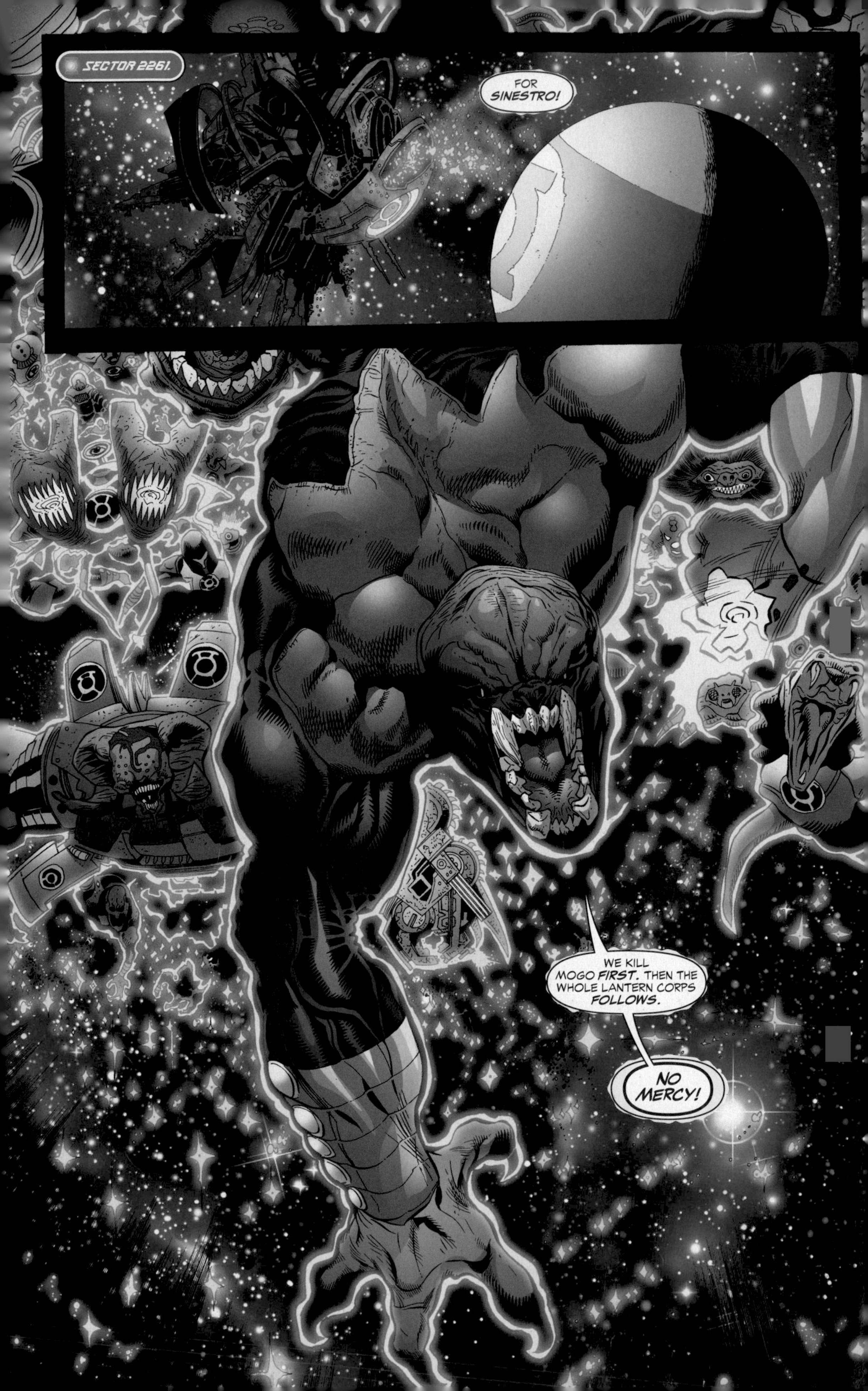
SECTOR 2261.
FOR SINESTRO!
WE KILL MOGO FIRST. THEN THE WHOLE LANTERN CORPS FOLLOWS.
NO MERCY!

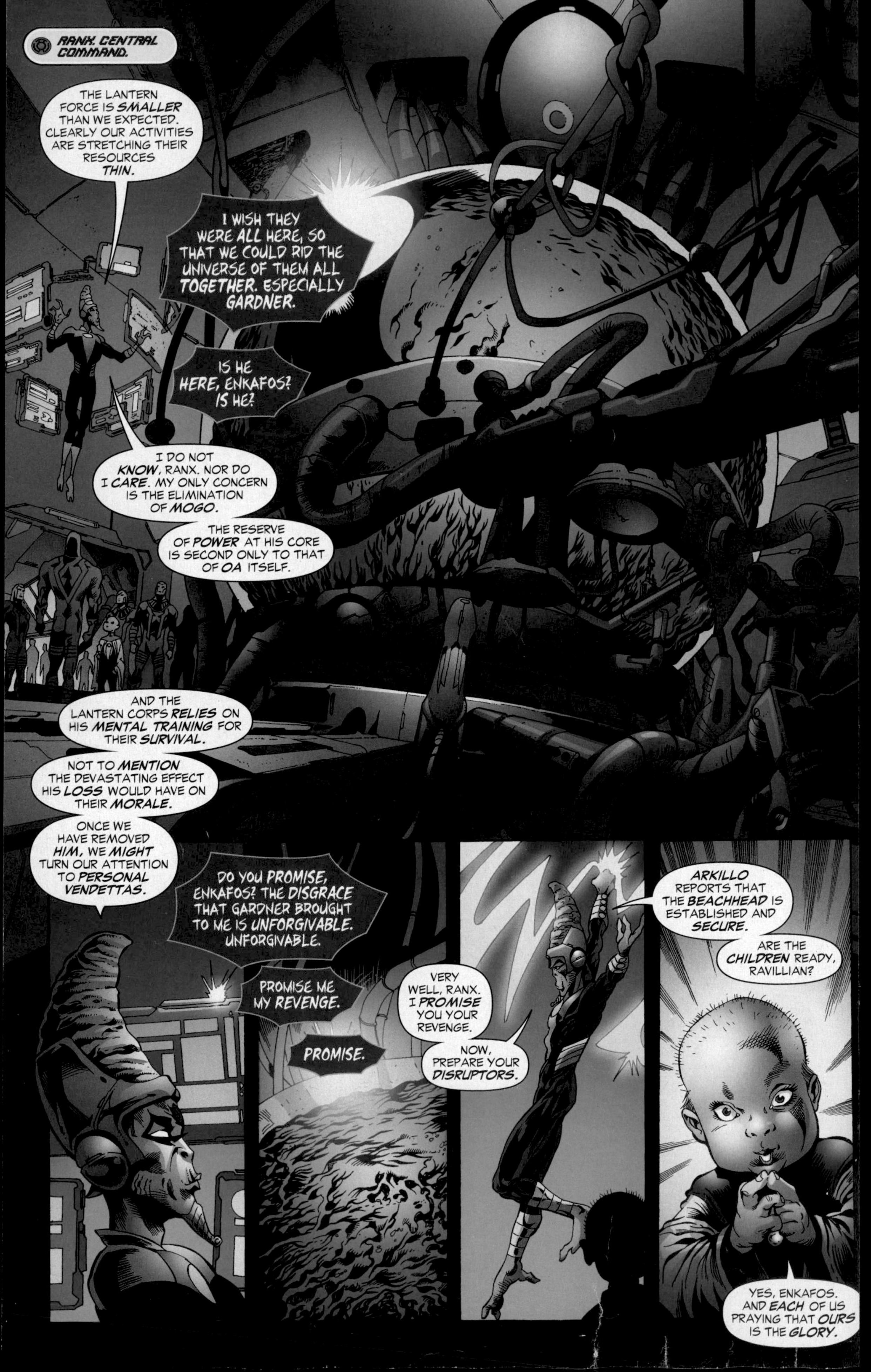
RANX. CENTRAL COMMAND.
THE LANTERN FORCE IS SMALLER THAN WE EXPECTED. CLEARLY OUR ACTIVITIES ARE STRETCHING THEIR RESOURCES THIN.
I WISH THEY WERE ALL HERE, SO THAT WE COULD RID THE UNIVERSE OF THEM ALL TOGETHER. ESPECIALLY GARDNER.
IS HE HERE, ENKAFOS? IS HE?
I DO NOT KNOW, RANX. NOR DO I CARE. MY ONLY CONCERN IS THE ELIMINATION OF MOGO.
THE RESERVE OF POWER AT HIS CORE IS SECOND ONLY TO THAT OF OA ITSELF.
AND THE LANTERN CORPS RELIES ON HIS MENTAL TRAINING FOR THEIR SURVIVAL.
NOT TO MENTION THE DEVASTATING EFFECT HIS LOSS WOULD HAVE ON THEIR MORALE.
ONCE WE HAVE REMOVED HIM, WE MIGHT TURN OUR ATTENTION TO PERSONAL VENDETTAS.
DO YOU PROMISE, ENKAFOS? THE DISGRACE THAT GARDNER BROUGHT TO ME IS UNFORGIVABLE. UNFORGIVABLE.
PROMISE ME MY REVENGE.
PROMISE.
VERY WELL, RANX. I PROMISE YOU YOUR REVENGE.
NOW, PREPARE YOUR DISRUPTORS.
ARKILLO REPORTS THAT THE BEACHHEAD IS ESTABLISHED AND SECURE.
ARE THE CHILDREN READY, RAVILLIAN?
YES, ENKAFOS. AND EACH OF US PRAYING THAT OURS IS THE GLORY.

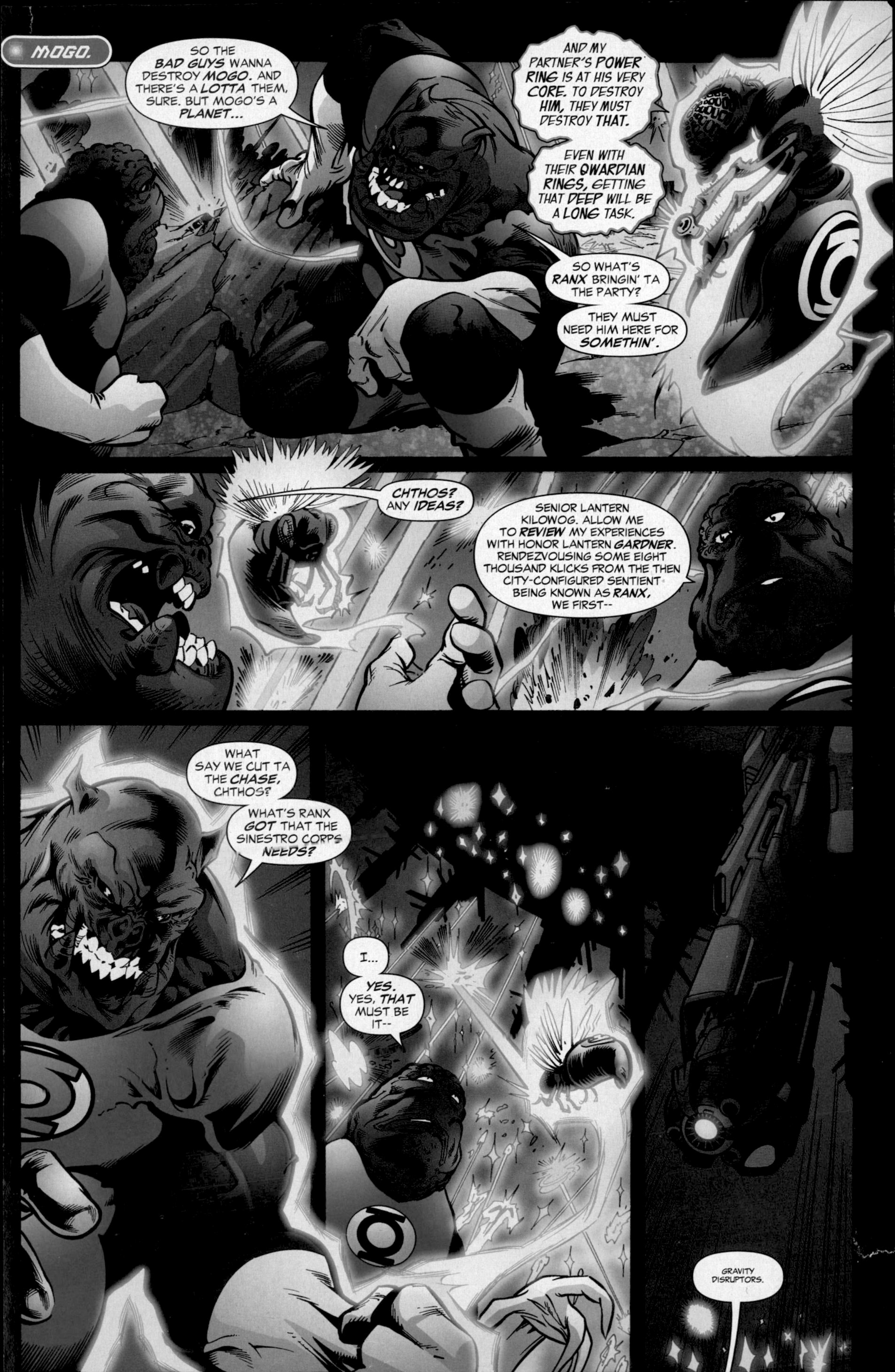
MOGO.
SO THE BAD GUYS WANNA DESTROY MOGO. AND THERE'S A LOTTA THEM, SURE. BUT MOGO'S A PLANET...
AND MY PARTNER'S POWER RING IS AT HIS VERY CORE. TO DESTROY HIM, THEY MUST DESTROY THAT.
EVEN WITH THEIR QWARDIAN RINGS, GETTING THAT DEEP WILL BE A LONG TASK.
SO WHAT'S RANX BRINGIN' TA THE PARTY?
THEY MUST NEED HIM HERE FOR SOMETHIN'.
CHTHOS? ANY IDEAS?
SENIOR LANTERN KILOWOG. ALLOW ME TO REVIEW MY EXPERIENCES WITH HONOR LANTERN GARDNER. RENDEZVOUSING SOME EIGHT THOUSAND KLICKS FROM THE THEN CITY-CONFIGURED SENTIENT BEING KNOWN AS RANX, WE FIRST--
WHAT SAY WE CUT TA THE CHASE, CHTHOS?
WHAT'S RANX GOT THAT THE SINESTRO CORPS NEEDS?
I...
YES. YES, THAT MUST BE IT--
GRAVITY DISRUPTORS.

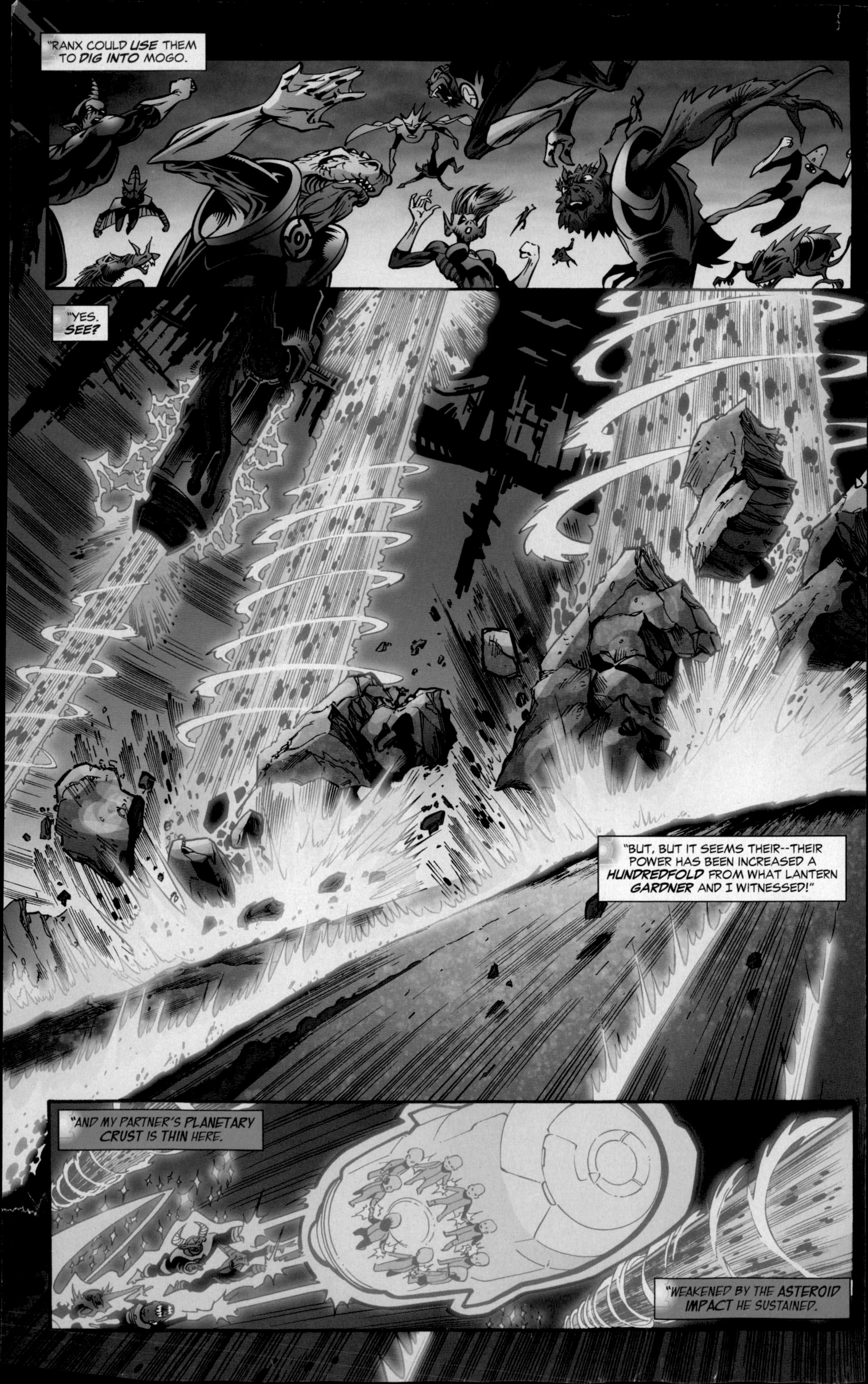
"RANX COULD USE THEM TO DIG INTO MOGO.
"YES. SEE?
"BUT, BUT IT SEEMS THEIR--THEIR POWER HAS BEEN INCREASED A HUNDREDFOLD FROM WHAT LANTERN GARDNER AND I WITNESSED!"
"AND MY PARTNER'S PLANETARY CRUST IS THIN HERE.
"WEAKENED BY THE ASTEROID IMPACT HE SUSTAINED.

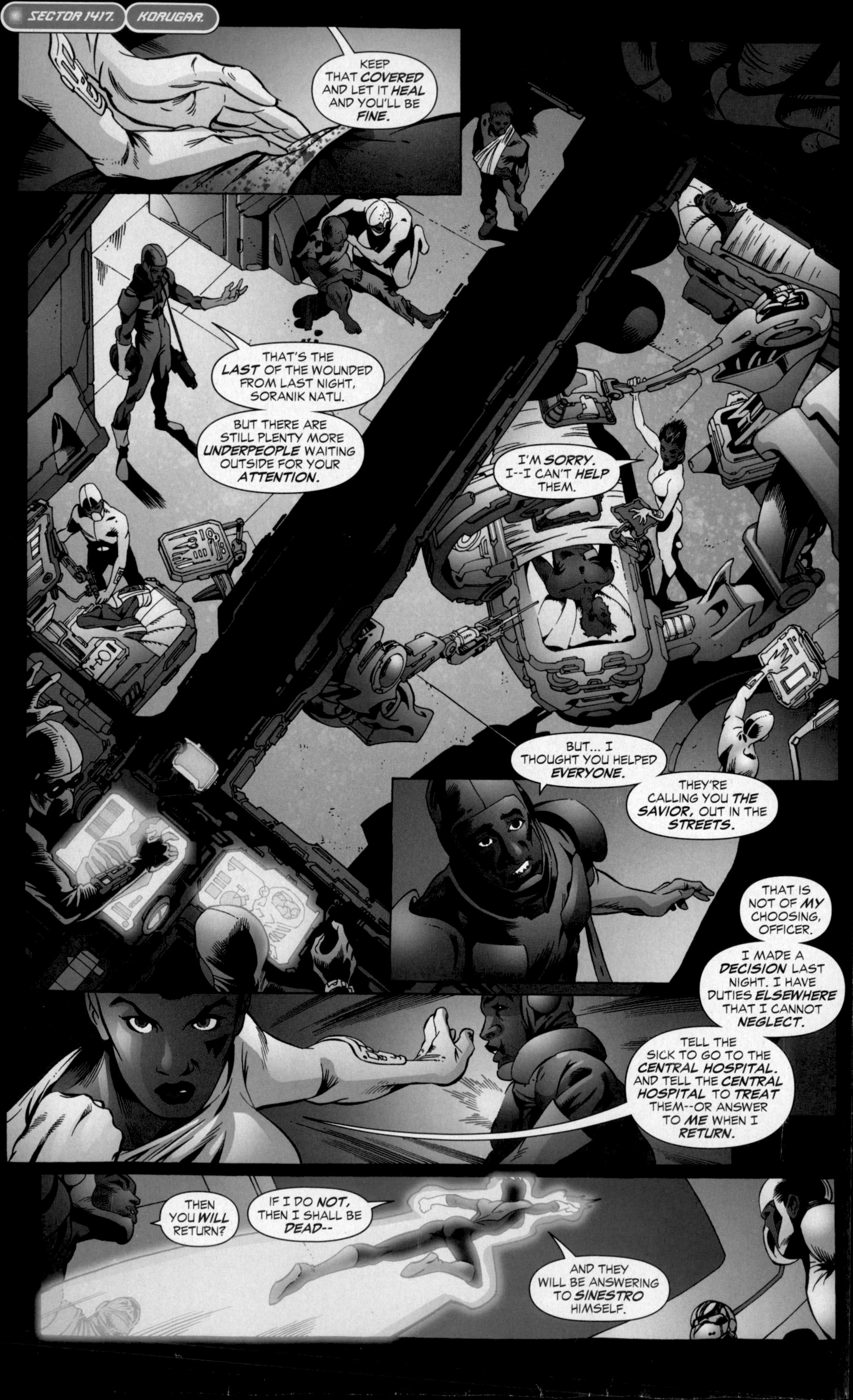
SECTOR 1417. KORUGAR.
KEEP THAT COVERED AND LET IT HEAL AND YOU'LL BE FINE.
THAT'S THE LAST OF THE WOUNDED FROM LAST NIGHT, SORANIK NATU.
BUT THERE ARE STILL PLENTY MORE UNDERPEOPLE WAITING OUTSIDE FOR YOUR ATTENTION.
I'M SORRY. I--I CAN'T HELP THEM.
BUT... I THOUGHT YOU HELPED EVERYONE.
THEY'RE CALLING YOU THE SAVIOR, OUT IN THE STREETS.
THAT IS NOT OF MY CHOOSING, OFFICER.
I MADE A DECISION LAST NIGHT. I HAVE DUTIES ELSEWHERE THAT I CANNOT NEGLECT.
TELL THE SICK TO GO TO THE CENTRAL HOSPITAL. AND TELL THE CENTRAL HOSPITAL TO TREAT THEM--OR ANSWER TO ME WHEN I RETURN.
THEN YOU WILL RETURN?
IF I DO NOT, THEN I SHALL BE DEAD--
AND THEY WILL BE ANSWERING TO SINESTRO HIMSELF.

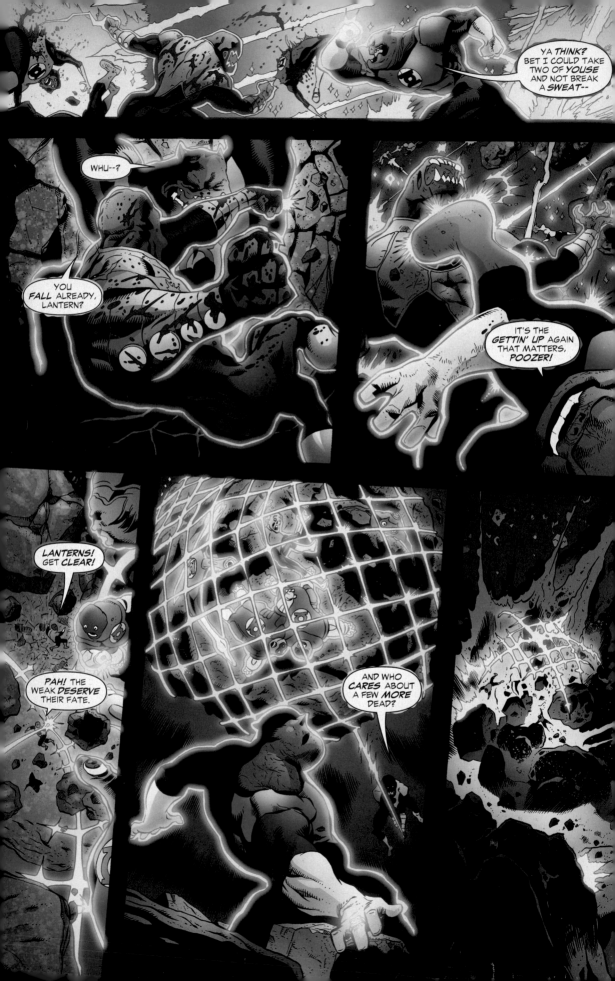

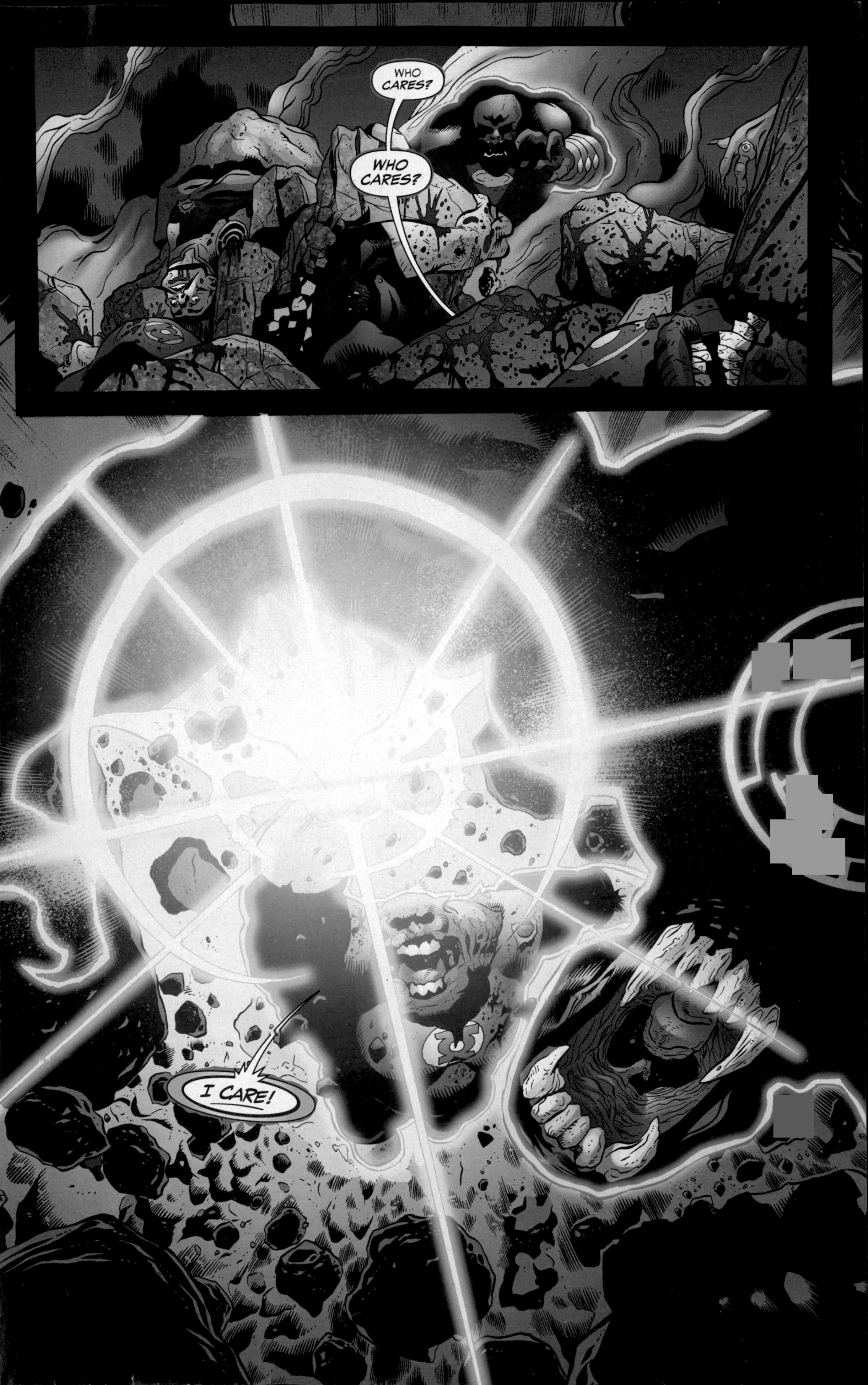
WHO CARES?
WHO CARES?
I CARE!

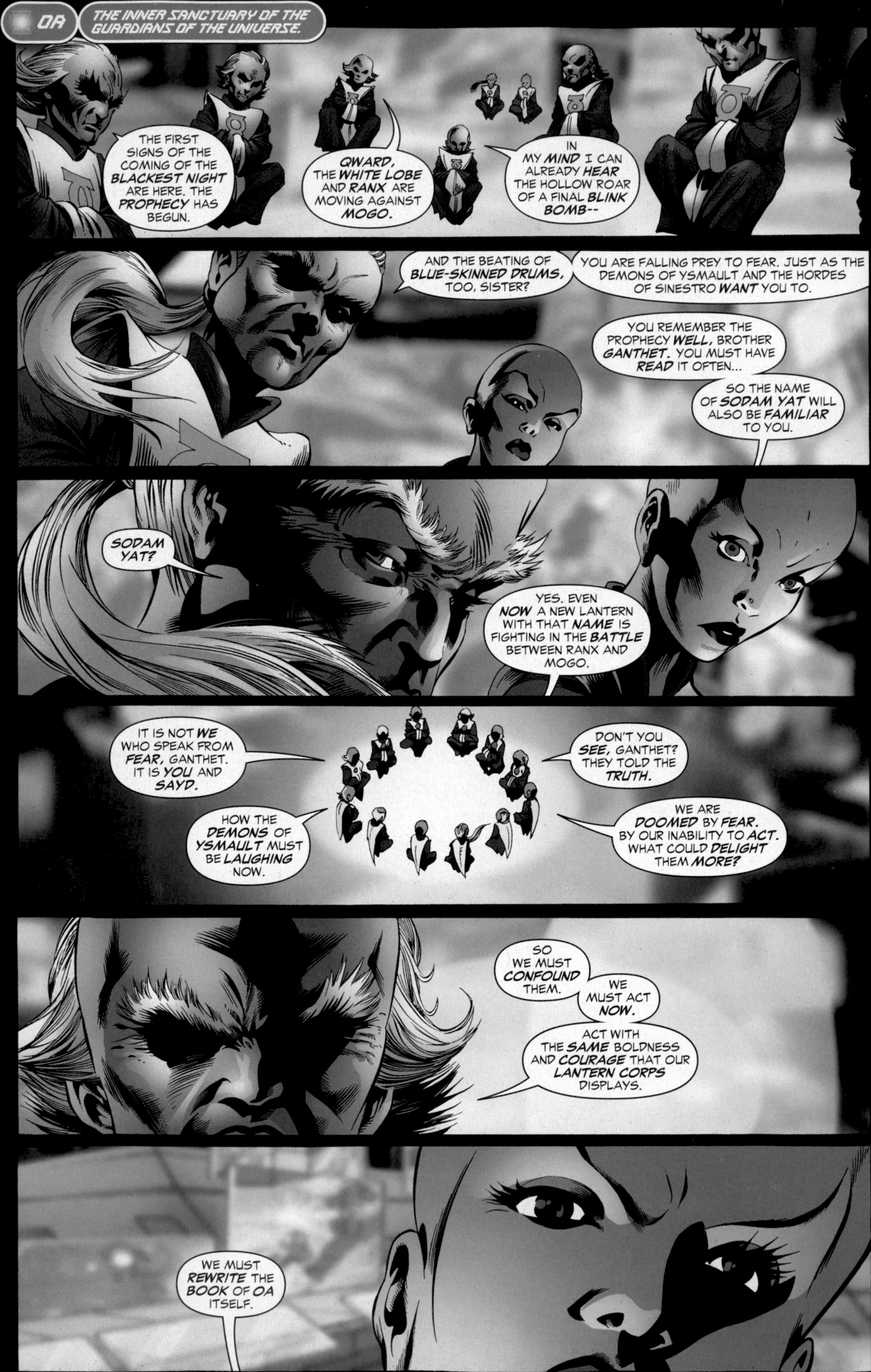
OA
THE INNER SANCTUARY OF THE GUARDIANS OF THE UNIVERSE.
THE FIRST SIGNS OF THE COMING OF THE BLACKEST NIGHT ARE HERE. THE PROPHECY HAS BEGUN.
QWARD, THE WHITE LOBE AND RANX ARE MOVING AGAINST MOGO.
IN MY MIND I CAN ALREADY HEAR THE HOLLOW ROAR OF A FINAL BLINK BOMB--
AND THE BEATING OF BLUE-SKINNED DRUMS, TOO, SISTER?
YOU ARE FALLING PREY TO FEAR. JUST AS THE DEMONS OF YSMAULT AND THE HORDES OF SINESTRO WANT YOU TO.
YOU REMEMBER THE PROPHECY WELL, BROTHER GANTHET. YOU MUST HAVE READ IT OFTEN...
SO THE NAME OF SODAM YAT WILL ALSO BE FAMILIAR TO YOU.
SODAM YAT?
YES. EVEN NOW A NEW LANTERN WITH THAT NAME IS FIGHTING IN THE BATTLE BETWEEN RANX AND MOGO.
IT IS NOT WE WHO SPEAK FROM FEAR, GANTHET. IT IS YOU AND SAYD.
DON'T YOU SEE, GANTHET? THEY TOLD THE TRUTH.
HOW THE DEMONS OF YSMAULT MUST BE LAUGHING NOW.
WE ARE DOOMED BY FEAR. BY OUR INABILITY TO ACT. WHAT COULD DELIGHT THEM MORE?
SO WE MUST CONFOUND THEM.
WE MUST ACT NOW.
ACT WITH THE SAME BOLDNESS AND COURAGE THAT OUR LANTERN CORPS DISPLAYS.
WE MUST REWRITE THE BOOK OF OA ITSELF.

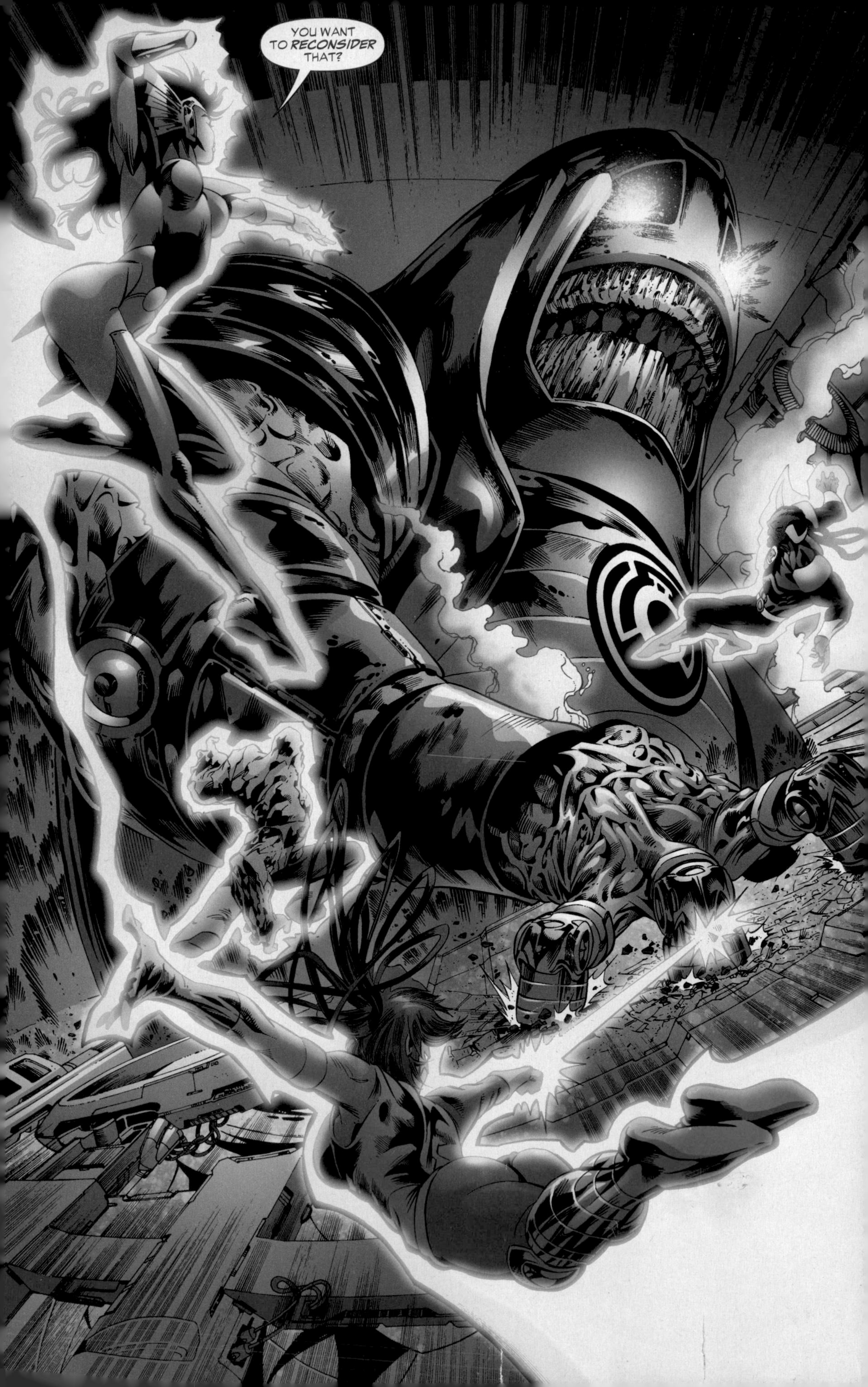
YOU WANT TO RECONSIDER THAT?

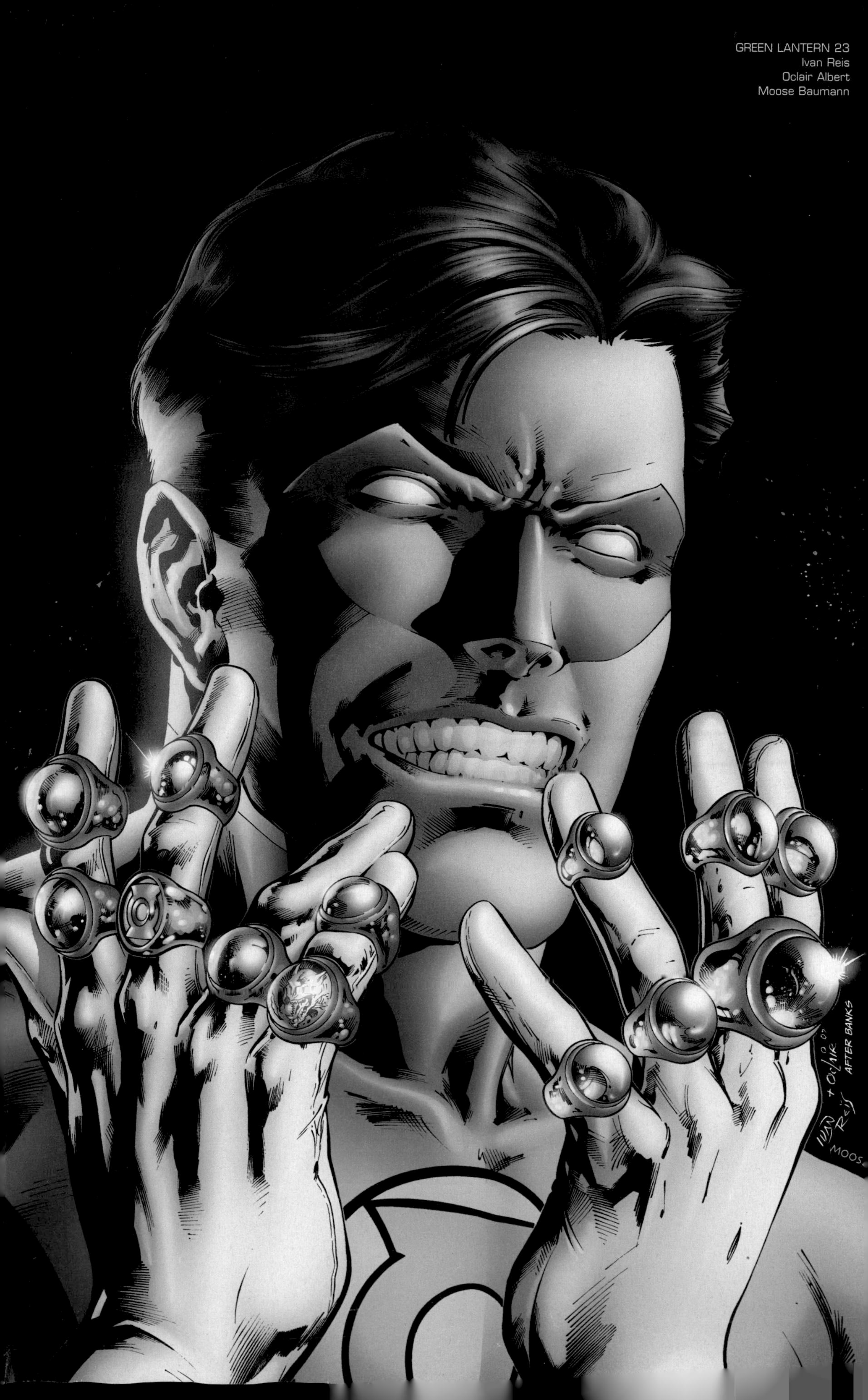
AFTER BANKS

GREEN LANTERN 23
Ivan Reis
Oclair Albert
Moose Baumann

THE SINESTRO CORPS WAR
Chapter Five
BROKEN LAWS

Writer: **Geoff Johns**
Penciller: **Ivan Reis**
Inker: **Oclair Albert**
Colorist: **Moose Baumann**
Letterer: **Rob Leigh**

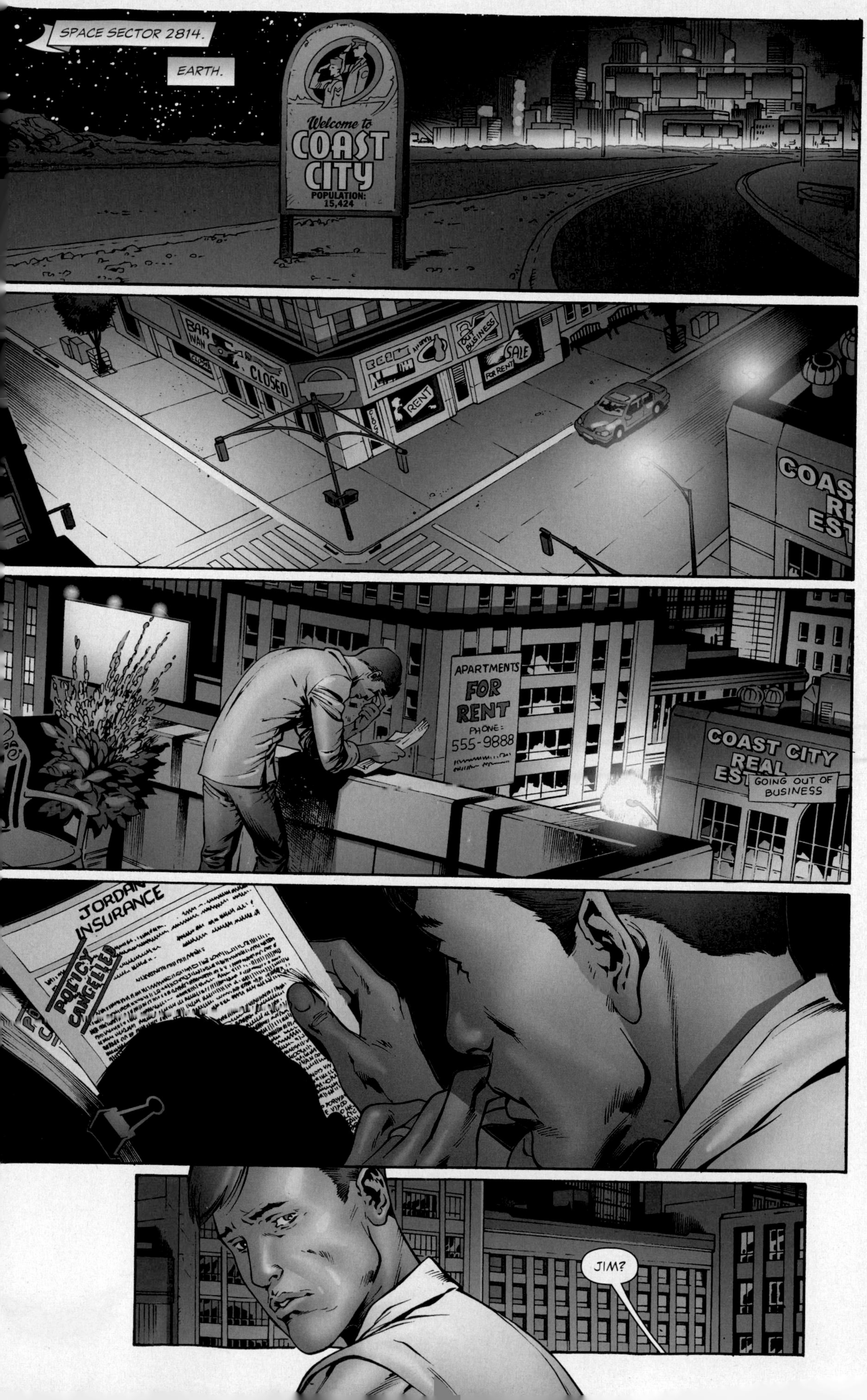
SPACE SECTOR 2814.
EARTH.
Welcome to COAST CITY POPULATION: 15,424
BAR
CLOSED
OUT OF BUSINESS
SALE
FOR RENT
RENT
COAST REAL EST
APARTMENTS FOR RENT PHONE: 555-9888
COAST CITY REAL EST
GOING OUT OF BUSINESS
JORDAN INSURANCE
POLICY CANCELLED
JIM?

HONEY, ARE YOU OKAY?

IT'S PAST MIDNIGHT. YOU NEED TO GET SOME SLEEP.

I NEED A LOT OF THINGS.

IT'S BEEN MORE THAN A YEAR SINCE REBUILDING STARTED. EIGHTY PERCENT OF HOUSING IS *UNOCCUPIED*. BUSINESS BUILDINGS ARE *VACANT*.

OUR KIDS' CLASSES HAVE MORE *EMPTY* DESKS THAN FULL ONES.

PEOPLE HAVEN'T MOVED TO COAST CITY LIKE EVERYONE WAS HOPING.

WE MOVED HERE BECAUSE WE BELIEVED IN YOUR BROTHER.

AND I STILL DO. BUT HAL CAN TAKE A *RISK*. HE DOESN'T HAVE *KIDS* TO LOOK AFTER.

I KNOW YOU'RE WORRIED--

I'M MORE THAN WORRIED, SUSAN. I'M *SCARED*.

DADDY!

JANE? WHAT HAPPENED, HOWARD?

SHE WOKE UP CRYING. I THINK SHE HAD A NIGHTMARE OR SOMETHING.

DADDY?!

WHAT IS IT, SWEETHEART?

IS...

...IS UNCLE HAL GOING TO *KILL* SOMEBODY?

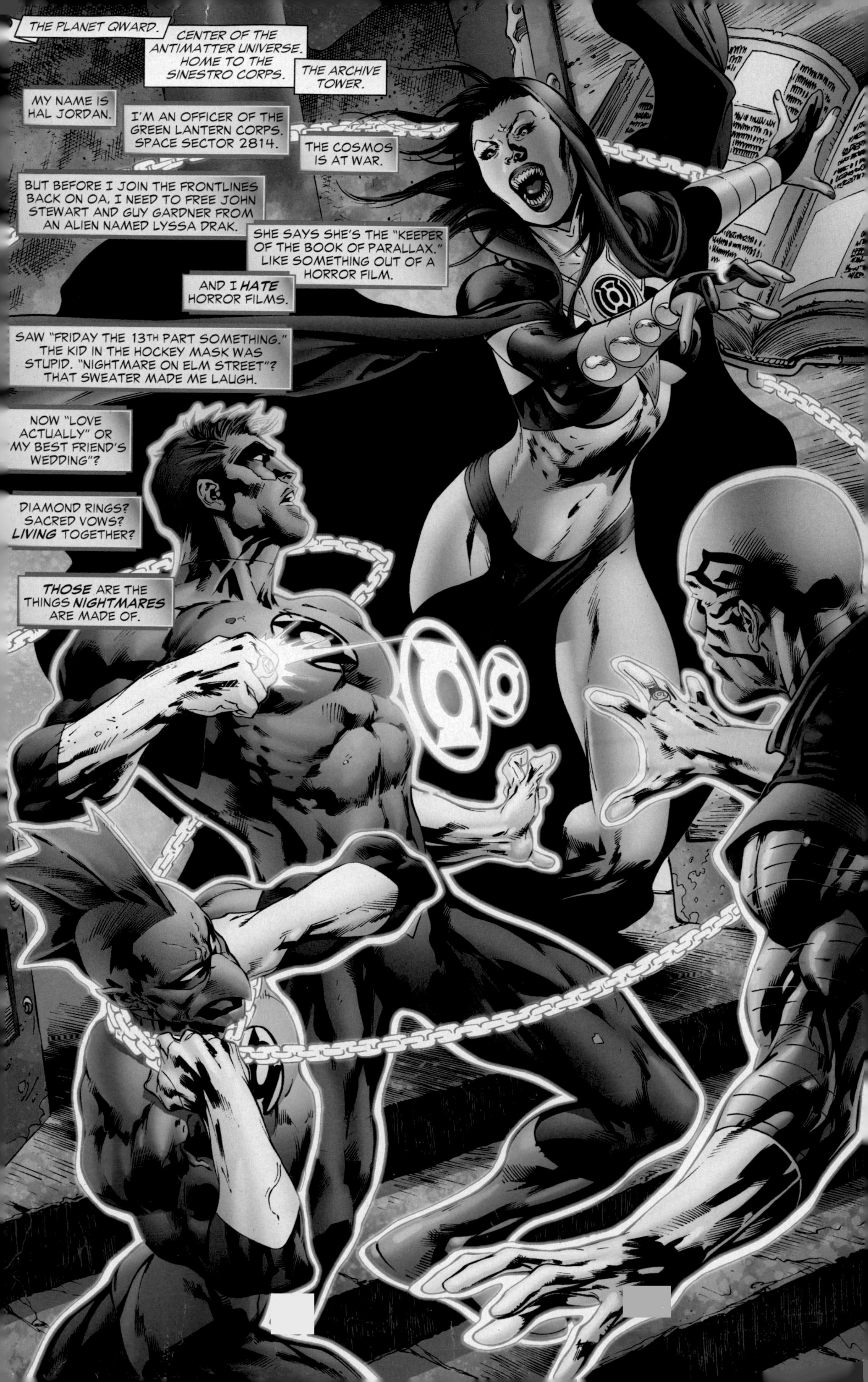
THE PLANET QWARD.
CENTER OF THE ANTIMATTER UNIVERSE. HOME TO THE SINESTRO CORPS.
THE ARCHIVE TOWER.
MY NAME IS HAL JORDAN.
I'M AN OFFICER OF THE GREEN LANTERN CORPS. SPACE SECTOR 2814.
THE COSMOS IS AT WAR.
BUT BEFORE I JOIN THE FRONTLINES BACK ON OA, I NEED TO FREE JOHN STEWART AND GUY GARDNER FROM AN ALIEN NAMED LYSSA DRAK.
SHE SAYS SHE'S THE "KEEPER OF THE BOOK OF PARALLAX." LIKE SOMETHING OUT OF A HORROR FILM.
AND I *HATE* HORROR FILMS.
SAW "FRIDAY THE 13TH PART SOMETHING." THE KID IN THE HOCKEY MASK WAS STUPID. "NIGHTMARE ON ELM STREET"? THAT SWEATER MADE ME LAUGH.
NOW "LOVE ACTUALLY" OR MY BEST FRIEND'S WEDDING"?
DIAMOND RINGS? SACRED VOWS? ***LIVING*** TOGETHER?
THOSE ARE THE THINGS ***NIGHTMARES*** ARE MADE OF.

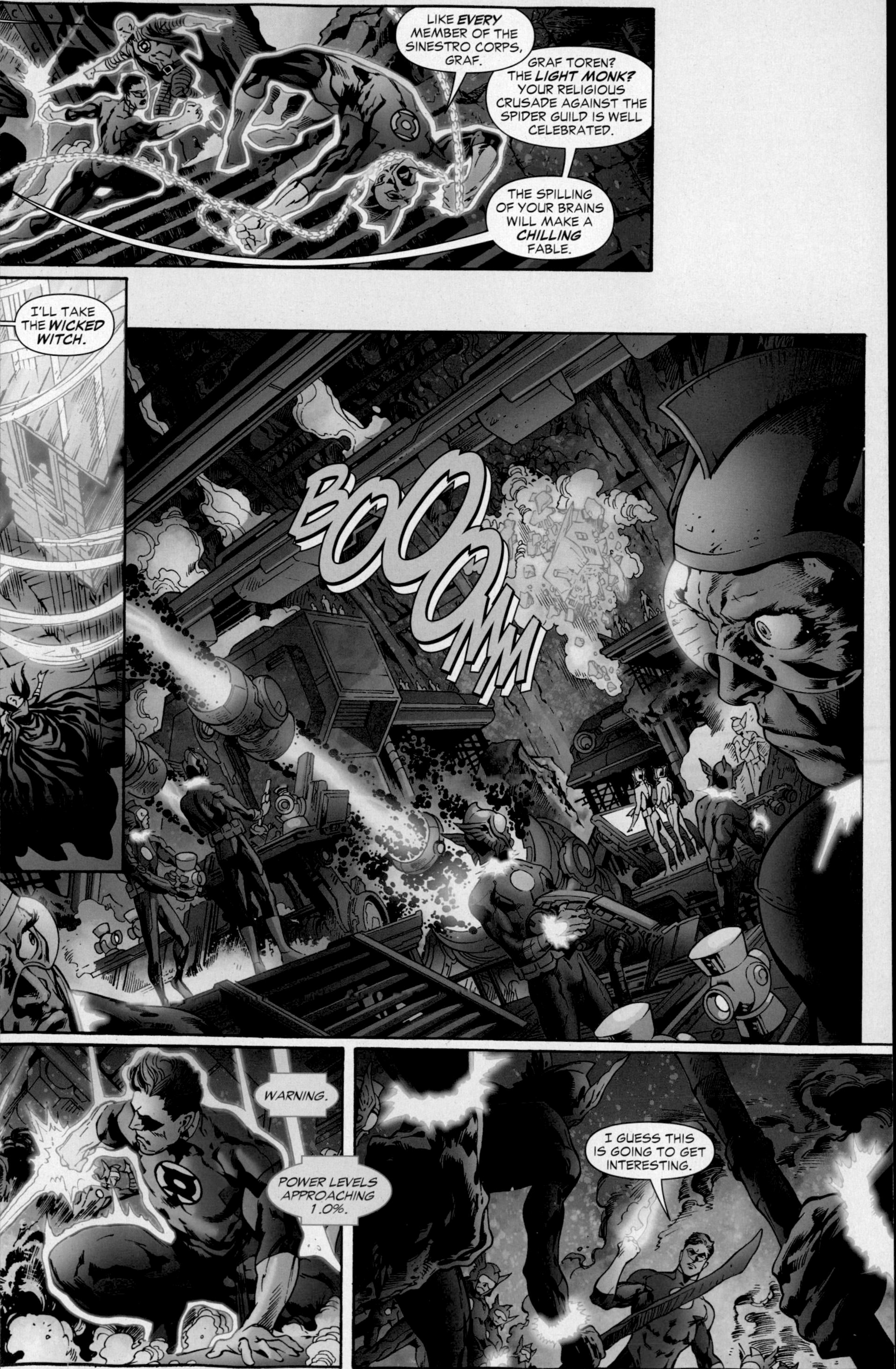
LIKE EVERY MEMBER OF THE SINESTRO CORPS, GRAF.
GRAF TOREN? THE LIGHT MONK? YOUR RELIGIOUS CRUSADE AGAINST THE SPIDER GUILD IS WELL CELEBRATED.
THE SPILLING OF YOUR BRAINS WILL MAKE A CHILLING FABLE.
I'LL TAKE THE WICKED WITCH.
BOOOMM
WARNING.
POWER LEVELS APPROACHING 1.0%.
I GUESS THIS IS GOING TO GET INTERESTING.

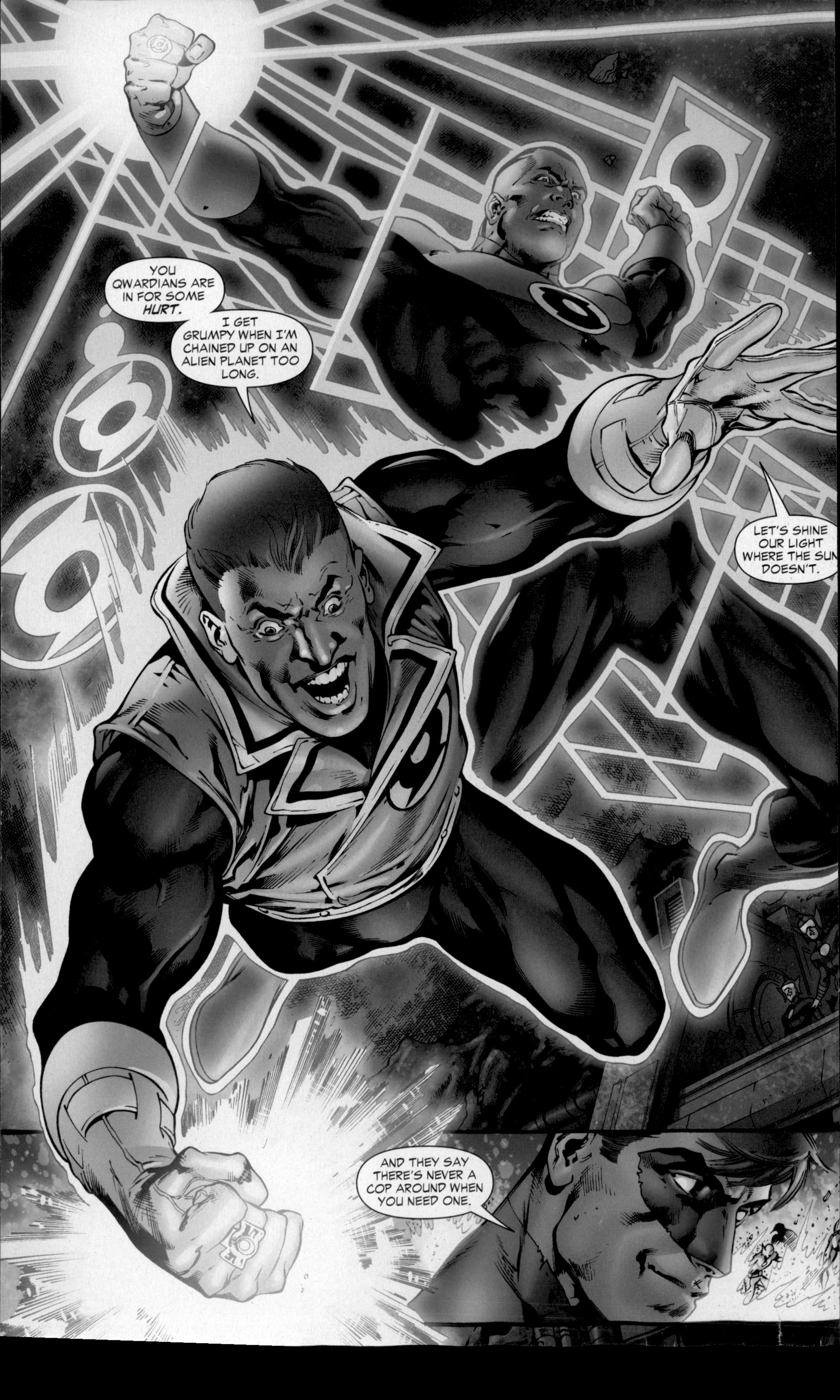
YOU QWARDIANS ARE IN FOR SOME *HURT*.
I GET GRUMPY WHEN I'M CHAINED UP ON AN ALIEN PLANET TOO LONG.
LET'S SHINE OUR LIGHT WHERE THE SUN DOESN'T.
AND THEY SAY THERE'S NEVER A COP AROUND WHEN YOU NEED ONE.

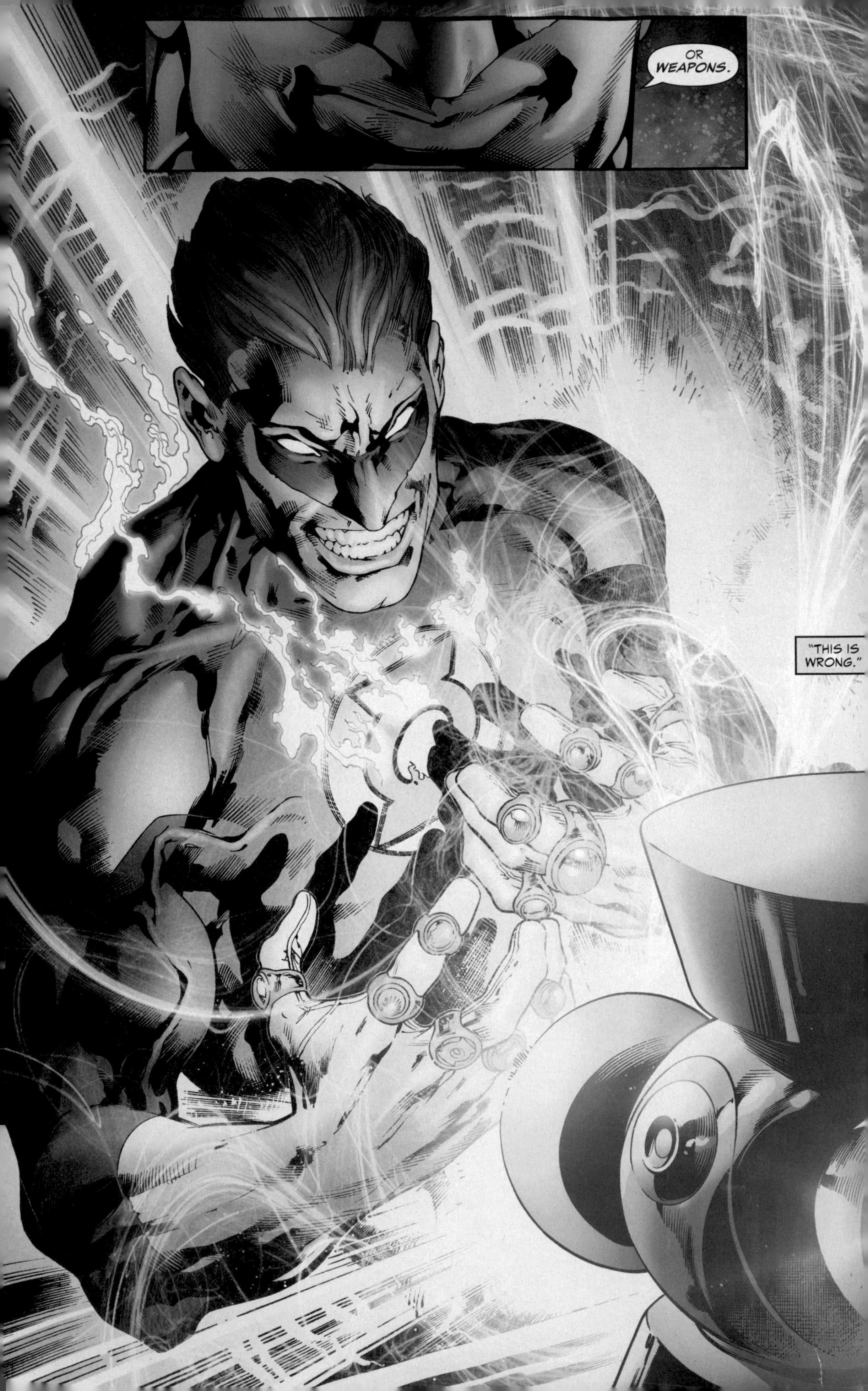
OR WEAPONS.
"THIS IS WRONG."

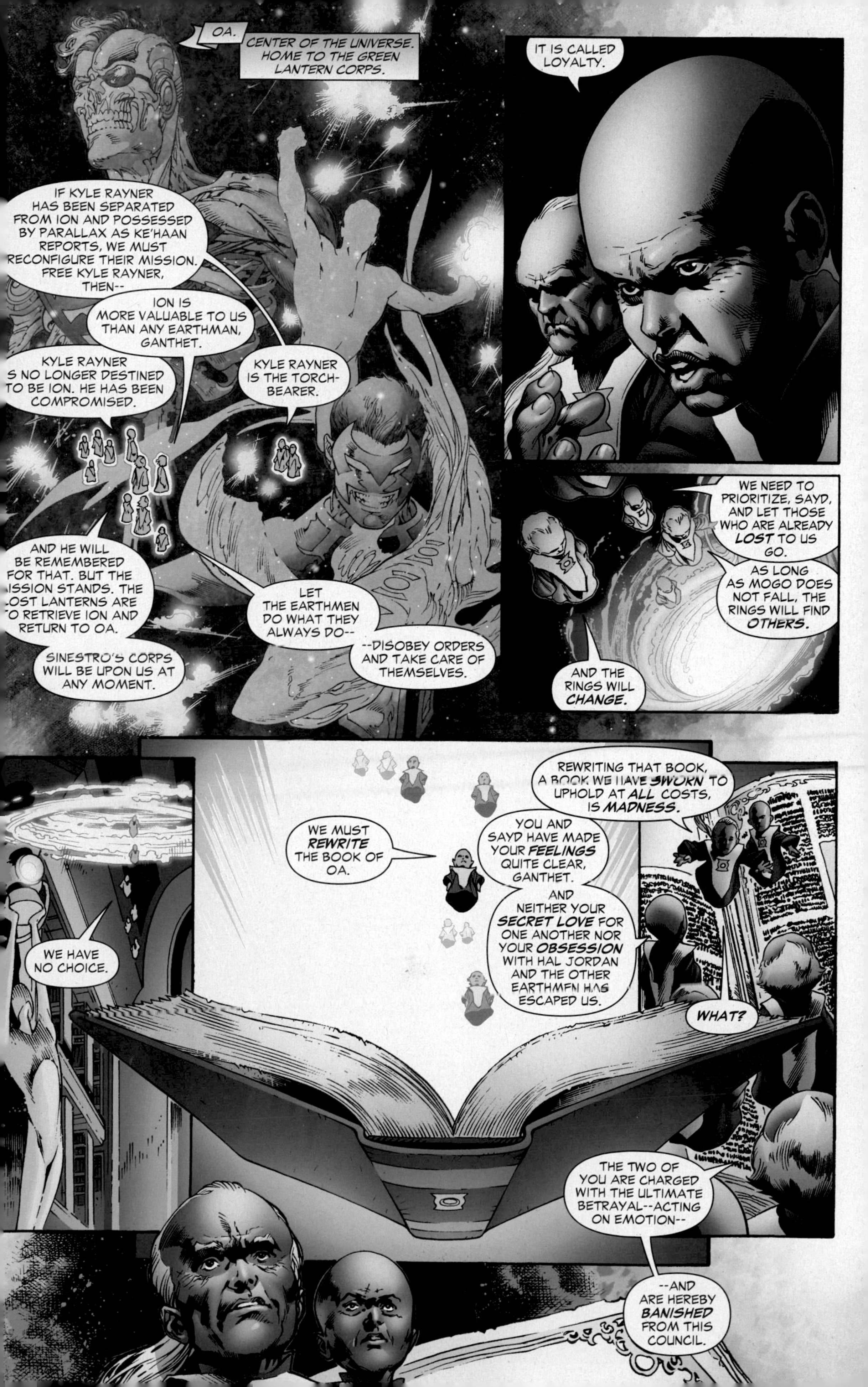
OA.
CENTER OF THE UNIVERSE. HOME TO THE GREEN LANTERN CORPS.
IT IS CALLED LOYALTY.
IF KYLE RAYNER HAS BEEN SEPARATED FROM ION AND POSSESSED BY PARALLAX AS KE'HAAN REPORTS, WE MUST RECONFIGURE THEIR MISSION. FREE KYLE RAYNER, THEN--
ION IS MORE VALUABLE TO US THAN ANY EARTHMAN, GANTHET.
KYLE RAYNER S NO LONGER DESTINED TO BE ION. HE HAS BEEN COMPROMISED.
KYLE RAYNER IS THE TORCH-BEARER.
AND HE WILL BE REMEMBERED FOR THAT. BUT THE ISSION STANDS. THE OST LANTERNS ARE O RETRIEVE ION AND RETURN TO OA.
SINESTRO'S CORPS WILL BE UPON US AT ANY MOMENT.
LET THE EARTHMEN DO WHAT THEY ALWAYS DO--
--DISOBEY ORDERS AND TAKE CARE OF THEMSELVES.
WE NEED TO PRIORITIZE, SAYD, AND LET THOSE WHO ARE ALREADY LOST TO US GO.
AS LONG AS MOGO DOES NOT FALL, THE RINGS WILL FIND OTHERS.
AND THE RINGS WILL CHANGE.
WE HAVE NO CHOICE.
WE MUST REWRITE THE BOOK OF OA.
REWRITING THAT BOOK, A BOOK WE HAVE SWORN TO UPHOLD AT ALL COSTS, IS MADNESS.
YOU AND SAYD HAVE MADE YOUR FEELINGS QUITE CLEAR, GANTHET.
AND NEITHER YOUR SECRET LOVE FOR ONE ANOTHER NOR YOUR OBSESSION WITH HAL JORDAN AND THE OTHER EARTHMEN HAS ESCAPED US.
WHAT?
THE TWO OF YOU ARE CHARGED WITH THE ULTIMATE BETRAYAL--ACTING ON EMOTION--
--AND ARE HEREBY BANISHED FROM THIS COUNCIL.

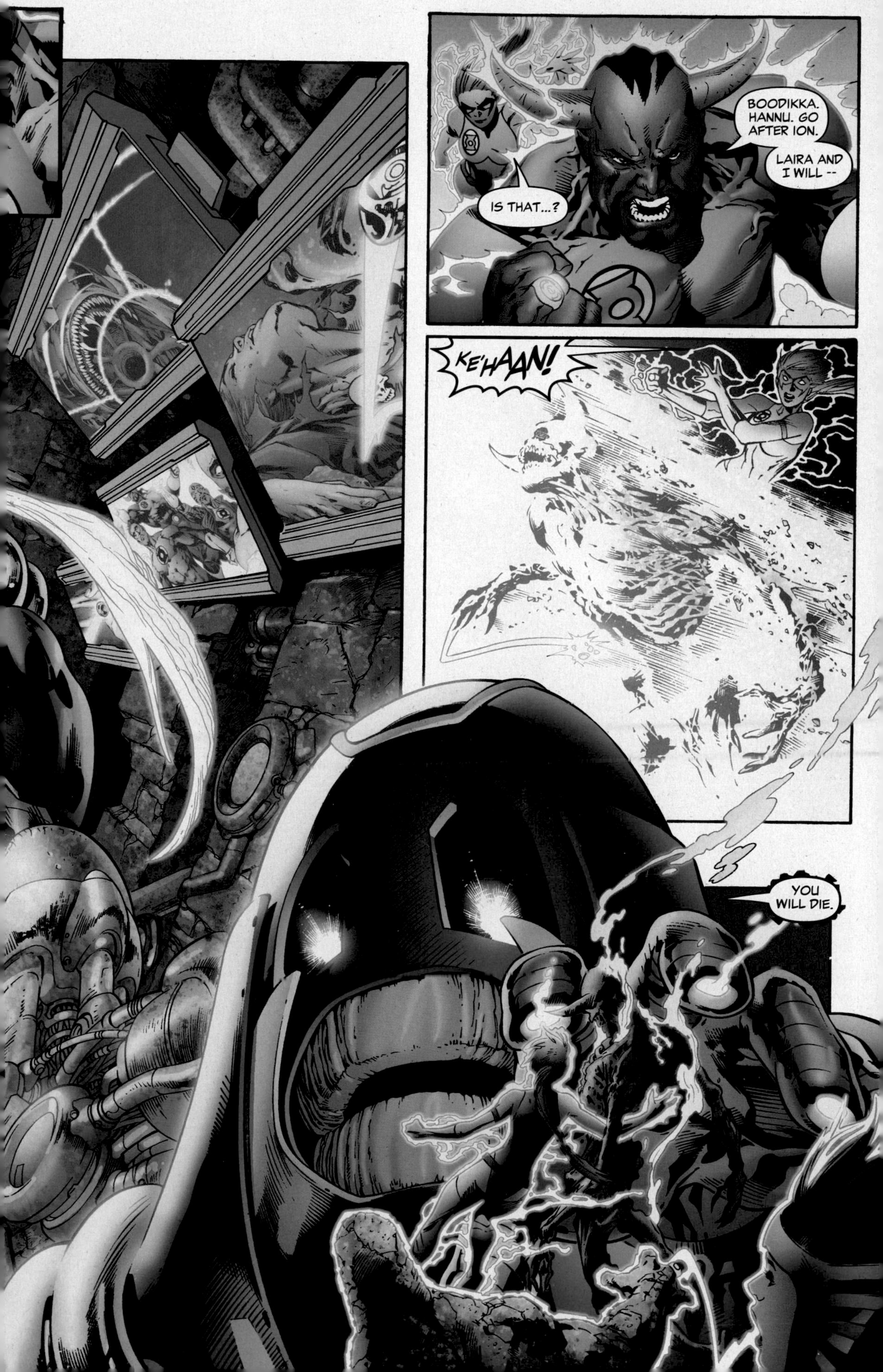
BOODIKKA. HANNU. GO AFTER ION.
LAIRA AND I WILL --
IS THAT...?
KE'HAAN!
YOU WILL DIE.

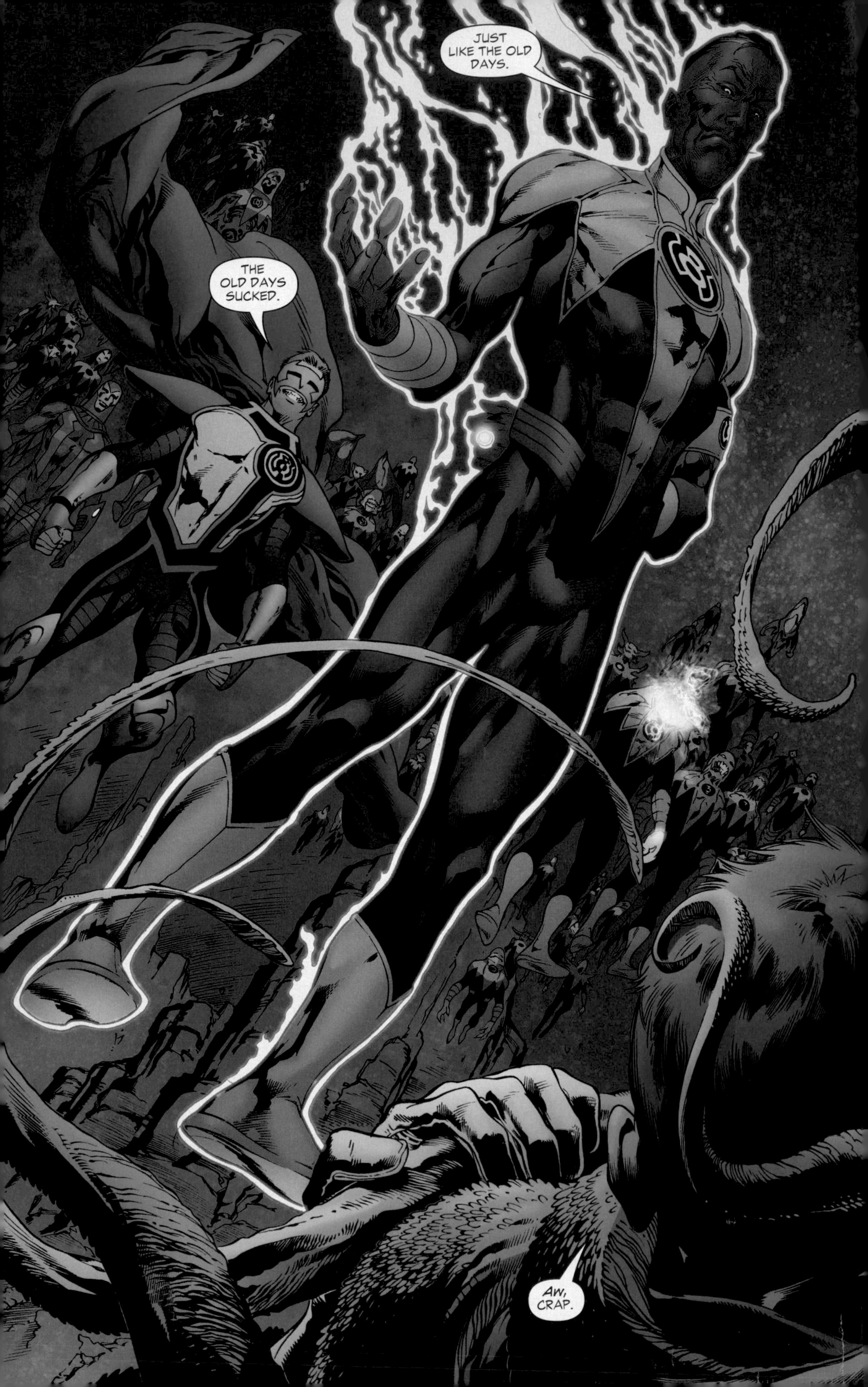
JUST LIKE THE OLD DAYS.
THE OLD DAYS SUCKED.
AW, CRAP.

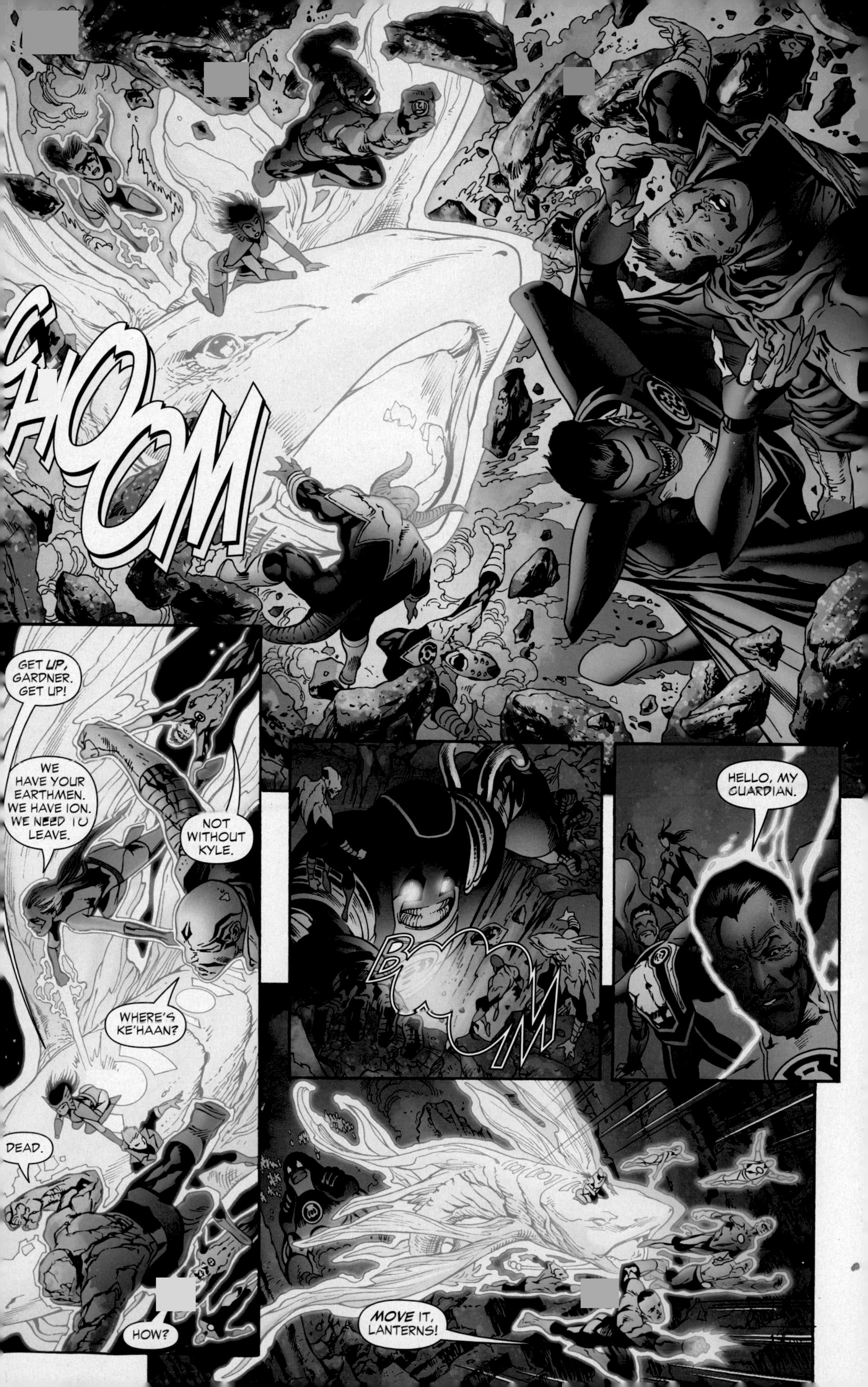

SHOOM
GET UP, GARDNER. GET UP!
WE HAVE YOUR EARTHMEN. WE HAVE ION. WE NEED TO LEAVE.
NOT WITHOUT KYLE.
WHERE'S KE'HAAN?
DEAD.
HOW?
BOOM
HELLO, MY GUARDIAN.
MOVE IT, LANTERNS!

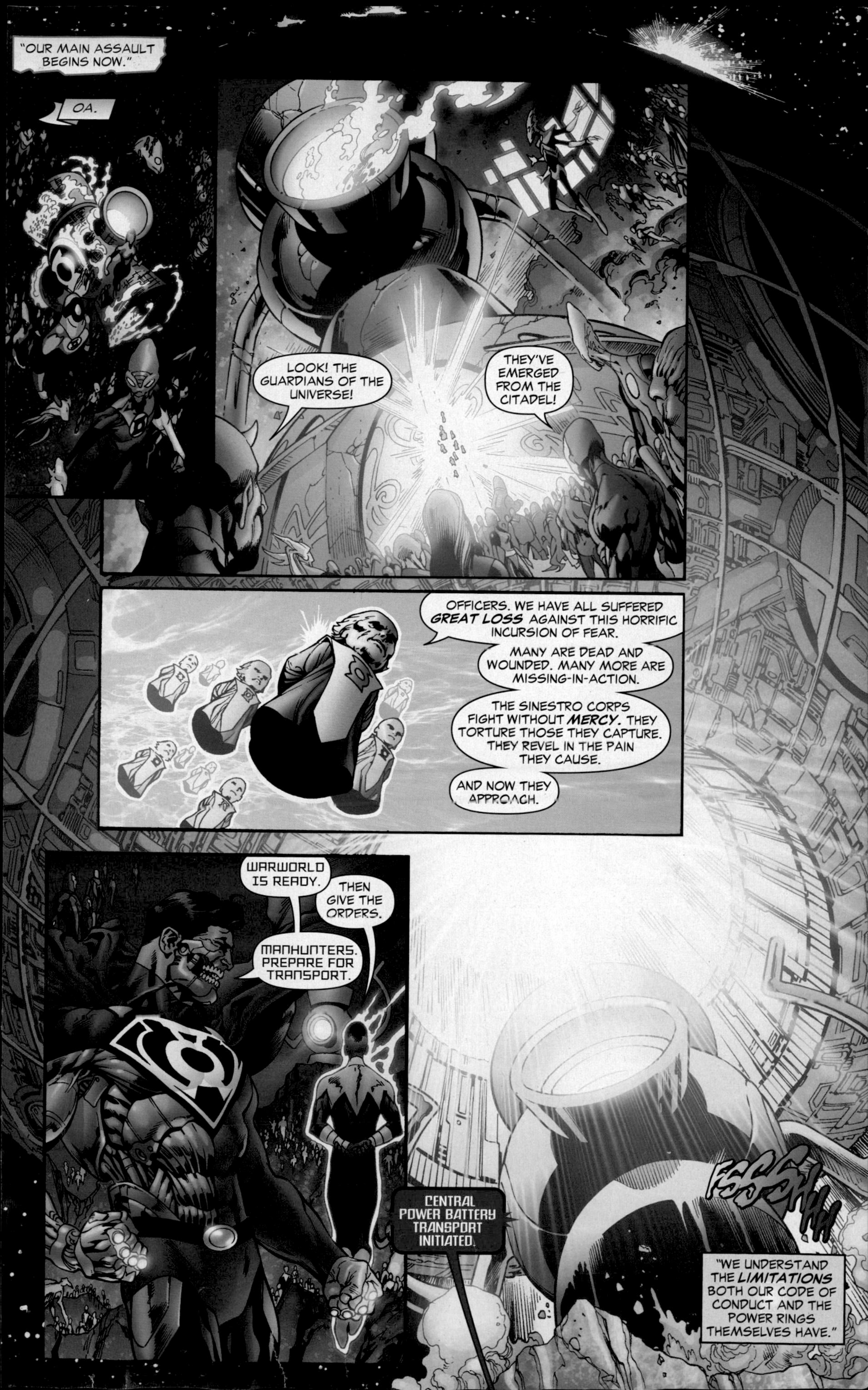
"OUR MAIN ASSAULT BEGINS NOW."
OA.
LOOK! THE GUARDIANS OF THE UNIVERSE!
THEY'VE EMERGED FROM THE CITADEL!
OFFICERS. WE HAVE ALL SUFFERED GREAT LOSS AGAINST THIS HORRIFIC INCURSION OF FEAR.
MANY ARE DEAD AND WOUNDED. MANY MORE ARE MISSING-IN-ACTION.
THE SINESTRO CORPS FIGHT WITHOUT MERCY. THEY TORTURE THOSE THEY CAPTURE. THEY REVEL IN THE PAIN THEY CAUSE.
AND NOW THEY APPROACH.
WARWORLD IS READY.
THEN GIVE THE ORDERS.
MANHUNTERS. PREPARE FOR TRANSPORT.
CENTRAL POWER BATTERY TRANSPORT INITIATED.
FSSSHHH
"WE UNDERSTAND THE LIMITATIONS BOTH OUR CODE OF CONDUCT AND THE POWER RINGS THEMSELVES HAVE."

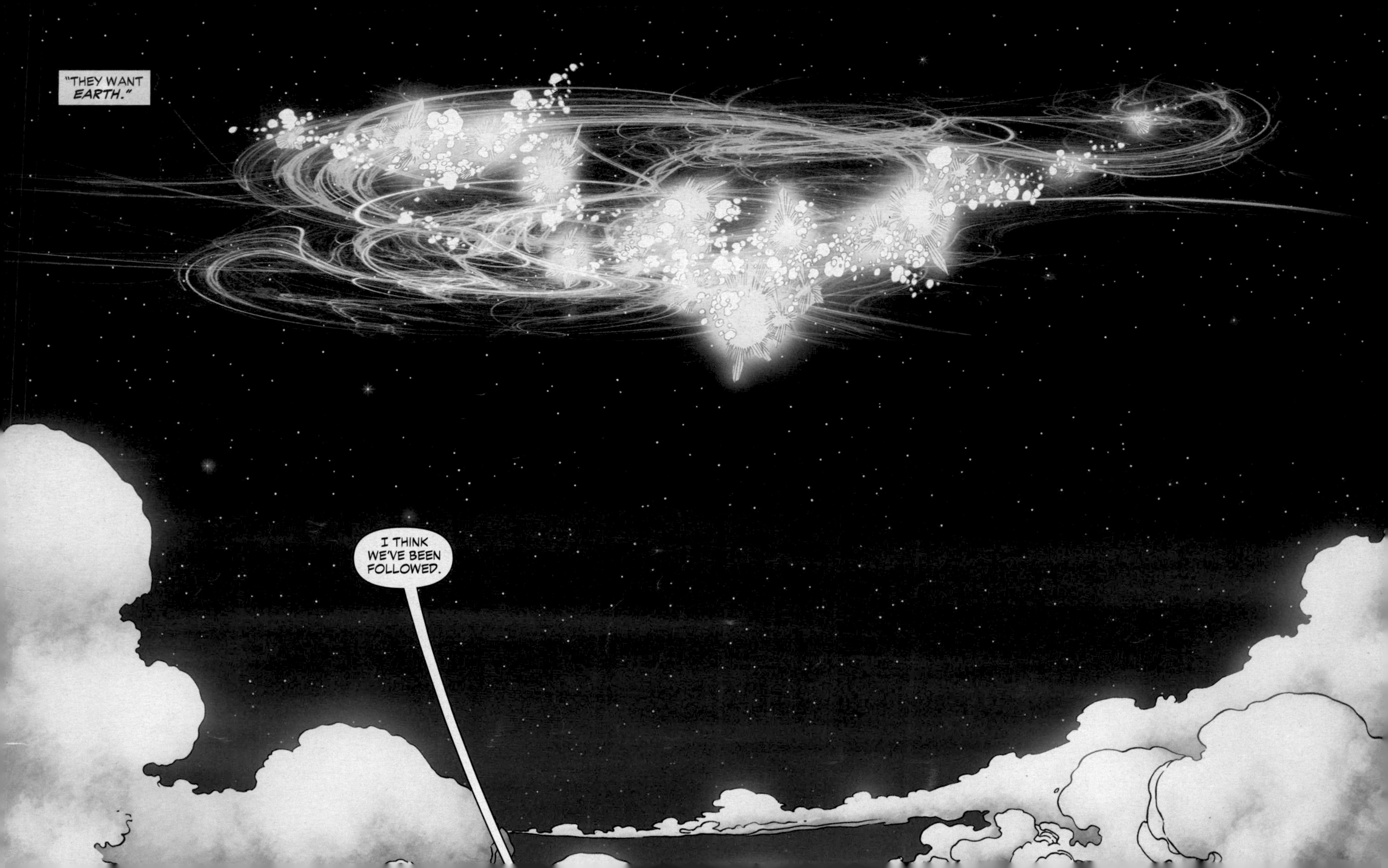
"THEY WANT EARTH."
I THINK WE'VE BEEN FOLLOWED.

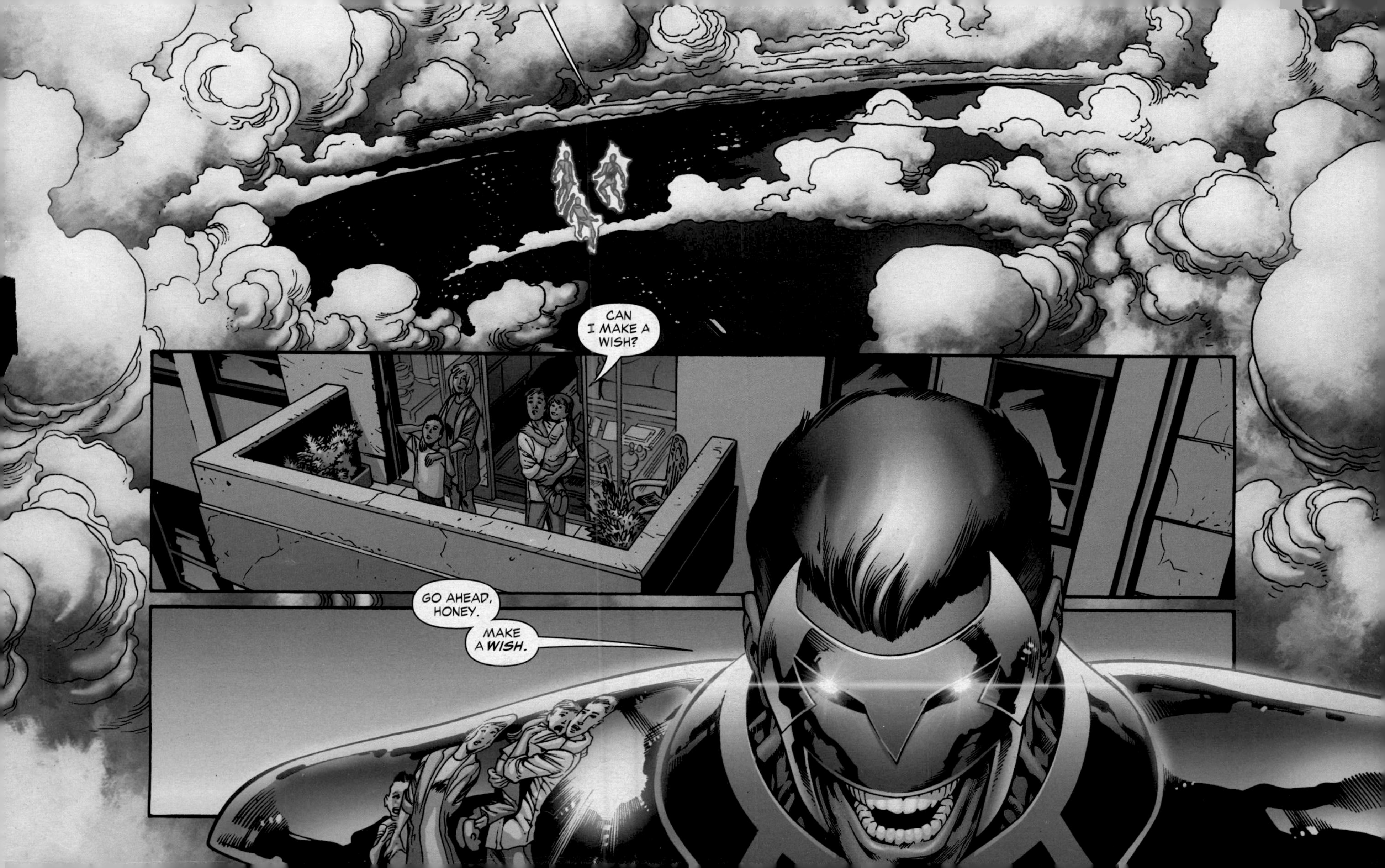
CAN I MAKE A WISH?
GO AHEAD, HONEY.
MAKE A WISH.